D1642735

GUIDE TO
THE USE OF LIBRARIES AND
INFORMATION SOURCES

Guide to the Use of Libraries and Information Sources

SEVENTH EDITION

Jean Key Gates

Professor Emerita
University of South Florida

McGraw-Hill, Inc.

New York St. Louis San Francisco Auckland Bogotá Caracas
Lisbon London Madrid Mexico City Milan Montreal New Delhi
San Juan Singapore Sydney Tokyo Toronto

This book is printed on acid-free paper.

1 2 3 4 5 6 7 8 9 0 DOC DOC 9 0 9 8 7 6 5 4 3

ISBN 0-07-023000-5

This book was set in Janson by Better Graphics, Inc.
The editors were Alison Husting Zetterquist, Laurie PiSierra, and Jean Akers;
the production supervisor was Denise L. Puryear.
The cover was designed by Rafael Hernandez.
R. R. Donnelley & Sons Company was printer and binder.

Cover photo: Draughton Library, courtesy of Auburn University, Ala.

Library of Congress Cataloging-in-Publication Data

Gates, Jean Key.
    Guide to the use of libraries and information sources / Jean Key
Gates.—7th ed.
        p.   cm.
    ISBN 0-07-023000-5
    1. Libraries—United States—Handbooks, manuals, etc.   2. Library
resources—United States—Handbooks, manuals, etc.   3. Reference
books—Bibliography.   4. Library science—United States—Handbooks,
manuals, etc.   I. Title.
Z710.G27   1994
025.5'6—dc20   93-14413

About the Author

Jean Key Gates is Professor Emerita of Library and Information Science at the University of South Florida where she designed and taught courses in basic information sources, information sources in the subject fields, foundations of librarianship, and contemporary publishing and printing.

Her professional career has included administration, secondary school and university teaching, academic librarianship, research, publishing, and service to the profession—locally and nationally.

Professor Gates received the B.A. degree from Hendrix College, the M.S. in L.S. degree from The Catholic University of America, and continued formal graduate study in special areas at the University of Arkansas, George Washington University, and The Catholic University of America.

The seventh edition of *Guide to the Use of Libraries and Information Sources* follows six highly successful editions that have been used in all English-speaking countries, translated into Spanish and Portuguese, and distributed by exclusive arrangement in Taiwan and in the Philippines.

Jean Key Gates is the author of *Introduction to Librarianship*, now in the third edition, and was the Consulting Editor of the prestigious McGraw-Hill Series in Library Education in which more than twenty volumes have been published. Other publishing projects include making indexes for her own and other publications and serving as educational advisor for six filmstrips to accompany early editions of *Guide to the Use of Books and Libraries*.

Professor Gates has been honored by Hendrix College, The Catholic University of America, and the University of South Florida for outstanding achievement in the field of library science and for distinguished service to her profession.

To
Students, teachers, and other users of
Guide since the first edition in 1962

Contents

Preface   *xi*

Part 1
The Library

1. A Brief History of Books and Libraries   *3*
2. The Parts of the Book   *25*
3. Academic Libraries   *29*

Part 2
The Organization and Arrangement of Library Materials

4. Classification   *37*
5. Library Catalogs   *55*

Part 3
General Information Sources

6. Reference and Information Sources   *58*
7. Dictionaries   *81*
8. Encyclopedias   *89*
9. Indexes   *96*

10. Biographical Dictionaries   108
11. Atlases and Gazetteers   118
12. Yearbooks and Handbooks   124
13. Bibliographies   129
14. Nonbook Information Sources   134
15. Government Publications   148

Part 4
Information Sources
in the Subject Fields

16. Subject Information Sources   159
17. Philosophy and Psychology   165
18. Religion and Mythology   173
19. The Social Sciences and Education   182
20. Language (Philology)   197
21. Science and Technology   205
22. The Fine Arts and Recreation   218
23. Literature   235
24. History and Geography   251

Part 5
Using Library Resources
for a Research Paper

25. The Research Paper   265

Indexes
    Subject Index   283
    Title Index   291

Preface

The purpose of the seventh edition of *Guide to the Use of Libraries and Information Sources* is to introduce the library of the 1990s with its numerous and varied kinds of materials, services, and equipment to students and other users in a way that will make them more knowledgeable about its contents and more able to use them effectively and advantageously. Particular attention is given to the academic library.

Books are not new to library users; learning how to use them efficiently is an ongoing need, and major attention is given to print sources in this edition as in previous editions because, at the present time, they constitute the largest part of the library's holdings. Many print sources are now available also in online and CD-ROM formats, and the number is increasing daily. Knowing how to use the print form will facilitate use of the electronic version. Too, many libraries have both versions.

Automated and electronic means of access to information sources *are* new. Most of today's students have grown up in the computer age, but using computers for games, for keeping personal files, and seeing them in use in business are very different from using them to find information for classes or for a research paper. It is the purpose of this edition of *Guide* to present automated and electronic sources in such a way that students will not be reluctant to use them; to introduce students and other library users to various options for searching these sources for information; to call attention to the differences in the operation of various systems; and to emphasize that the ability to use electronic—as well as print sources—is vital to students' ability to find the information they need during their college years and after.

Information sources—print and nonprint—are discussed as general or specialized (subject) according to kinds: dictionaries, encyclopedias, indexes, audiovisual materials, government publications, databases, CD-ROMs, and others. Electronic sources are interfiled with print sources. Emphasis is placed on what they are, the purposes each kind of source serves, the kinds of questions the various resources are designed to answer, how to choose them for given purposes, and how to use them.

In general, each chapter includes a definition of terms, a brief statement of historical development, discussion, and appropriate examples.

The selection of titles—print and nonprint—to illustrate the several kinds of library materials is based on a critical study of the titles, supported by reviews in a number of selective and evaluative bibliographies, including:

"Book Reviews: Reference." *Library Journal.* New York: Bowker, 1876– . Semimonthly, February–June, September–November; monthly, January, July, August, December.

Booklist. Chicago: ALA, 1905– . Semimonthly; monthly in August.

Choice. Chicago: ALA, 1964– . Monthly; bimonthly July and August.

Rettig, James. "Current Reference Books." *Wilson Library Bulletin.* New York: Wilson, 1972– . Monthly.

Sheehy, Eugene P. *Guide to Reference Books.* 10th ed. Chicago: ALA, 1986. *Supplement.* Ed. Robert Balay. 1992.

The titles given as examples are only a selected sample of the many now available, and each person will wish to add titles and to replace with new titles some of those that have been included. Listings of titles in this seventh edition have been brought up to date by new editions and new titles published since 1989.

This book is not a manual for the study of a particular library. It is designed to serve as a textbook for college freshmen and other students who want or need instruction in the use of libraries and library materials. It can be used to advantage by reference librarians and by any person who is interested in learning what a library is and how to use it.

Technical library terminology is used only when it seems essential for clarity. The language is, with few exceptions, that of the student and the nonspecialist.

I am indebted to many authors, publishers, and holders of copyrights for permission to use their material. I should like to express my appreciation to my family and friends for their support; to my professional colleagues who answered questions or volunteered suggestions regarding this revision; and to cooperative librarians in many libraries, especially the University of South Florida Library, who helped locate needed materials.

I am grateful to my editors, Laurie PiSierra and Alison Husting Zetterquist, for their suggestions and encouragement, and to my editing supervisor, Jean Akers, for her patience and cooperation.

Jean Key Gates

GUIDE TO
THE USE OF LIBRARIES AND
INFORMATION SOURCES

PART

1

The Library

CHAPTER

1

A Brief History
of Books and Libraries

The earliest system for storing information and transmitting it from one person to another was language. By the use of words, history, rituals, stories, prayers, and medical and other knowledge were passed on from one generation to another. When people realized that spoken words could be represented by visual symbols, they invented their second means for the preservation and transmission of knowledge: writing—the chief medium used for this purpose for more than 5000 years.

The first writings were crude pictures carved on rocks, stone, bark, metal, and clay, or whatever materials were at hand. They were of three kinds: (1) pictographic, representing an object; (2) ideographic, representing the idea suggested by the object; and (3) phonographic, representing the sound of the object or idea. Some of these ancient inscriptions can be interpreted. Crude picture writing was done on other materials which were at hand: vegetable fiber, cloth, wood, bark, animal skin, clay, and metal. However, only the writings on clay, metal, and stone have survived.

Most historians agree that all our systems of writing came from these crude carvings and picture writings.

The story of books and libraries from earliest times to the present is closely interwoven with the story of writing and other methods of preserving and transmitting information and knowledge, with the materials and the physical forms which have been used for these purposes, and with the methods of preserving them and of making them accessible for use. For with the first "book" came the necessity for a place to keep it, to make it accessible for use, and to pass it on to succeeding generations.

3

Writing, Books, and Libraries

ANTIQUITY

The Sumerians, Babylonians, and Assyrians

From about 3600 to 2357 B.C. the Sumerian civilization flourished in the Tigris-Euphrates Valley, and as early as 3100 B.C. Sumerian historians began to record their current history and to reconstruct the story of their past.

The system of writing of the Sumerians—perhaps their greatest contribution to human culture—is the oldest system known. The word "cuneiform," which describes their style of writing, is from *cuneus*, the Latin word for "wedge." The materials used were soft clay and a wedge-shaped stylus of metal, ivory, or wood. When the scribe had finished writing, the clay was baked until it was hard as stone. These pieces of baked clay, small enough to be held in the hand of the scribe, are called "tablets" and were the first books.

To the Sumerians, writing was first of all a tool of trade and commerce. In addition, it was an instrument for recording religious works: prayers, ritual procedure, sacred legends, and magic formulas. On these clay tablets are also preserved the records of the first schools, the first social reforms, the first tax levies, and the first political, social, and philosophical thinking. It was several hundred years before the Sumerians produced literature, but among the tons of tablets and cylinders removed from the ruins of Sumer's ancient cities are some containing literary works almost 1000 years older than the *Iliad*. They constitute the oldest known literature.

By 2700 B.C., the Sumerians had established private and religious, as well as government, libraries. Among these libraries was one at Telloh which had a collection of over 30,000 tablets.

Sumer's culture passed to Babylonia in Lower Mesopotamia, a civilization which lasted until 689 B.C. and which produced Hammurabi and his notable code of laws. In both Sumerian and Babylonian writing, the characters represented syllables rather than letters.

The Babylonians used writing in business transactions and in recording noteworthy events; thus their books were devoted to government, law, history, and religion. It is believed that there were many libraries in the temples and palaces of Babylonia. While none of these survives, the tablets of one of the most important ones, the library of Borsippa, were copied in their entirety by the scribes of Assurbanipal, king of Assyria (d. ca. 626 B.C.), who preserved them in his library at Nineveh. These duplicates of the tablets from Borsippa are the chief sources of our knowledge of Babylonian life.

The kingdom of Assyria, which existed at the same time as Babylonia, also inherited Sumeria's language and method of writing, but modified the written characters until they resembled those of the Babylonians. The most important library in Assyria was established at Nineveh by Assurbanipal. Tens of thousands of clay tablets were brought to this great royal library by the king's scribes, who traveled throughout Babylonia and Assyria to copy and translate the writings they found. The catalog of the Nineveh library was a listing of the contents of each cubicle or alcove, painted or carved on the entrance, where the clay tablets were arranged according to subject or type. Each tablet had an identification tag.

Among the most famous surviving specimens of cuneiform writing are the Code of Hammurabi,[1] now in the Louvre Museum in Paris, and the Gilgamesh Epic, part of which is the Babylonian story of the great flood. The key to this system of writing is the Behistun Inscription, which is located on the side of a mountain in Iran (Persia). Written in three languages (Persian, Babylonian, and Elamite), it was deciphered by Sir Henry Rawlinson when he was consul at Baghdad in 1844.

The Egyptians

The civilization of ancient Egypt flourished simultaneously with the Sumerian, Bablyonian, and Assyrian civilizations. The earliest known writings of the Egyptians date from ca. 3000 B.C. The writing material was the papyrus sheet,[2] and the instrument for writing was a brushlike pen made by fraying the edges of a reed.

Papyrus was far from satisfactory as a writing material, for there was constant danger of punching through it in the process of writing. Also, it was susceptible to damage from water and dampness, and when it was dry, it was very fragile and brittle. In spite of these limitations, however, papyrus was the accepted writing material throughout the ancient Mediterranean world and is known to have been used as late as A.D. 1022.

The form of the book in ancient Egypt was the roll, usually a little more than 12 inches high and about 20 feet long, made from papyrus sheets pasted end to end. The style of writing was hieroglyphic, a word derived from the Greek *hieros*, meaning "sacred," and *glyphein*, meaning "to carve." Hieroglyphic writing, as old as the earliest Egyptian dynasty, was used as late as A.D. 394.

The Egyptians developed an alphabet of twenty-four consonants, but they did not adopt a completely alphabetic style of writing. They mixed

---

[1] The Code of Hammurabi was not written on clay but was carved on a diorite cylinder. Diorite is a granular, crystalline, igneous rock.

[2] To make a papyrus sheet, the marrow of papyrus stalks was cut into thin strips and laid flat, side by side, one layer crossways over the other. The two layers were treated with a gum solution, pressed, pounded, and smoothed until the surface was suitable for writing, and then sized to resist the ink.

pictographs, ideographs, and syllabic signs with their letters and developed a sketchy kind of writing for manuscripts, but the sacred carvings on their monuments were hieroglyphic.

Egyptian scribes were trained in the temple schools to learn to draw at least 700 different characters (hieroglyphs).

Writing was done in columns without spaces between words, without punctuation marks, and usually without titles; the text began at the extreme right and continued right to left. Egyptian rolls included religious, moral, and political subjects. The Prisse Papyrus in the Bibliothèque Nationale in Paris—the oldest Egyptian book known—is believed to have been written before the end of the third millennium (2880) B.C.; it contains the proverbial sayings of Ptahhotep. The longest Egyptian manuscript in existence, more than 130 feet long, is the Harris Papyrus, a chronicle of the reign of Rameses II.

The key to hieroglyphic writing is the Rosetta Stone, which was discovered near the mouth of the Nile in 1799 by a young officer of Napoleon's expeditionary force in Egypt. In 1821 this flat slab of slate, bearing an inscription in three styles of writing—hieroglyphic, demotic (popular), and Greek—gave to Jean François Champollion, the French Egyptologist, the clue needed to decipher the Egyptian hieroglyphics. It is now preserved in the British Museum in London.

Little is known about Egyptian libraries. There may have been private and temple libraries as well as government archives. Records indicate that a library existed at Gizeh in the 2500s B.C., and it is known that Rameses II founded one at Thebes about 1250 B.C. Rolls were kept in clay jars or in metal cylinders with an identifying key word on the outside or on the end, or they were stacked on shelves.

Other Semitic peoples

In addition to the Babylonians and the Assyrians, other Semitic peoples inhabited that part of the near east known as the "fertile crescent."[3] Among them were the Phoenicians. Phoenicia was the name given in ancient times to a narrow strip of land about 100 miles long and 10 miles wide between Syria and the sea.

The Phoenicians were traders, and an important item in their wares was papyrus, which they imported from Egypt and exported to all the countries along the Mediterranean. It is believed that wherever the Phoenicians took papyrus, they also took the Egyptian alphabet. History gives them major

---

[3] The region bounded by the Taurus and the mountains of Armenia and Iran, the Persian Gulf, the Indian Ocean and the Red Sea, Egypt and the Mediterranean (*Cambridge Ancient History*, I 1924, 182).

credit for spreading the knowledge and use of the alphabetic characters which had been developed in Egypt, Crete, and Syria and which form the basis of Greek and of all European writing. The Phoenicians were not a literary people; writing and books were to them merely means of keeping their numerous commercial accounts, and in time they developed a cursive, flowing style of writing and replaced the cumbersome clay tablets with papyrus sheets.

The Chinese

The art of writing was known in China as early as the third millennium B.C. Materials on which the Chinese wrote included bone, tortoiseshell, bamboo stalks, wooden tablets, silk, and linen, and their writing instruments were the stylus, the quill, and the brush pen, depending upon the particular writing material used. The style of writing involved the use of characters, mainly ideographic, and book forms were the tablet and the roll. Little is known about their libraries.

The Greeks

In the early part of the second millennium B.C., Crete became the center of a highly developed civilization which spread to the mainland of Greece and, before the end of the fifteenth century B.C., throughout the entire Aegean area. The Cretans developed the art of writing from a pictographic system to a cursive form, now called "Linear A," and by the fifteenth century B.C. to a system now called "Linear B." Many scholars believe that the language of Linear B tablets is an early form of Greek which was spoken by the Mycenaeans who occupied Knossos about 1460 B.C. and eventually overthrew the Minoan kingdom. After 1200 B.C. the Mycenaean world ceased to exist and the script disappeared. A period of illiteracy is believed to have existed from this time until the Greeks adopted the consonantal twenty-two-letter alphabet of the Phoenicians in the eighth century B.C.

Of the seventh and sixth centuries B.C., only fragments of literature remain, but these fragments show the beginnings of new forms of poetry, notably the elegy and the choral lyric, and the birth of philosophy and scientific research. The fables of Aesop date from this period.

The fifth century was the golden age of Greek civilization, a period characterized by the highest form of literary creativity: the tragedies of Sophocles, Aeschylus, and Euripides; the lyric poetry of Pindar; the histories of Thucydides and Herodotus; the comedies of Aristophanes; and the philosophy of Socrates. This period, also referred to as the "Classical Age," extended through the fourth and into the third centuries B.C., finding expression in the works of Plato and Aristotle, as well as in drama, poetry, oration, and music.

During the Hellenistic period, which dated from the death of Alexander in 323 B.C. to the Roman conquest, the literary activities of the preceding century continued and there was a new emphasis on scientific knowledge (in the works of Euclid and Archimedes), on art, and on rhetoric.

In ancient Greece the materials used to receive writing were leaves or bark of trees, stone or bronze for inscriptions, and wax-coated wooden tablets for messages or notes. From the sixth century B.C., papyrus, which the Phoenicians brought from Egypt, was the usual writing material. In Hellenistic Greece, parchment and vellum came into use.[4]

The use of parchment and vellum made necessary the development of a new kind of writing instrument, the broad-pointed pen made from a reed or a quill. Parchment proved to be a better medium for writing than papyrus because it was smooth on both sides and was less likely to tear. Papyrus competed with it for three centuries, however, and only in the fourth century after Christ did parchment become dominant.

The forms of Greek books were the roll, the wax tablet, and the codex, in which the papyrus or parchment leaves of the manuscript were fastened together as in a modern book. The subject matter of Greek books included literature, history, science, mathematics, philosophy, religion, and politics.

Early Greek writing resembled that of the Phoenicians, who had brought them the alphabet, but gradually the Greeks changed the forms of the letters, added vowels, changed some consonants to vowels, developed lowercase letters, and began writing from left to right. The first books did not have spaces between words or punctuation marks of any kind. Change from one topic to another was indicated by a horizontal dividing stroke called the *paragraphos*, and if the roll had a title, it was located at the end. Before the conquest of Greece by the Romans, Greek grammarians had introduced some forms of punctuation.

Aristotle (384-322 B.C.) is said to have been the first person to collect, preserve, and use the culture of the past. The story of his library is told by Strabo. In Hellenistic Greece there were private, governmental, and royal libraries.

The greatest libraries were in Alexandria in Egypt. The Museion, founded by Ptolemy I (323-285 B.C.) as an essential part of the academy of scholars under his patronage, is reported to have reached a total of 200,000 rolls within five years. It is said that foreigners were required, upon entering the Alexandria harbor, to surrender any books in their possession, later receiving copies in exchange for the originals. By the time of the Roman conquest, it contained 700,000 rolls, including manuscripts from all parts of the known world, written in Egyptian, Hebrew, Latin, and other languages.

---

[4] Parchment was the skin of animals, principally that of the sheep or the calf, prepared for writing. Vellum, which is made from the skin of calves, is heavier than parchment and more expensive. It is probably the most beautiful and the most lasting material ever used for books.

The second library, the Serapeum, founded by Ptolemy III (r. 246-221 B.C.) and located in the Temple of Serapis, grew to more than 100,000 volumes. Although there is not complete agreement regarding the fate of the Alexandrian libraries, many historians date the destruction of the Museion from Julius Caesar's campaign in Alexandria in 47 B.C. and that of the Serapeum from the reign of Theodosius the Great (A.D. 379-395), whose edicts against paganism resulted in the destruction of many pagan temples.

Second in importance to the libraries at Alexandria was the one at Pergamum, founded by Eumenes II (197-159 B.C.). Pergamum became outstanding for patronage of arts and letters, and book production was so intense that an embargo was placed by the Egyptians on the exportation of papyrus, with the hope of discouraging the copying of books. This act led to the increased production of parchment for use as a writing material.

According to Plutarch, Calvisius, a friend of Caesar, charged that Antony gave to Cleopatra the entire library at Pergamum, which contained 200,000 distinct volumes.[5]

The Romans

The Romans continued the Greek tradition in books. Through commerce with Greece, Rome had early adopted the Greek alphabet, and Greek culture became important in Rome following the first Punic war (264-241 B.C.). By the time of the Roman conquest of Greece, the Romans were under the influence of the Greeks to the extent that they read and studied their literature, philosophy, and science, sent their sons to Athens to be educated, and at times spoke Greek. Latin literature began in the second century B.C.

The materials which the Romans used for writing were papyrus, parchment, vellum, wood tablets coated with wax, the stylus, the split-point reed, and the split-feather quill.

The Romans developed a style of handwriting unlike the ordinary cursive writing for use in literary works. Much like the Greek, it consisted largely of capital letters. By the end of the fourth century after Christ, another style, called "uncial script," which involved the use of large, somewhat rounded letters was the standard book script and continued as such until the end of the eighth century.

The forms of the book in ancient Rome were the roll, the wax tablet, the diptych (two boards hinged together at one side with waxed surfaces on the inside for writing), and the codex.

Since the roll was relatively inconvenient to write upon and to read, it was superseded inevitably by the more usable form, the codex, which was used to some extent by the Greeks and which is known to have been in use

---

[5] *Plutarch's Lives of Illustrious Men*, corrected from the Greek and revised by A. H. Clough (Boston: Little, Brown, 1930) 674.

among the Christians in the second century after Christ. From that time the codex generally was used for Christian works, even though the papyrus roll was continued in use for pagan works.

Roman books included all known fields of knowledge: law, science, mathematics, philosophy, politics, and religious and secular literature. The earliest known fragment of a manuscript book is the Papyrus Rylands, a tiny piece of a papyrus leaf of the Gospel according to St. John, dated (from the style of writing) in the first half of the second century after Christ. The Codex Vaticanus of the fourth century after Christ is the oldest extant manuscript of antiquity.

Roman generals brought back entire libraries from the campaigns in Greece, and these libraries, considered spoils of war, became their private collections.

Julius Caesar drew up plans for public libraries, but his plans were not carried out until the reign of Augustus, when Asinius Pollio established the first public library in Rome between 39 and 27 B.C. By the middle of the fourth century after Christ there were at least twenty-eight public libraries in Rome, and they were used by any person, slave or free, who could read.

The Ulpian Library, founded by Trajan—a scholarly collection housed in two structures, one for Latin and one for Greek works—was second in importance among ancient libraries only to those at Alexandria and Pergamum. In Roman libraries, Greek works were kept on one side of the library, and Latin works were placed on the other side; they were arranged according to subject on shelves or in bins. Except in rare cases, books had to be used in the reading rooms.

THE MIDDLE AGES

Monasteries

With the disintegration of the western Roman Empire[6] came the decline of classical literature, and all libraries, including Christian collections, suffered at the hands of the barbarians.It was in the monasteries that literature was preserved and developed during the Middle Ages.

In the last half of the sixth century, under the leadership of Cassiodorus, the monastery became a center for all studies and for the preservation of all writings, both religious and secular. In southern Italy, Cassiodorus established the monastic community of Vivarium. He set up a great library which

---

[6] Emperor Diocletian (A.D. 284-305) had divided the Roman Empire into eastern and western spheres. In 330, Constantine, then emperor of both the east and the west, moved the capital from Rome to Constantinople. When the western part of the Roman Empire fell in 476, the eastern part (called the "Byzantine Empire") was entering upon a period of progress which was to last 1000 years.

included manuscripts of the great literature of the past—Greek and Latin, pagan and Christian—and established a scriptorium (writing room) for the copying of Christian and secular literature, thus assuring the preservation of much ancient writing which would otherwise have been lost during those troubled times.

After Cassiodorus, intellectual activity came to a standstill in western Europe, except in Ireland. In the sixth century, numerous Irish monasteries came into existence and in their scriptoria a national script and a national art evolved and the first great development of manuscript books was begun— books which were characterized by superb calligraphy and illumination[7] and fine workmanship. Irish manuscript art reached its height in the *Book of Kells*, a manuscript of the Gospels, written in the eighth century and believed to be the most richly decorated manuscript ever produced in an Irish scriptorium.

Irish missionaries established monastic centers in Scotland, northern England, and continental Europe, including Lindisfarne in Northumbria, Luxeuil in France, and Bobbio in northern Italy.

During the eighth century, missionaries from the English church also established monasteries on the continent. Most notable of the English missionaries was St. Boniface, whose greatest monastery was at Fulda in Germany.

The reign of Charles the Great, or Charlemagne (768-814), marked by his efforts to raise the educational level of his subjects, brought to western Europe a period of educational and cultural growth. Alcuin, master of the school at York in Northumbria, was chosen by Charlemagne to direct his educational program. In 782, as head of the Palace School in Aachen, Alcuin began the task of establishing educational centers and disseminating learning throughout the Frankish Empire. Scriptoria were established in monasteries and a carefully planned system of selecting, collecting, and copying religious and secular literature was begun. When Alcuin retired from the Palace School to the monastery of St. Martin at Tours, he made the monastery a center of learning, and the works copied in the scriptorium served as models for copyists for many generations. This revival of learning during the time of Charlemagne is called the "Carolingian Renaissance."

In the scriptoria of countless monasteries in continental Europe, Ireland, and England, as well as in the Byzantine Empire and the Moslem world, manuscripts were copied and recopied by the monks and by secular scribes who were often brought in for special tasks. These manuscripts tell us much of what we know of the ancient world. In these institutions were preserved the books of the Bible; the epics of Homer; the poetry of Virgil; the Greek dramas; and the scientific, legal, and philosophical works of the great minds of antiquity.

---

[7] Decorations of ornamental letters, scrolls, and miniatures—small paintings in color.

The chief materials used by the monks for writing were plain or dyed parchment or vellum, quill pens, and many kinds of colored inks. The forms of the book were the roll and the codex.

Early monastic libraries were small. Manuscripts were expensive: a large Bible was bought for 10 talents (about $10,000), and a missal was exchanged for a vineyard. A monastery library would have many copies of the Bible, the service books of the church, lives of the saints, early Christian writings, law, poetry, and some classical works.

Books were kept in chests or cupboards, or they were brought out and chained to desks for safety. Most of the reading was done standing up. In general, books were arranged by subject or kind—religious or secular, Greek or Latin, At first, catalogs were rough checklists. Later, a fuller and more precise description of a book and its contents was given in the listing.

Universities

From the fall of Rome to the twelfth century, education was in the hands of the monastery, and instruction was chiefly theological. Some instruction was given to sons of noblemen and, in some cases, to promising children of the poor. In trading centers there were schools to train clerks.

By the middle of the twelfth century, men were going to school to study Latin grammar and other basic subjects. The rise of cathedral schools, the study of Latin grammar, the appearance of writing in the vernacular (the language of the masses), and the increasingly favorable social and economic conditions gave rise to the universities.

The university of this period was a group of teachers organized as a kind of guild and empowered by either religious or civil government to grant degrees. The outstanding universities of the Middle Ages were the universities of Bologna, Paris, Prague, Heidelberg, Oxford, and Cambridge.

Book dealers (*stationarii*) and their scribes were an important part of every medieval university. They were appointed or controlled by the university to guarantee the authenticity of texts. They kept in stock correct editions of books used for instruction and rented them to the students. Dealers in parchment and vellum were licensed by the university. Since the universities constituted both the chief supply of books and the chief demand for them, they became the main centers of the book trade and of the publishing (copying) business. Book forms were the roll and the codex.

There was little need for libraries as long as the students could rent the texts they needed. However, as the number of students increased, the universities were forced to establish libraries. In time, books were given by individuals to the universities for the use of students.

Each college within a university had its own library. Arrangement and organization were similar to those of the larger monastery libraries except that books were divided according to the subject taught. They were arranged according to size or accession, sometimes on shelves rather than in chests. The more important books were still chained to the desks.

The Renaissance

In Italy during the fourteenth century, Petrarch and Boccaccio were laying the foundations for a new revival of learning. They searched medieval monasteries for old manuscripts, and many long-lost Latin works were recovered. The fall of Constantinople in 1453 aided the revival of learning by dispersing to Europe many works of ancient Greek and Latin literature. This period, the Renaissance (also called the "age of humanism"), was characterized by the unceasing search for missing ancient Greek and Latin works and the intense effort to read and understand them and to imitate their style and form. Florence became the center of the Italian Renaissance, and under the Medici saw the most brilliant development of culture since the Golden Age of Greece.

Printing with movable types

The zeal for learning which characterized the Renaissance brought a demand for books which could no longer be satisfied by handwritten copies. The need for a new and faster medium for transmitting knowledge was urgent. In northern Europe by the middle of the fifteenth century, this medium had been developed: printing with movable types

The success of printing depended upon a cheap substance on which to print, an ink which would adhere to type, a press which could apply heavy pressure over a larger frame, and a general knowledge of metal technology.

By the second quarter of the fifteenth century, these needs had been met. Paper was a cheap and plentiful material on which to print. Discovered in China in the second century but used little by the Chinese, paper had traveled west along the trade routes. It was brought to Persia in the eighth century; it was displacing papyrus in Egypt in the ninth century; the Moslems used it in Spain in the eleventh and twelfth centuries; it was manufactured in southern Italy in 1270; and by the end of the fourteenth century, it was manufactured in France and Germany. The material used in making paper was linen rags.[8]

A suitable ink was developed by adapting the oil paints which the artists of the time were using.

---

[8] The linen rags were softened to a pulp and molded into sheets on a wooden frame. The sheets were drained, pressed and pressed again, hung to dry completely, and then sized to make them impervious to ink.

The screw presses which were used for pressing olives and grapes and in binding manuscript books were used to apply pressure over a large frame.

The general knowledge of metal technology, which was essential to the success of printing, was borrowed from the goldsmiths and silversmiths. Carving of woodblocks for wood-block printing and engraving on metal by goldsmiths and silversmiths had reached a high degree of perfection. This knowledge was easily transferred to the process of making metal types.

Perhaps no event in human cultural history exceeds in importance the invention of printing with movable types.[9] Learning, which was formerly confined to monasteries or available only to the student, particularly the wealthy student, was now within reach of any person who wished to pursue it.

Movable word types made of clay originated in China but were used very little. It is to Johann Gutenberg, born in Mainz, Germany, about 1400, that credit is given for the development of printing with movable types. His creative genius combined the available materials and supplied the remaining essentials which made possible the printing of the famous 42-line Bible, commonly called the "Gutenberg Bible," between 1450 and 1456. This was the first book printed with movable types.

The printed book was new only in the way it was made; it was not new in appearance. The types were similar to manuscript writing. Space was left for illumination and rubrication,[10] which were done by hand. The first illustrations were woodcuts. This similarity to the handwritten book continued for more than a hundred years.

The first printed works are called "incunabula" (from the Latin *incunabulum*, meaning "cradle"), indicating that printing was in its infancy. The subject matter of early printed books included the Bible and other religious works, textbooks, histories, travel books, and literature of all kinds.

During the last quarter of the fifteenth century, printing spread to all major cities of Europe. More than 20,000 different works and editions of this period survive. The first book printed in the English language was the *Recuyell of the Histories of Troy*, printed between 1474 and 1476 by William Caxton, who learned the art of printing in order to be able to print his own translation of this work.

---

[9] The Babylonians and the Egyptians had used metal or wooden seals to print on soft clay or on wax; the Romans printed symbols on coins and stamped official documents with a carved seal; as early as the fifth and sixth centuries, the Chinese used carved seals to print short mottoes and charms. The full-page woodcut, printed from a wooden block on which the text and illustrations had been carved, was the next step in printing. By the ninth century, the Chinese produced a complete book printed in this manner. This kind of book was called a block book. The *Diamond Sutra*, a block book printed in A.D. 868, has survived. By the tenth century, printing in this manner was common in China. In Europe there were woodcut prints by the fourteenth century.

[10] Rubrication was writing or underlining in a color (e.g., red) a heading or a part of a book or a manuscript.

The sixteenth century is notable for the rise of a large number of printing families, each with its own specialty. The House of Estienne, for example, printed Greek and Latin classics. The French printer Geoffroy Tory was responsible for introducing the accent, the apostrophe, and the cedilla into the French language; and in Venice, Aldus Manutius developed a system of punctuation marks. By 1700 the printed book had reached its present form, with a title page, illustrations, a table of contents, and even a kind of index.

The invention of printing provided an unparalleled and effective impetus to the rebirth of learning. Precious manuscripts of the past, formerly copied one at a time by hand, could be reproduced in multiple copies and passed on to those who eagerly sought them. By making written works quickly available, the printing press also encouraged the production of new literature, and in this way it helped to create the "professional literati." The printing press and the increased dissemination of printed materials contributed significantly to the spread of the Reformation, and the stimulus which it gave to mapmaking hastened the era of discovery and exploration.

1500 TO 1900

Europe

Books after 1500 varied widely both in format and in content. There were many large volumes, many very small ones. Bookbindings ranged from ornate, bejewelled, gold-tooled leather to plain vellum and, eventually, paper. Printing types ceased to be copies of manuscript writing and assumed an identity all their own. In the sixteenth and seventeenth centuries periodicals were published; in the late seventeenth century newspapers appeared.

The contents of books during these centuries included religious and classical subjects, as well as science, superstition, travel, and romance.

The nineteenth century brought new mechanical developments, including stereotyping and the cylinder press. The first successful effort to set type mechanically and thus speed up printing was the invention of the linotype machine by Ottmar Mergenthaler in 1866. Other inventions followed.

In the nineteenth century there was much fine printing, especially in England. Wood came into use as a material for paper, books were bound with cloth, and copyright legislation was enacted.

In Europe, libraries flourished during the period from 1500 to 1900. Italy was outstanding for the number and quality of libraries in the sixteenth century. The Laurentian Library in Florence, the Ambrosian Library in Milan, and the Vatican Library in Rome were the most important.

In France, the Bibliothèque Nationale (which had its origins in the collections formed by the kings of France and dates from Francis I) was moved to Paris by Charles IX (1560-1574) and was greatly expanded and enlarged by Louis XIV (1643-1715).

Germany had the finest libraries of the nineteenth century. State libraries and university libraries were outstanding for size, content, and organization. There were also circulating libraries with catalogs, popular reading rooms, and children's collections.

The libraries of Oxford University, Cambridge University, and the British Museum (the National Library) were the most important in England.

The Austrian Royal Library, the royal library at Brussels, and the university libraries at Ghent and Louvain were other important libraries founded between 1500 and 1900.

America

Among the valued possessions which the early settlers brought to America or imported as necessities as soon as they were settled were books. Even though a printing press was in operation in Massachusetts as early as 1639, books had to be imported from England and the Continent for many generations. The earliest book known to have been printed in colonial America was *The Bay Psalm Book*, printed in 1640.

Important private libraries of the early colonial period were those of Elder Brewster of the Plymouth Colony (about 400 different works), John Winthrop (over 1000 volumes), and John Harvard (more than 300 volumes). Outstanding eighteenth-century libraries were those of Cotton Mather of Boston (between 3000 and 4000 volumes), James Logan of Philadelphia (more than 2000 volumes), and William Byrd II of Virginia (3600 titles).

In 1731, Benjamin Franklin and a group of his friends in Philadelphia established the first subscription library, a voluntary association of individuals who contributed to a common fund to be used for the purchase of books, which every member had the right to use but whose ownership was retained by the group. Subscription libraries (also called "social libraries") of several forms and names flourished for more than a century. Their collections, at first largely moral and theological in content, in time included history, biography, literature, travel, and scientific materials.

The first colleges in the American colonies—Harvard (1638), William and Mary (1695), Yale (1700), and Princeton (1746)—began with, or were accompanied by, gifts of books. Although the Massachusetts General Court voted in 1636 to set aside £400 for the establishment of a "schoole or colledge," Harvard was not opened until 1638, when John Harvard bequeathed to the new college one-half of his estate and his entire library of 320 volumes. Yale College began with forty books. Each of the eleven clergymen who met in 1700 for the purpose of forming a college brought a number of books which he gave "for the founding of a college in this colony" (Connecticut). Most of the volumes in the early college libraries were books on theology, but there were also copies of the classics and of philosophical and literary works. By 1725 the Harvard Library had 3000 books, and was the largest college library in the colonies.

Before the Revolution nine colleges were formed in the colonies, and by the time of the Civil War more than 500 colleges and twenty-one state universities had been established.

In the early college libraries there was no effort to make books available to students; rather, it seemed, books were protected from the students. This protective attitude continued throughout the nineteenth century, and as late as the 1850s, some college libraries were open only one hour every two weeks, others one hour twice a week, and a few one hour a day. In some libraries, attempts were made to classify books into three groups: memory, judgment, and imagination; or history, philosophy, and poetry. In others, books were arranged according to appearance, accession, or donor. The location symbol for books gave the physical location only and did not indicate the subject class to which the book belonged. Catalogs were printed lists, with little information about the books.

Following the Revolution, historical societies were formed to collect materials important in the history of the state or territory and a library was an essential part of each society. The Library of Congress (LC) was established in 1800 to serve the needs of the Congress,[11] and in the following decades state and territorial libraries were organized to collect and preserve publications of the state or territory and to serve the needs of the state or territorial government.

The first tax-supported town library in the United States was established in Peterborough, New Hampshire, in 1833. But it was not until 1854, when the Boston Public Library was opened to the public, that the free, public, tax-supported library became a part of American life.

By 1890 the public library had become an established institution in America, and the organization and development of libraries was given added impetus after that time by the state library commissions, which were established to aid in founding libraries and in improving and extending their services.

In 1876 the American Library Association was organized to promote libraries and librarianship throughout the United States. That same year Melvil Dewey published the first edition of his *Decimal Classification*, and eleven years later organized—at Columbia University—the first library school for the training of professional librarians, which he served as director. At the close of the nineteenth century in the United States, there was a developing interest in all libraries and in the training of persons for library positions. Financial aid during the last quarter of the nineteenth century and

[11] See pp. 45-46.

into the first quarter of the twentieth century came from gifts of private philanthropy. The greatest individual benefactor of libraries was Andrew Carnegie, whose gifts totaled over $41 million. Other benefactors included the Rockefeller Foundation, the Ford Foundation, and individual philanthropists who have opened their collections of rare books to the public. Examples of rare-book libraries are the Pierpont Morgan Library in New York City and the Folger Shakespeare Library in Washington, D.C.

THE TWENTIETH CENTURY

During the first half of the twentieth century, libraries maintained a steady growth, continuing to perform the traditional services: building collections, circulating materials, giving reference service, etc. Collections were small. By the time of World War II, there were more than 1500 academic libraries in the United States. The major concern of the academic library at that time was to acquire and preserve materials. The textbook was the chief method of instruction, and there was little need for library materials.

New emphases on learning in the late forties and fifties, such as the teaching of science, mathematics, and foreign languages, called for new methods of instruction and new materials; and libraries began to acquire various kinds of nonprint sources: audio, visual, audiovisual, and microforms.

From 1956–1965, Congress passed a succession of legislative acts to provide financial aid to public, school, academic, and research libraries: the Library Services Act (1956) and the Library Services and Construction Act (1964) for public libraries; the Elementary and Secondary Education Act (1965) for schools; and the Higher Education Act and Higher Education Facilities Act (1965) for college, university, and research libraries. The aid provided by all of this legislation resulted in tremendous growth of all libraries, both in collections and in facilities.

Evolving space technology in the 1960s spurred interest in science and technology and added to research already being conducted in those areas. The increasing importance and use of information resulting from research was seen in the rapid development of facilities for the purpose of identifying, collecting, evaluating, and disseminating information and in the numerous methods being used in an effort to speed up those processes.

Information quickly became vital not only in science and technology but in all disciplines, resulting in a flood of publications. This explosion of information—books, reports, papers, journals, etc.—called for faster and more ways of managing it and more efficient means of access to it. Libraries, like all other agencies concerned with information handling, turned to technology. The technology was available in the form of the electronic digital computer.

The electronic digital computer

In 1946, the first electronic digital computer, ENIAC,[12] was switched on at the Army Proving Grounds in Aberdeen, Maryland, for the purpose of providing computational assistance in the national defense program. It was large enough to fill a two-car garage, weighed about 30 tons, and cost about half a million dollars.[13] Yet so highly regarded were the demonstrated capabilities and the assumed potential of ENIAC that "the age of automation" is usually thought of as dating from that time.

The enormous size and cost of computers limited their use for more than a decade to large businesses, corporations, and government agencies that could afford them. Within a decade, over 5000 mainframe computers were used worldwide. The development of the microcomputer in 1985 brought the computer into the office. The personal computer, the PC, became "the basic building block of the information society."[14] It offered entertainment at first but is now used in businesses; homes; research, education, and library activities; and information centers.

Discovery of new uses for the computer and auxiliary machines has continued, and today few, if any, areas of life are untouched by the many constructive things being done by them. Along with the development of new uses, there has been steady improvement in the performance and capabilities of computers, especially in their calculation speed, their storage capacity, their compactness and flexibility, and the relative economy of their operation.

The term information retrieval came into use when technology grew in importance and when demands for specific bits of utilitarian information accelerated. The term covers a variety of recovery-of-information activities such as reference retrieval via library catalogs, document retrieval, and data or fact retrieval.

Over the years, libraries have used various technologies to acquire, organize, store, and disseminate information and knowledge, including the telephone, typewriter, paper tape, punched cards, copy machines, microforms, audio, visual, and audiovisual forms. Computers were first used in carrying on the routine library tasks such as bookkeeping, payroll, personnel files, maintaining inventories, and making lists.

In the early 1960s, the Library of Congress began to study the possibility of using computer technology to catalog library materials. By 1966, the success of this effort, Machine Readable Cataloging (MARC), led to

---

[12] Electronic Numerical Integrator and Computer.

[13] See Tom Forester, ed., *The Information Technology Revolution* (Oxford: Basil Blackwell, 1985) xiii. Today the same amount of computing power is contained in a pea-sized silicon chip.

[14] Forester, xv.

computerized cataloging, the establishment of cooperative cataloging databases, and the online public access catalog (OPAC), which is in wide use in academic libraries today.

Other electronic devices have followed: online searching of commercial databases; the CD-ROM (Compact Disk Read-Only Memory), on which are stored indexes; reference sources of various kinds and books; electronic journals; electronic books; E-mail; telecommunications electronic bulletin boards; and many more—all of which have found their place in the library.

So rapid is the move to electronic formats that there are many who predict the library of the future will be paperless: everything will be in digital form and access will be by computer or computer controlled devices.[15] Others see the library of the future as a blending of old and new technologies: the traditional library elements existing with the new, each serving its own purposes. The library will continue to adopt and utilize new technologies as it has already adopted and is utilizing such new technologies as the film, television, microfilm, the computer, the CD-ROM, the electronic book and journal, E-mail, telefacsimile, and others.[16]

Today, there are more than 115,000 libraries in the United States— public, academic, school, and special, with collections ranging from under 20,000 to more than a million volumes.[17] New library construction continues, and in 1993 there are 780 new library building projects in progress.[18]

Emphasis in libraries is on access to information, and many experiments and efforts are underway to achieve it. Among the notable experiments is American Memory, inaugurated by the Library of Congress in 1989. This six-year pilot program is the first step in the long-term effort of the Library of Congress to provide access to the collections of the library by electronic means to local library users all over the United States. The collections will be available in the form of compact disks and video disks and, in the future, they will be accessible online.[19]

[15] See Lauren Seiler and Thomas Surprenant, "When We Get the Libraries We Want, Will We Want the Libraries We Get?" *Wilson Library Bulletin* 65 (September 1991): 29–31, 157.

[16] Susan Berg Epstein, "Technology, Building, and the Future," *Library Journal* 116 (December 1991): 112–114.

[17] Mary Jo Lynch, et al., *Libraries in an Information Society* (Chicago: ALA, 1987): 10.

[18] Bette-Lee Fox, et al., "Building a Better Tomorrow," *Library Journal* 117 (December 1992): 68.

[19] James H. Billington, "Library of Congress to Open Collections to Local Libraries in Electronic Access Plans," *American Libraries* 22 (1991): 706–709.

Bibliography

Augarten, Stan. *Bit By Bit: An Illustrated History of Computers.* London: Allen, 1985.

Bieler, Ludwig. *Ireland, Harbinger of the Middle Ages.* London: Oxford UP, 1963.

Billings, Harold. "The Bionic Library." *Library Journal* 116 (15 Oct. 1991): 38–45.

Brooke, Christopher. *The Monastic World 100–1300.* New York: Random, 1974.

Bury, J. B., S. A. Cook, and F. E. Adcock, eds. *The Cambridge Ancient History.* 2d ed. Vol. I: *Egypt and Babylonia to 1580 B.C.* New York: Cambridge UP, 1924.

Chiera, Edward. *They Wrote on Clay.* Chicago: U of Chicago P, 1938.

Durant, Will. *The Story of Civilization.* Vols. I–V. New York: Simon, 1944–1966.

Evans, Joan, ed. *The Flowering of the Middle Ages.* New York: McGraw, 1966.

Forester, Tom. *High-Tech Society: The Story of the Information Technology Revolution.* Cambridge: MIT, 1987.

———. *The Information Technology Revolution.* Cambridge: MIT, 1985.

Fox, Bette-Lee, et al. "Between a Recession and a Hard Place." *Library Journal* 116 (December 1991): 58–89.

Gates, Jean Key. *Introduction to Librarianship.* 2d ed. McGraw-Hill Series in Library Education. New York: McGraw, 1976.

———. *Introduction to Librarianship.* 3d ed. New York: Neal-Schuman, 1990.

Goodrum, Charles A. *Treasures of the Library of Congress.* New York: Abrams, 1980.

Grant, Michael, ed. *The Birth of Western Civilization: Greece and Rome.* New York: McGraw, 1964.

Grun, Bernard. *The Timetables of History: A Horizontal Linkage of People and Events.* New York: Simon, 1979.

Harris, Michael H. *History of Libraries in the Western World.* Metuchen: Scarecrow, 1984.

Herodotus. *The History of Herodotus.* Trans. George Rawlinson. New York: Tudor, 1941.

Hessel, Alfred. *History of Libraries.* 2d ed. Trans. Reuben Peiss. New York: Scarecrow, 1955.

Hobson, Anthony. *Great Libraries.* New York: Putnam's, 1970.

Hoffert, Barbara. "Books Into Bytes." *Library Journal* 117 (1 Sept. 1992): 130–135.

Jackson, Sidney L. *Libraries and Librarianship in the West: A Brief History.* McGraw-Hill Series in Library Education. New York: McGraw, 1974.

TABLE 1.1
Highlights in the history of books and libraries

PEOPLE OR PERIOD	APPROXIMATE DATES	KIND OF WRITING; MATERIALS USED	FORMS OF THE BOOK	KINDS OF LIBRARIES	EXAMPLES OF LIBRARIES	EXAMPLES OF WRITING
Prehistory		Pictographs Landmarks Word of mouth				Cave paintings
ANTIQUITY Sumerians Babylonians Assyrians	3600 B.C. 626 B.C.	Cuneiform Clay Stylus	Clay tablet Clay cylinder	Temple Government Private Royal	Telloh Borsippa Nineveh	Code of Hammurabi
Egyptians	3000 B.C.	Hieroglyphic writing Papyrus sheets Reed brush, inks Alphabet of 24 consonants	Roll	Temple Government Private	Gizeh Thebes	Prisse Papyrus Harris Papyrus Inscriptions
Phoenicians	2756 B.C.	Alphabet of 22 consonants Papyrus	Roll Sheet			
Chinese	3d millenium B.C.	Ideographic charac- ters Bone, bamboo, silk, linen	Tablet Roll	Temple		
Greeks (Crete) Greeks	2d millenium B.C. 6th century B.C.— 146 B.C.	Linear A Linear B Phoenician alphabet; added vowels Papyrus, vellum, parchment, wax- coated boards	Tablet Roll Wax tablet Codex	Private Royal Government	Alexandrian library Library at Pergamum Aristotle's library	
Romans	753 B.C. — 476 A.D.	Greek alphabet Papyrus, vellum, parchment, wax- coated boards, quill	Roll Codex Diptych Wax tablet	Private Government Public Christian Pagan	Ulpian library	
MIDDLE AGES Monasteries Western Europe	400 A.D.– 12th century after Christ	Alphabet Handwriting: different styles at each monastery	Roll Codex	Church Monastery Royal Private		Book of Kells

Period / Place	Materials / Technology	Formats	Ownership / Library types	Institutions	Examples
Ireland England 12th century–15th century Renaissance	Plain and dyed vellum, parchment; illumination Handwritten books Parchment, vellum	Roll Codex	Private Royal Church Monastery University	University of Paris	Book of Hours Greek and Latin works
Invention of printing with movable types 15th century	Printing with movable types Parchment Vellum Paper	Handwritten books; printed books; printed leaflets; calendars	Public Private Government Royal		Gutenberg Bible
1500–1900 Europe	Printing Paper	Handwritten books; printed books; periodicals; maps; pamphlets; newspapers	National Private Public University Royal	Vatican library Oxford Cambridge British Museum Bibliothèque Nationale	
America 1607–1776	Printing with movable types (1639) Paper	Printed books Almanacs Magazines Government publications Pamphlets Broadsides	College University Private Subscription	Harvard Yale William and Mary Princeton	Bay Psalm Book
America 18th and 19th centuries	Printing Paper	Printed book Paperbacks Broadsides Pamphlets Almanacs Magazines Maps Government publications	College University Private Public Government	Library of Congress Boston Public Library	Printing with movable type
America 20th century	Printing Paper Film Tapes Disks Computer printing Microforms Magnetic tape Optical disks Digitized text	Printed books Periodicals Audio, visual, audio-visual forms Microforms Databases Videoforms CD-ROMs Electronic books and journals CD-I	Academic Special Public School Research Private Government Rare-book archives	Library of Congress School, public, academic, research, and special libraries	Printed book Compact disks Electronic books and journals

Johnson, Elmer D. *A History of Libraries in the Western World*. New York: Scarecrow, 1965.

Kramer, Samuel Noah. *From the Tablets of Sumer*. Indian Hills: Falcon Wing's P, 1956.

McMurtrie, Douglas C. *The Book: The Story of Printing and Bookmaking*. New York: Oxford UP, 1943.

Piggott, Stuart, ed. *The Dawn of Civilization*. New York: McGraw, 1961.

Platt, Colin. *The Atlas of Medieval Man*. New York: St. Martin's, 1980.

Plutarch's Lives of Illustrious Men. Corrected from the Greek and rev. A. H. Clough. Boston: Little, Brown, 1930.

Posner, Ernst. *Archives in the Ancient World*. Cambridge: Harvard UP, 1972.

Rice, David Talbot, ed. *Dawn of European Civilization*. New York: McGraw, 1966.

Seiler, Lauren, and Thomas Surprenant. "When We Get the Libraries We Want, Will We Want the Libraries We Get?" *Wilson Library Bulletin* 65 (June 1991): 29–31, 157.

Shera, Jesse H. *Foundations of the Public Library: Origins of the Public Library Movement in New England from 1629–1855*. Chicago: U of Chicago P, 1949.

Tenopir, Carol. "Predicting the Future." *Library Journal* 116 (1 Oct. 1991): 70–72.

Thompson, James Westfall, *Ancient Libraries*. Berkeley: U of California P, 1940.

———. *The Medieval Library*. New York: Hafner, 1957.

Ver Steeg, Clarence L. *The Formative Years: 1607–1763*. The Making of America Series. New York: Hill, 1964.

Vervliet, Hendrik D. L., ed. *The Book through Five Thousand Years*. London: Phaidon, 1972.

Wright, Louis Booker. *The Cultural Life of the American Colonies*. The New American Nation Series. New York: Harper, 1957.

CHAPTER

2

The Parts of the Book

In order to understand and appreciate the importance, significance, and usefulness of each of the physical parts of a book, one needs only to recall the lack of aids to the reader in the early forms of the book.[1] Each of the parts of the book has been added because it contributes to the usefulness of the book and to the ease of use by the reader.

Physical Divisions of the Book

The physical divisions of the book can be grouped as follows: (1) the binding, (2) the preliminary pages, (3) the text, and (4) the auxiliary or reference material.

BINDING

The binding holds the leaves of the book together, protects them, and makes them easy to handle. It may be plain or decorated, and it may bear the author's name and the title. It has two important parts, the spine and the endpapers.

The spine is the binding edge of the book and carries the title or a brief form of it, the author's name, the publisher, and the call number if it is a library book.

The endpapers are pasted to the covers to make them stronger; they may carry useful information, such as tables, maps, graphs, and rules.

---

[1] See Chapter 1.

PRELIMINARY PAGES

The preliminary pages precede the body of the book and include the fly-leaves, the half-title page, the frontispiece, the title page, the copyright page, the dedication, the preface, the table of contents, lists of illustrative materials, and the introduction.

The flyleaves are blank pages next to the endpapers; they are the first and last leaves in the book.

The half-title page precedes the title page and serves as protection for it; it gives the brief title of the book and the series title if the book belongs to a series.[2] The series is important because it is included in the description of a work in a bibliography,[3] e.g.;

Lunt, William Edward. *History of England.* 4th ed. Harper's Historical Series. New York: Harper, 1957.

The frontispiece is an illustration relating to the subject matter of the book; it precedes the title page. Not all books have a frontispiece; it is most commonly found in a biographical work in which it is usually a picture of the biographee. A frontispiece is frequently found in an art book; it may be a reproduction of a painting or other work or a painting or photograph of an artist.

The title page is the first important printed page in the book; it includes the following items:

1. Title; that is, the name of the work
2. Subtitle, a descriptive phrase which clarifies or explains the main title
3. Author's name and, usually, facts concerning his or her status, such as academic position, academic degrees, or the titles of other works by the same author
4. Name of the editor, if there is one
5. Name of the illustrator or translator, if there is one
6. Name of the person who wrote the introduction, if other than the author
7. Edition,[4] if it is other than the first
8. Imprint, which includes the place of publication, the publisher, and the date of publication

[2] A series is a number of separate works issued successively and related to each other in subject, form, authorship, or publication.

[3] A bibliography is a list of works used in writing a book, a paper, or an article, or a list of works recommended for further reading. See also pp. 129–130 and the section on bibliography in Chapter 25.

[4] An edition is the total number of copies of a book or other publication printed from one set of type. A revised edition is a new edition in which the text of the original work has been changed or new material has been added. A revised edition will have a new copyright.

The title page is the authoritative source of information which is used in listing a source in a bibliography. If the title page is destroyed, facts of authorship, publication, etc., must be arrived at by tedious scientific processes such as a study of the kind of paper used and the watermark.[5]

Nonprint and nonbook sources do not have title pages in the same form that books have them, but they do have comparable sources of authoritative information. On a disk, descriptive (bibliographical) information is found on the label or the slipcase: title, performer, recording company, copyright date, contents, and production facts such as length in minutes, number of revolutions per minute (rpms), etc. On a filmstrip or film, it is found in the title frames at the beginning which give the title, subtitle, producer, photographer, place, publisher or distributor, and date. The label on a cassette gives title, performer(s), producer, place, date, and a contents note. On a microfilm or microfiche, the opening frames give author, title, producer or publisher, place, and date.

The back (verso) of the title page gives the date of the copyright,[6] the names of the copyright owners, and other information, including restrictions on photocopying.

The dedication page follows the title page and bears the name or names of the person or persons to whom the author dedicates the book.

The preface introduces the author to the reader and gives his or her reasons for writing the book; it indicates those for whom the book is intended, acknowledges indebtedness for services and assistance, and explains the arrangement, symbols and abbreviations used, and any special features.

The table of contents is a list of the chapters of the book with page numbers; it may be so detailed that it serves as an outline of the book.

The lists of illustrative material may include illustrations, maps, or tables.

The introduction describes the general subject matter and plan of the book.[7]

---

[5] A watermark is a marking in paper made by pressure of a design in the paper when it is molded into sheets, and visible when the paper is held up to the light.

[6] Copyright is the exclusive right to publish, reproduce, and sell a literary or an artistic work. The new copyright law, which took effect January 1, 1978, provides that for works already under statutory protection (created before January 1, 1978) the copyright term is twenty-eight years, renewable for forty-seven years. For works created after January 1, 1978, the new law provides a term lasting for the author's life and an additional fifty years after the author's death. (See Public Law 94-553 for additional information about copyright. See also p. 31.)

[7] The introduction may be written by the author, by a person of importance who has encouraged the author to write the book, or by one who considers the book an important contribution. It may be an elaboration of the preface, or it may be the first chapter in the book.

TEXT

The text is made up of the numbered chapters and constitutes the main body of the book.

AUXILIARY OR REFERENCE MATERIAL

The auxiliary or reference material follows the text and may include an appendix or appendixes, a bibliography, a glossary, notes, and one or more indexes.

An appendix may contain material referred to, but not explained, in the text (such as biographical or geographical information), or it may contain the text of a statement referred to in the text (such as the Library Bill of Rights).

A bibliography may be a list of the books, articles, and other materials which the author has used in writing the book, or it may be a list of materials recommended for further reading. A bibliography at the end of an article or a book, or as a separate publication, is an invaluable aid in research. It directs the user to additional sources which will be useful and points out different types of sources, such as books, journals, newspapers, and nonbook material, which might provide needed information.

The glossary is a section which lists and explains or defines all technical terms or foreign words not explained in the body of the book.

All footnotes, if they are not placed at the bottom of each page, may be placed in a section for notes. This section may contain explanations of certain passages in the text and descriptive information about the sources listed.

An index is a list of topics discussed in the text, arranged alphabetically with page references. An index may have subdivisions of the topics and cross references. The detailed subdivisions of the index are useful in limiting a subject or in suggesting headings under which to search in other sources such as the library catalog, indexes, and reference books for additional information on a topic.

Not all books have all the parts which have been discussed in the preceding paragraphs, nor do the parts always follow the order given in this chapter.

CHAPTER

3

Academic Libraries

Libraries in institutions of higher learning—academic libraries—are as varied and distinctive as the institutions which they serve. There are the libraries in community colleges and in four-year colleges, and there are the central libraries in the universities and the more specialized libraries in colleges within the universities. In each kind of institution, the purposes, staff, buildings, program of services, equipment, and physical facilities of the library are determined by the extent and nature of the curriculum, the size of the faculty and student body, the methods of instruction, the variety of graduate offerings, the needs of faculty and graduate students for advanced research materials, the amount of financial support, and whether or not the library is a part of an area, state, or regional cooperative system in which certain materials, equipment, and services may be shared.[1]

Function and Organization

Academic libraries differ from each other in many respects but they all have the same basic function, which is to aid the parent institution in carrying out its objectives. The library contributes to the realization of these objectives and supports the total program by acquiring and making available the books, materials, and services which are needed.

In carrying out its responsibility in the academic program effectively, the library[2] performs certain activities and offers certain services.

---

[1] See pp. 20, 30–31.
[2] "The library" refers to the professional staff and the personnel under its direction.

1. It selects and acquires books and materials through purchases and gifts.
2. It prepares these materials for the use of students, faculty, and others
    who require them. This preparation includes:
    a Classifying materials according to the classification system in use by
    the library.[3]
    b Cataloging these materials; that is, providing descriptive informa-
    tion about each one as to author, title, facts of publication, number
    of pages, illustrative material, and subject matter
    c Stamping, pasting, typing, and lettering
3. It makes these materials easily accessible physically through open
    shelves or other efficient means and bibliographically through catalogs,
    bibliographies, indexes, and thesauri.[4]
4. It circulates materials from the general collection and from the reserve
    collection. (Reserve materials are those in which class assignments have
    been made; they are kept together in one place and administered under
    special rules and regulations.)
5. It gives reference service. The reference staff answers questions that
    range from simple questions requiring only simple answers to questions
    that require lengthy searches of a number of different sources. The
    reference librarians assist the user in locating materials; give guidance in
    choosing materials for given purposes; aid the user in learning to use the
    various library materials: the catalog, the indexes, reference materials,
    microforms and other nonbook materials and the equipment they re-
    quire; suggest additional sources which might answer a question or
    provide additional information; provide assistance in defining a ques-
    tion or limiting a topic for a term paper and suggest sources which are
    helpful in the research for and the preparation of the term paper; and
    prepare bibliographies and reading lists on various subjects and make
    them available to library users.
6. It offers both formal and informal instruction in the use of the library.
    Regularly scheduled classes in the use of the library, which are taught
    by the reference staff, may be required or the courses may be electives.
    They usually carry one or two hours of college credit. The reference
    staff also gives lectures on specific topics and on special types of
    materials.
7. It borrows and lends materials on interlibrary loan. An interlibrary
    loan is a transaction in which library material, or a copy of the material,
    is made available by one library to another upon request. Since a
    library cannot own all materials, it borrows needed items through

[3] See Chapter 4.
[4] A thesaurus (plural, "thesauri") is a detailed list of subject headings.

interlibrary loan (ILL) from another library for the use of students and faculty members. Each library has a borrowing policy, that governs the kinds of material it will lend; the conditions under which material will be borrowed or loaned; the length of time material may be kept; the responsibility of the borrower regarding copyright[5]; the form of the ILL request; etc. Information regarding the purpose of ILL and the library's policies is provided by the reference department.

8. It provides adequate and comfortable physical facilities for study, including carrels and such aids as printing and photocopying devices. In some libraries, especially in community college libraries, facilities for graphic, photographic, audio, and video production are provided.

9. It may make bibliographical searches by computer through commercial databases. A fee may be charged for these searches.

10. It administers the total library program, including the budget, the organization and supervision of the various library activities, the maintenance of the building and equipment, and the public relations activities.

In most libraries, these activities are divided into departments such as the acquisitions department, the cataloging department, the circulation department, and the reference department, all of which are under the administrative head of the library. These departments may be subdivided according to specific activities, such as technical processes, or according to specific materials, such as audiovisual and other nonbook materials; they may be combined; and they may be given different names. Many academic libraries have departmental branches in the respective departments, such as a collection of materials in the history department. Others, especially university libraries, are organized departmentally according to subject areas, such as the education library or the engineering library, each with its own staff, collection, catalog, and services. In this type of organization, materials in each departmental catalog are also entered in the main catalog of the university library. Academic libraries may have other special departments or divisions,

---

[5] The copyright law which became effective January 1, 1978, established the conditions under which photocopies or reproductions of copyrighted works may be made. One specified condition is that the photocopy or reproduction is not to be "used for any purpose other than private study, scholarship, or research." If a user makes a request for or uses a photocopy or reproduction for any other purpose, that user may be liable for copyright infringement. Libraries are required by law to place a notice to this effect on photocopying machines, at places where orders for copies are accepted by libraries, and on all printed forms supplied by libraries for ordering copies. Other conditions of copyright are found in Section 107 and Section 108 of PL 94-553. The librarian will be able to explain the user's responsibility as well as the library's responsibilities in the matter of photocopying.

such as the rare-book room, the periodicals department, the government documents room, the curriculum laboratory, and so on.[6]

Kinds of Materials Provided

The quantity and diversity of library materials will vary according to the size, purpose, and the program of the college, but in most college libraries materials will include:

1. Reference sources of a general nature and reference sources in the subject fields, with emphasis upon the subject areas included in the instructional program.[7] These reference sources include dictionaries, encyclopedias, indexes, yearbooks, handbooks, atlases, gazetteers, bibliographies, reference histories like the *Cambridge Ancient History* and the *Cambridge History of American Literature*, and nonbook sources such as microforms.
2. A collection of materials containing:
    a Book and nonbook materials which relate to and supplement each curriculum offered, such as history, education, foreign languages, and mathematics.
    b Important general materials not relating to a specific subject area and important sources in subject fields not included in the college curriculums
    c Books and nonbook materials for voluntary and recreational reading, viewing, and listening
3. Periodicals and newspapers—current issues, bound volumes, and issues on microfilm and microfiche.
4. Pamphlets and clippings.
5. Audiovisual materials, which include pictures, motion picture films, slides, filmstrips, music, phonograph records, tape and disk recordings, maps, globes, cassettes, videotapes, and videocassettes.
6. Microfilm, microcards, microfiche, and other microforms.
7. Government publications.
8. Programmed materials.
9. Archival materials pertaining to the institution.

---

[6] In some institutions, the library is a department of a larger learning resources division which has, in addition, a language laboratory, classrooms, audiovisual department, and television studios.

[7] The academic library must support not only the traditional programs, but also such programs as independent study, tutorial, honors and seminar-type experiences, programs of study abroad, residence-hall libraries, year-round study, off-campus courses, and advanced research.

10. Equipment for the use of these materials, such as microreaders and listening and viewing equipment.
11. Terminals for on-line catalog and other searches—computer or CD-ROM.

Staff

The academic library is administered and staffed by professional librarians who have a broad, general education and the specializations which are required in each area of service offered by the library, such as specialties in the subject fields, in languages, in audiovisual and other nonbook materials, in guidance of readers, and in computer and other technologies. They have an understanding of the educational philosophy and teaching methods of the institution and work with the faculty in selecting and evaluating materials to support the instructional program. They keep up with trends in higher education, curriculum development, methods of teaching, and new materials and new sources of materials. They may teach a course in their specialty and they may participate in team teaching.

Rules and Regulations

In order that all students will have an equal opportunity to use the library materials, certain rules and regulations are established in all libraries. These rules govern the kinds of materials which are circulated, the length of time they can be borrowed, the fines charged for overdue books, the use of library facilities—reading rooms, listening rooms, conference rooms, and other special areas—interlibrary loans, photocopiers, computer searches, and the hours of service.

Orientation Visit

A part of the first-year orientation program in most colleges and universities is a visit to the library. In many libraries students are given a handbook which includes information about the physical arrangement of the library, the kinds of materials it provides, the classification system in use, the nature of the library catalog, the rules governing the use of the library, and the schedule of the hours the library is open.

PART

2

*The Organization
and Arrangement
of Library Materials*

CHAPTER

 4

Classification

Classification is the systematic arrangement of objects, ideas, books, or other items which have like qualities or characteristics into groups or classes. The like characteristics may be size, color, type, form, content, or some other feature.

Historical Development of the Classification of Books

Ever since there have been books, there has been the problem of organizing and arranging them so that they can be used easily and conveniently. Clay tablets were arranged on narrow shelves according to subject or type. Papyrus rolls were placed in clay jars or metal cylinders which were labeled with a few key words describing their content. Parchment rolls were divided by author or title or by major subject or form groups and were placed in bins or on shelves. In medieval monasteries, manuscripts were classified as religious or secular, Latin or Greek; or they were divided according to subject matter, and all books on a subject were kept in the same chest. Books in medieval university libraries were divided according to the subjects taught and were arranged by size and the date acquired on shelves or in chests. After the advent of printing, books were classified as manuscript books or printed books or as Latin, Greek, or Hebrew. In the college libraries of colonial America, the organization was by location symbol—alcove 1, shelf A, book 6—with subject or language divisions within the alcoves.

Since the time of Aristotle, philosophers and nonphilosophers alike have been devising schemes for the classification of knowledge. In his *Advancement of Learning*, published in 1605, Sir Francis Bacon developed a plan for

37

classifying knowledge into three large divisions: history, poetry, and philosophy. These large divisions were then subdivided into specific classes, with further subdivisions within the classes.

Thomas Jefferson adapted Bacon's plan for the classification of knowledge for use in his personal library at Monticello; and when he sold his library of 6700 volumes to the United States to replace the Library of Congress which had been destroyed by the British in 1814,[1] his classification system went along with it and was used by the Library of Congress until 1864—and, with modifications, until the end of the nineteenth century, when the development of a new classification system was begun.[2]

When Melvil Dewey, a student library assistant at Amherst College in 1872, decided to organize the contents of the college library, his first step was to develop a classification system. After studying the schemes for classifying knowledge which had been devised by Aristotle, Bacon, Locke, and other philosophers, as well as some more recently published library classification schemes, he decided to group books according to subject matter. Like his predecessors, Dewey divided all knowledge into main classes which he subdivided into specific classes and into further subdivisions within each class, always proceeding from the general to the specific.

Purposes and Characteristics of Library Classification Systems

The chief purpose of a classification system in a library is to provide a basis for organizing books and materials so that they can be found quickly and easily by those persons who use the library; it is also a means of bringing materials on the same subject together so that they can be used easily and conveniently. Since ease of use is the basic concern, library classification schemes place materials in those categories from which they are most likely to be called for by those who need them. In addition, such schemes provide for the form of the material as well as for the subject matter; for example, dictionaries, encyclopedias, handbooks, periodicals, and other book forms have specified numbers.

The first step in classifying according to subject is to arrange all knowledge into major classes, bringing together into one class the parts which are related and arranging the parts in some logical order, usually from the

[1] The Library of Congress was housed in the Capitol building when it was burned by the British in 1814.

[2] See p. 45.

general to the particular. The several classes so formed constitute the classification scheme.

To be used, these classes must follow a definite and established plan so that they can be referred to again and again. Such a plan is called a "schedule." Classes and subdivisions within the classes are arranged in logical order.

Each class of the schedule and each subdivision within each class must be given a symbol so that all the materials in which a particular subject is discussed can have the same number. The symbols used are letters of the alphabet, Arabic numerals, or a combination of these.

Library classification systems follow the generally accepted ideas of what major classes of knowledge are: philosophy, religion, science, history, language, literature, art, and so on. A general class number or letter is assigned to these large classes; for example in the Dewey Decimal Classification System, 900 is Geography and History; 973 is History of the United States; 973.3 is the Period of Revolution; and 973.3113 is the Boston Tea Party. The shortest numbers belong to the largest subjects, and the longest numbers are assigned to the smallest or the most specialized areas. For example, 621 is the number for applied physics; 621.381528 is the number for transistors.

In addition to a definite and established schedule of classes, there must be an index to all materials which are classified according to this schedule so that these materials can be found quickly and easily. The index to all the classified materials in a library is the catalog,[3] which gives the location symbol for each publication. This location symbol is the call number, composed of the classification number and the book number (see pp. 40-43; 49-50).

Theoretically, a classification system should be so organized that material on any one subject can be found in only one place. Some subjects, however, have so many aspects, so many phases, so many contributing factors that it may not be possible to place all sources relating to such a subject in only one class. For example, on a given subject, such as the great depression, historical information may be found in History, economic data in Economics, sociological facts in Sociology, cultural information in Literature.

It is important to remember that even though books are classified according to the subject that is given the greatest emphasis, they may, to some extent, treat other subjects.[4]

---

[3] The catalog may be a card catalog, a book catalog, a computer printout, a microfiche catalog, an online catalog (to a data base) or some other form, and it is supplemented by files, bibliographies, and indexes.

[4] See Figure 5.6.

Dewey Decimal Classification System[5]

HOW THE DEWEY DECIMAL SYSTEM WORKS

In the Dewey Decimal Classification System, Arabic numerals are used decimally to signify the various classes of subjects.

Dewey divided all knowledge, as represented by books and other materials, into nine classes, which he numbered 100 to 900. Materials too general to belong to a specific group—encyclopedias, newspapers, magazines, and the like—he placed in a tenth class, which preceded the others as the 000 class. Each of the nine subject classes was organized as follows: The first of the ten divisions of every subject was given to the general books in the subject:[6]

700 CLASS:	The Arts, fine and decorative arts
700	The arts
701	Philosophy and theory
702	Miscellany
703	Dictionaries, encyclopedias, and concordances
704	Special topics of general applicability
705	Serial publications
706	Organizations and management
707	Educational research related topics
708	Galleries, museums, private collections
709	Historical, geographical, persons [biographical] treatment

The remaining nine classes were assigned to specific subject areas, moving within each class from the general to the specific. The 620 class and selected subdivisions illustrate the general-to-specific organization:[7]

620	Engineering and allied operations
621	Applied physics
621.38	Electronics and communications engineering
621.381528	Transistors

[5] Certain selections in this section have been reproduced from *Dewey Decimal Classification and Relative Index*, devised by Melvil Dewey, 20th ed., ed. by John P. Comoromi, et al., 4 vols. (Albany: Forest Press, 1989). Each quoted selection is documented.

[6] *Dewey*, 700 Class, *passim*.

[7] *Dewey*, vol. 3, 14–15, *passim*.

621.382	Communications engineering
621.38235	Facsimile Transmission Telefacsimile
621.38456	Cellular telephones
621.38804	Color television
621.388332	Video recordings
621.389324	Cassettes
621.39	Computers
621.3976	CD-ROM

The ten classes of the Dewey Decimal Classification System,[8] as listed in the Second Summary, the 100 Divisions are:

Second Summary: *The 100 Divisions*[9]

000 Generalities
010 Bibliography
020 Library & information sciences
030 General encyclopedic works
040
050 General serials & their indexes
060 General organizations & museology
070 News media, journalism, publishing
080 General collections
090 Manuscripts & book rarities

100 Philosophy & psychology
110 Metaphysics
120 Epistemology, causation, humankind
130 Paranormal phenomena
140 Specific philosophical schools
150 Psychology
160 Logic
170 Ethics (Moral philosophy)
180 Ancient, medieval, Oriental philosophy
190 Modern Western philosophy

200 Religion
210 Natural theology

---

[8] The Dewey Decimal System is the most widely used classification system in the world; it is used in more than 135 countries, translated into over thirty languages, used by 95 percent of all public and school libraries, 35 percent of all college and university libraries, and 20 percent of all special libraries. *Dewey*, vol. 1, p. xxvi.

[9] *Dewey*, vol. 1, p. x.

220 Bible
230 Christian theology
240 Christian moral & devotional theology
250 Christian orders & local church
260 Christian social theology
270 Christian church history
280 Christian denominations & sects
290 Other & comparative religions

300 Social sciences
310 General statistics
320 Political science
330 Economics
340 Law
350 Public administration
360 Social services; association
370 Education
380 Commerce, communications, transport
390 Customs, etiquette, folklore

400 Language
410 Linguistics
420 English & Old English
430 Germanic languages   German
440 Romance languages   French
450 Italian, Romanian, Rhaeto-Romanic
460 Spanish & Portuguese languages
470 Italic languages   Latin
480 Hellenic languages   Classical Greek
490 Other languages

500 Natural sciences & mathematics
510 Mathematics
520 Astronomy & allied sciences
530 Physics
540 Chemistry & allied sciences
550 Earth sciences
560 Paleontology   paleozoology
570 Life sciences
580 Botanical sciences
590 Zoological sciences

600 Technology (applied sciences)
610 Medical sciences   medicine
620 Engineering & allied operations
630 Agriculture

640 Home economics & family living
650 Management & auxiliary services
660 Chemical engineering
670 Manufacturing
680 Manufacture for specific uses
690 Buildings
700 The arts
710 Civic & landscape art
720 Architecture
730 Plastic arts, Sculpture
740 Drawing & decorative arts
750 Painting & paintings
760 Graphic arts   printmaking & prints
770 Photography & photographs
780 Music
790 Recreational & performing arts
800 Literature & rhetoric
810 American literature in English
820 English & Old English literatures
830 Literatures of Germanic languages
840 Literatures of Romance languages
850 Italian, Romanian, Rhaeto-Romanic
860 Spanish & Portuguese literatures
870 Italic literatures   Latin
880 Hellenic literatures   Classical Greek
890 Literatures of other languages
900 Geography & history
910 Geography & travel
920 Biography, genealogy, insignia
930 History of ancient world
940 General history of Europe
950 General history of Asia   Far East
960 General history of Africa
970 General history of North America
980 General history of South America
990 General history of other areas

CALL NUMBER IN THE DEWEY DECIMAL SYSTEM

The class number and the book or author number make up the call number of a book or other type of material. A book (or any other type of information source) is classified according to the subject matter it covers and is given the number in the classification schedule which stands for the subject. The class number for a dictionary of music is 780.3; since there are many dictionaries of music and since all of them will be placed in the 780.3 number, it is necessary to have a means of distinguishing one from another. This distinction is made by assigning a book number (or author number) as well as a class number, using the initial of the author's last name plus Arabic numerals. Author numbers are usually taken from a table called the Cutter table [10] in which numerals, used decimally, are assigned to letters of the alphabet in the order of the alphabet, thus providing for alphabetical arrangement by author. Examples of names and numbers they would be given from the Cutter table are:[11]

Bane	B215		Bond	B711
Bartholomew	B287		Borg	B732
Beard	B368		Boyle	B792
Best	B561		Brunswick	B911
Bing	B613		Burdett	B951
Blake	B636		Butler	B986
Bloomfield	B655		Byron	B996

The title of a publication may be represented in the call number by the first letter of the title, excluding articles. This letter, in lowercase, is placed immediately following the book number and serves to distinguish between books on the same subject written by the same author. Thus the call number for *A Dictionary of Music* by Beard is 780.3 B368d, whereas the call number for *A Concise Dictionary of Music* by Beard in 780.3 B368c.

The arrangement of classified materials on the shelves follows the outline of the classification system. They will appear on the shelves in this order:

745.4	745.4441	745.5	745.537	745.54
H883n	F352d	V882a	P359w	N134b
745.674	745.7	810	810.9	810.903
L152g	B121f	D191s	Ar658a	L181t
810.91	810.917	810.93	810.95073	810.974
B582c	D193s	C111a	N564r	F692h

---

[10] Many libraries use the table which was developed by C. A. Cutter about the time Dewey was devising his classification system. This accounts for the fact that the author or book number is also referred to as the "Cutter number." Adaptations of this and other tables are in use. All are used for the purpose of arranging books within a class alphabetically by author.

[11] *C. A. Cutter's Cutter-Sanborn Three-Figure Author Table.* (Chicopee, Mass.: Huntting n.d.). Some libraries use a two-figure table.

In some libraries, fiction and biography are not classified. Books of fiction may be given the designation F or Fic plus an author number and arranged alphabetically on the shelves by author. An example is Fic M621 for *The Covenant* by James Michener.

Biography, instead of being given a class number, may be marked B and arranged in alphabetical order by the subject of the biography—for example, B R781 for a biography of Franklin Delano Roosevelt.

Special symbols are sometimes added to the call number to indicate that the book is shelved in a particular location or that it is a particular kind of material. For example, the symbol R or Ref with the call number signifies that the book is a reference book and that it is located in the reference collection. J or C above or below the call number might mean that the book is in the children's collection. H.H. or a similar symbol with the call number may indicate that the book is one of a memorial gift collection which is kept together in one place. For nonbook materials, the words Kit, Video, Transparency, Filmstrip, or Phonodisc may be added to the call number.[12]

Library of Congress Classification System

The Library of Congress was founded in 1800 by and for the Congress of the United States. The earliest classification of books in the library—as in many other libraries of the time—was by size. When Congress purchased Thomas Jefferson's private library in 1815,[13] his classification system and catalog were included. Jefferson's classification, based on a modification of Francis Bacon's division of knowledge, was used by the Library of Congress until 1864, and with some adaptations until the end of the century.

In 1897, when the Library of Congress was moved from the Capitol building to its own building, the collections contained more than 1.5 million items and the library was receiving more than 100,000 items each year. It was then that a new system of classification was begun, designed specifically for the Library of Congress.[14] This system of classification is still being developed; it is under constant study, classes are revised whenever it is necessary, and new classes are added.

The functions of the Library of Congress, the nature of its collections at that time and its expected acquisitions, and the ways the collections were to be used, determined the organization and the details of the classification system. Since the library was to serve the Congress, it was assumed that the

[12] See also Figure 14.1.

[13] See p. 38.

[14] See L. E. La Montagne, *American Library Classification with Special Reference to the Library of Congress* (Hamden: Shoe String, 1961).

holdings in the branches of knowledge most used by lawmakers—the social sciences—would be very large and diverse, and adequate provision had to be made for these fields. It was also expected that the library would receive, through purchase, national and international exchange, gifts, copyright deposit, and other sources, much material which university and other scholarly libraries would not ordinarily acquire. Therefore, because of the range and diversity of materials, a comprehensive and minute classification system was needed. The primary concern in devising the new system was that it should meet the requirements of Congress. In addition, it must provide for the organization of large amounts of diverse material, both scholarly and popular.

In spite of the fact that it was designed specifically for the Library of Congress collections and is particularly suited to very large collections, the Library of Congress Classification System is used widely in America and in other countries, and increasingly, academic and public libraries are adopting it.

HOW THE LIBRARY OF CONGRESS SYSTEM WORKS

The Library of Congress Classification System combines letters of the alphabet and Arabic numerals. Starting from a base of twenty-six letters, it offers, in theory, 676 subject divisions—compared with 100 divisions (from a base of 10) in the Dewey Decimal Classification System. At the present time, the letters I, O, W, X, and Y are not used but are reserved for further expansion. [15]

Unlike the Dewey Decimal Classification System, in which each class follows the same form, no two classes of the Library of Congress Classification System are identical in their divisions. Each subject class has been given individual treatment and has been developed according to the kind of material the Library of Congress had or expected to acquire in that subject area. There are not any memory devices or constant form numbers because not all classes have all forms of materials. Each class is, in fact, a separate classification. There are, however, some basic features which are characteristic of all classes.

1. In the Library of Congress classification, general materials, such as periodicals, dictionaries, directories, and so on, appear early in the class, for example: [16]

---

[15] See pp. 50–53 for a listing of the main classes and selected subdivisions.

[16] Subject Cataloging Division, Processing Department, *Library of Congress Classification, Class M: Music and Books on Music*, 3d ed. (Washington: LC, 1978), *passim*.

ML   Literature of music
ML 1   Periodicals
ML 12   Directories
ML 25   Societies
ML 29   Foundations
ML 32   Institutions
ML 100   Dictionaries, encyclopedias
ML 111   Bibliographies

2. The classes in the Library of Congress classification, like those in other classification systems, proceed from general to particular:[17]

TK 7800   Electronics
TK 7871.3   Lasers
TK 7874   Microelectronics
TK 7881.7   High fidelity systems
TK 7885   Computer engineering computer hardware
TK 7888.3   Digital computers
TK 7889   Special Computers
TK 7889.I26 IBM Personal Computer

3. Main classes are marked with a single letter.[18]

P   Language and literature

4. Principal subdivisions are denoted by an added letter:

PN   Literary history and collections (General)
PR   English literature
PS   American literature

---

[17] Subject Classification Division Processing Department, *Library of Congress Classification, Class T, Technology*. 1st ed. (Washington: LC, 1971) *passim*. Rita Runchock and Kathleen Droste, eds., *Class T, Technology*. *Library of Congress Classification Schedules: A Cumulation of Additions and Changes Through 1991* (Detroit: Gale, 1991) 92.

[18] Subject Cataloging Division, Processing Department, *Library of Congress Classification, Class P, Subclasses PN, PR, PS, PZ, General Literature, English and American Literature, Fiction in English, Juvenile Belles Lettres*, 2d ed. (Washington D.C.: LC, 1979) *passim*.

5. Further subdivision is by use of Arabic numerals in ordinary sequence, beginning at 1 in each of the main divisions and going as high as 9999 in some classes.

PN 1	International periodicals
PN 2	American and English periodicals
PN 3	French periodicals
PN 1560	The performing arts
PN 1992	Television broadcasts
PN 6109.9	Collections of poetry by women authors
PN 6700	Collections of comic books

6. Decimal letters and numbers may also be used in the class number to subdivide a subject alphabetically by subject or form or by state or country:

PN 6110	Special collections of poetry
PN 6110.C7	Collections of college verse
PN 6110.H8	Humor
PN 6110.S6	Sonnets
PN 6511	Oriental proverbs
PN 6519.A7	Arabic
PN 6519.C5	Chinese
PN 6519.J3	Japanese

A class number may have both a decimal number and a decimal letter and numeral:

PN 1993.5	History of motion pictures
PN 1993.5.A1	General history of motion pictures
PN 1993.5.U65	History of motion pictures in Hollywood, California

7. The decimal letter and Arabic numeral combinations are used for persons as subjects and authors as well as for subjects which are not persons:

PS 708.B7	William Bradford (author of the colonial period)
PS 595.C6	Collection of cowboy verse

In no other classification is alphabetical suborder within the class so commonly used. But the alphabetical designation is not uniform in every class; for example, C7 in another class is not college verse, and in another class J3 is not Japanese proverbs.

Usually two letters and four figures are the limit of the length of a class number, but the class number may be expanded by the use of decimal letters and numbers, as has been noted.

Through the combination of letters and numerals, the Library of Congress classification provides for the most minute grouping of subjects. In general, because of the specificity of the class number, only a brief author number is used. It is taken from a modified Cutter table[19] and allows for alphabetical arrangement by author within a subject class. Author numbers, used decimally, may be made up of a letter and one numeral or a letter and two or three numerals.

CALL NUMBER IN THE LIBRARY OF CONGRESS SYSTEM

The Library of Congress classification numbers range in length from one letter and one numeral (P 1) to two letters, four numerals, one decimal number, and a decimal letter and number combination (PN 1993.5.U65). The classification proceeds from general to specific, and the longest numbers belong to the most specialized subjects.

All numbers before the decimal are read in ordinary sequence; all those following the decimal are read decimally. Therefore, PN1993.5.U65S4 will come before PN1994.C5. Class number and author number make the call number. The last letter-and-numeral combination is the author number. Examples of class numbers and author numbers are:

PN1	PN86	PN86	PN1993.5.U65	(class number)
A86	K57	K7	S4	(author number)
PN1994	PN6099	PN6099	PN6110.C7	(class number)
C5	L27	L4	T47	(author number)

Books are arranged on the shelf according to the classification and, within each class, alphabetically by author. The following examples show the way the call number looks on the spine of a book and how the books would be arranged on the shelf:

[19] See p. 44.

PN	PN	PN	PN	PN	PN	PN
1	56.5	56.5	86	86	1990.4	1991.3
A86	.C48	.C5	K57	K7	.D5	.U6
	W39	W16			V57	B78

PN	PN	PN	PN	PN
1992	1993	1994	6099	6110
T4	.5.U65	C5	L4	.C7
	S4			A86

Because of the length and the complexity of Library of Congress classification numbers, and because collections in which the system is used are generally quite large, the researcher can save time by beginning a search for materials with the library catalog. In fact, as library collections increase and become more diversified and as all classification systems become more complicated, the necessity for using the catalog increases. However, if library users will learn the letter designations and the range of numbers for the fields in which they are working and will remember the general to specific arrangement, they can soon be able to go directly to those sections and browse. In all literatures, a large number of the subdivisions are devoted to individual authors; for example, the subclasses in English literature (PR) from PR1509 through PR6076 are devoted to individual authors from the beginning to about the middle of the twentieth century.

A listing of the classes and a selected list of subclasses from the Library of Congress Classification System follows.[20]

A			General Works
	AE	1–90	Encyclopedias (General)
	AI	1–21	Indexes (General)
	AY	10–2001	Yearbooks. Almanacs. Directories
B			Philosophy. Psychology. Religion
	B	1–5739	Philosophy (General)
	BF	1–940	Psychology
	BL	1–2790	Religions. Mythology. Rationalism
	BM	1–990	Judaism
	BP	1–610	Islam, Bahaism, Theosophy, etc.
	BR	1–1725	Christianity
C			Auxiliary sciences of history
	C	1–51	Auxiliary sciences of history (General)

[20] From the Library of Congress, Subject Cataloging Division, Processing Services, *LC Classification Outline*, 6th ed. (Washington, D.C.: LC, 1990).

	CB	3–481	History of civilization
	CC	1–960	Archaeology (General)
	CT	21–9999	Biography
D			History: General and Old World
	D	1–1075	History (General)
	DA	1–995	Great Britain
	DC	1–947	France
	DD	1–905	Germany
	DE	1–100	The Mediterranean region. Greco-Roman world
	DK	1–973	Soviet Union
	DS	1–937	Asia
	DT	1–3415	Africa
	DU	1–950	Oceania (South Seas)
	DX	1–301	Gypsies
E–F			History: America
	E	11–29	America (General)
		51–99	Indians. Indians of North America
		186–199	Colonial history
		456–655	Civil War
	F	2201–2239	South America (General)
G			Geography. Anthropology. Recreation
	G	1–9980	Geography (General), Atlases, Maps
	GB	3–5030	Physical geography
	GN	1–890	Anthropology
	GR	1–7070	Folklore
	GV	1–1860	Recreation. Leisure
H			Social Sciences
	H	1–99	Social Sciences (General)
	HC	10–1085	Economic history and conditions. National production
	HG	1–9999	Finance
	HJ	9–9995	Public finance
	HM	1–299	Sociology (General and theoretical)
	HQ	1–2039	The family. Marriage. Woman
	HX	1–970.7	Socialism. Communism. Anarchism
J			Political science
	JF	1321–2112	Government. Administration. General works. Comparative works
	JK	1–9993	United States Law (General)

K			
	KF	1–9827	Federal law. Common and Collective state law
L			Education
	L	7–991	Education (General)
	LB	5–3640	Theory and practice of education
M			Music
	M	1–5000	Music
	ML	1–3930	Literature of music
N			Fine Arts
	N	1–9165	Visual arts (General)
	NA	1–9428	Architecture
	ND	23–3416	Painting
	NX	1–820	Arts in general
P			Language and literature
	P	1–1091	Philology and linguistics (General)
	PA	1–8595	Classical languages and literature
	PC	1–5498	Romance languages
	PD	1001–1350	Germanic languages
	PJ		Oriental languages and literatures
	PN	1–6790	Literary history and collections (General)
	PQ		Romance literatures
	PR	1–9680	English literature
	PS	1–3576	American literature
	PT		Germanic literatures
	PZ	5–90	Fiction and juvenile belles lettres
Q			Science
	Q	1–385	Science (General)
	QA	1–939	Mathematics
	QB	1–991	Astronomy
	QC	1–999	Physics
	QD	1–999	Chemistry
	QE	1–996.5	Geology
	QH	1–278.5	Natural history (General) Biology (General)
	QK	1–989	Botany
	QL	1–991	Zoology
	QM	1–695	Human anatomy
	QP	1–981	Physiology
	QR	1–500	Microbiology
R			Medicine
	R	5–920	Medicine (General)

	RB	1–214	Pathology
	RK	1–715	Dentistry
	RT	1–120	Nursing
S			Agriculture
	S	1–954	Agriculture (General)
	SB	1–1110	Plant culture
	SD	1–668	Forestry
	SF	1–1100	Animal culture
	SK	351–579	Wildlife management. Game protection
T			Technology
	T	1–995	Technology (General)
	TA	1–2040	Engineering (General) Civil engineering (General)
	TK	1–9971	Electrical engineering. Electronics Nuclear engineering
	TP	1–1185	Chemical technology
	TS	1–2301	Manufactures
	TX	1–1107.4	Home economics
U			Military Science
	U	1–900	Military Science (General)
	UA	10–997	Armies: Organization, description, facilities, etc.
	UD	1–495	Infantry
V			Naval Science
	V	1–995	Naval science (General)
	VA	10–750	Navies: Organization, description, facilities, etc.
	VD	7–430	Naval seamen
	VE	7–500	Marines
	VK	1–1661	Navigation. Merchant marine
Z			Library science
		4–8	History of books and bookmaking
		40–115.5	Writing
		116–265	Printing
		662–1000.5	Libraries and library science
		719–871	Libraries
		1001–8999	Bibliography

The library user should keep in mind that some types of materials may be arranged by some method other than subject. In depository libraries, where government publications are housed, the publications are usually arranged according to the Superintendent of Documents Classification System, which is an arrangement by publishing agency (see Chapter 15). In the Educational Resources Information Center (ERIC) files—which contain educational research reports on microfiche—the fiche are filed by Educational Documents number, e.g., ED 191022, ED 191023, ED 191024, ED 191025. The library user may need to look into several kinds of catalogs, indexes, bibliographies, or files in order to locate all the materials in the library on a given subject.

CHAPTER

 5

Library Catalogs

Originally, the word "catalog" meant a list or an enumeration. It has come to mean a systematic or methodical arrangement of items in alphabetical or other logical order, with the addition of brief descriptive information such as price, size, and color. A library catalog, then, is a systematic listing of the books and materials in a library with descriptive information about each one: author, title, edition, publisher, date, physical appearance, subject matter, special features, and location. It is an index to the library materials which it includes just as the index of a book is the key to the contents of that particular book.

Not all the materials in a library are listed in the library catalog; for example, individual articles in periodicals are not listed in the catalog but are located by using indexes,[1] periodicals may not be listed in the catalog but may be in a special file called the "serials file";[2] government documents, pamphlets, clippings, audiovisual materials, microforms, and other special types of materials are sometimes not included in the catalog but are located by means of bibliographies, lists, or special catalogs and files.[3]

The function of all these bibliographical tools—card catalogs, other forms of catalogs, indexes, bibliographies, and special catalogs, lists, and files—is to make the total resources of the library fully and easily accessible to the users.

---

[1] See pp. 98–105.

[2] A serial is a publication issued in successive parts, usually at regular intervals, and, as a rule, intended to be continued indefinitely. Examples are periodicals, newspapers, yearbooks and annual reports, and so on.

[3] See Chapter 14, Nonbook Information Sources, and Chapter 15, Government Publications.

Common Characteristics of Library Catalogs

All library catalogs, regardless of form, have some things in common:

1. They provide aids for the user: labels on the outside and guide cards on the inside of the trays in the card catalogs, an index on the cabinet of the COM reader, and printed instructions and illustrations to aid in using the online catalog and the CD-ROM catalog.

2. They have many cross references: a *see* reference refers from a heading that is *not* used to one that *is* used; a *see also* reference refers from a heading that *is* used to another that *is also* used.

Highway law	Music festivals
see	see also
Highways	Concerts
Modern languages	Middle Ages
see	see also
Languages, Modern	Chivalry
Computers	Hurricanes
see	see also
Computing machines (Computers)	Typhoons
Clemens, Samuel Langhorne 1835–1900	Folk-songs
see	see also
Twain, Mark 1835–1900	Ballads

3. The catalog records in all library catalogs give the same kinds of information about the items they describe: author, title, imprint,[4] collation,[5] notes, subject headings, and other information. At the present time catalog cards are available from several sources: Library of Congress, commercial firms, Ohio Computer Library Center (which prints cards by computer), and local processing centers. Most libraries make some of their own cards. Therefore, catalog cards do not always look alike, but they do give the same kinds of information. (See Figures 5.1 and 5.2)

The library catalog is the reader's chief means of discovering and locating material in the library.

---

[4] Publisher, place of publication, date of publication.

[5] The collation indicates the number of volumes or pages, the number and kinds of illustrations, and the size of the book.

1. It points out the location of the books and other types of materials the library holds by giving the location symbol or call number.
2. It lists in one place, in alphabetical order, all books (and nonbook materials, if they are included in the catalog) by a particular author or on a particular subject, regardless of their locations in the library.
3. It provides several ways of finding materials, listing them by author, title, subject; by coauthor, translator, or illustrator, if there is one; and often by series, if the work belongs to a series.

Forms of Library Catalogs

All library catalogs provide the same kinds of information: about the item cataloged, author, title, facts of publication, number of pages, special features such as illustrations and bibliographies, and subject matter. They differ in the way the information is presented. (See Figures 5.1 and 5.2). The library catalog may be a book catalog, a computer output microform (COM) catalog, a card catalog, an online catalog accessed by computer, or a CD-ROM (compact disk read-only memory) catalog.[6]

BOOK CATALOGS

Some library catalogs are in the form of printed books. This form of catalog has always been in use to some extent and was at one time the generally accepted form. It was discarded because, as libraries grew in size, the printed catalog was soon out of date since cards for new materials could not be interfiled alphabetically. Photocopying devices, modern photographic equipment and microphotography, and the computer have made book catalogs easily and economically available again and many libraries use this form of catalog.

Book catalogs may be used for books, for nonbook materials, or for both. They may be divided—author, title, or subject—or all entries may be filed in one alphabet. Some libraries use a book catalog for only one kind of material, e.g., periodicals.

In a book catalog which is reproduced photographically, the entries are simply photographic reproductions of printed or typed catalog cards displayed in page format. In computer-produced catalogs, the entries may

---

[6] See pp. 59-66 for a discussion of the card catalog; pp. 66-70 for a discussion of the online catalog; pp. 70–71 for a discussion of the CD-ROM catalog.

consist of full information or of only two lines, depending upon the amount of information which was fed into the computer. The computer not only can make multiple copies of a catalog but can also interfile new entries in the old alphabet with each printing.

Advantages claimed for the book catalog are that it is easier to use; a large number of entries can be seen at a glance (e.g., all books by an author follow each other on one or more pages); duplicate copies of the catalog can be made and put in every room of the library; and so on. Disadvantages are the difficulties in keeping it up to date and the necessity for consulting more than one volume.

COM CATALOGS

A large number of academic libraries—as well as public and other kinds of libraries—have COM catalogs. A COM catalog (or COMcat) is produced directly from machine-readable records. In this process, the catalog card which is in digital form on a computer-generated tape is converted into print on a microform, either microfilm or microfiche.[7]

In the COM (microfiche) catalog, the information on a catalog card is reduced 42 times or 48 times. At a reduction of 42 times, a fiche contains 207 frames, and each frame can contain twelve or thirteen catalog cards (more or less, depending on the amount of information on a card), or approximately 1035 titles. If the catalog card information is reduced 48 times, a fiche can contain approximately 1350 titles. A library collection of 200,000 titles could be stored on about 160 fiche. Access to the microfiche is by means of a reader especially designed for that purpose. The reader has a large screen on which the cards are displayed. A COM reader (terminal) takes up little space (about 20 by 19 by 15 inches with a 12- by 14-inch screen). The fiche are stored outside the reader—usually in slots on each side and in numerical order, arranged alphabetically.

Some COM catalogs are on microfilm—16-mm or 35-mm—onto which the catalog cards are photographed in microimages. Each frame can contain up to 100 lines of print, and up to 174,000 titles can fit on a 6-inch roll of microfilm.[8] In a COM catalog which uses microfilm, the film roll is inside the reader; an index on the outside of the reader cabinet provides access to the contents. An entire library catalog can be contained in one COM (microfilm) catalog. Like the microfiche catalog, the microfilm catalog must be read with a reader especially designed for it.

[7] See pp. 137-138
[8] See pp. 137-138

The COM catalog may be an author catalog, having only author cards; a title catalog, having only title cards; a subject catalog, having only subject cards, or a dictionary catalog, with all kinds of cards in one alphabetical arrangement.[9] In some libraries, the total holdings of the library are in the COM catalog. In other libraries, the COM catalog supplements the card—or other—catalog. In libraries which are changing to a COM catalog and in libraries in which the COM catalog supplements the card catalog, it is often necessary to look in both catalogs to complete a search for information.

All COM catalogs have the same advantages: they require small space; they are easy and economical to duplicate, and a library can have a COMcat in every department and on every floor; they are easy to use.

CARD CATALOGS

Card catalogs are made up of 3- by 5-inch cards on which the cataloging information is printed, typewritten, or photocopied. The cards are filed alphabetically in trays or drawers.

A library card catalog may be a single alphabetical arrangement, or it may be divided into author, subject, and title catalogs.

1. An author catalog includes only the author or main entry cards.
2. A title catalog is made up of title entries only.
3. A subject catalog is made up exclusively of subject entries.
4. A dictionary catalog has all entries—author, title, subject, and other entries—filed in one alphabet.

Large libraries usually have three separate catalogs: author, title, and subject. In general, small libraries have a dictionary catalog. It is important to know how the catalog in your library is arranged in order to avoid making mistakes such as looking in the title catalog for an author.

Kinds of Entries (Cards) in the Catalog

An entry is a single listing of a publication. Most publications have at least two entries in the catalog: (1) They are entered under author, and (2) they are entered under title or subject. Most publications other than fiction are listed under author, title, and subject. In addition, a work may be entered in the catalog under coauthor, editor, translator, and illustrator.

[9] See pp. 64-66

AUTHOR ENTRY

The author entry (Figure 5.1) is the basic cataloging record and is called the "main entry." In general, it gives the following information:

1. Author's full name, inverted (some cards give the dates of the author's birth and death, if applicable)
2. Title and subtitle of the work
3. Edition, if it is not the first
4. Coauthor, illustrator, translator
5. Imprint, which includes place of publication, publisher, and date of publication
6. Collation, which includes number of pages or volumes, illustrative material, and size in centimeters
7. Series to which the work belongs, if it is one of a series

FIGURE 5.1

Author card or main entry: (1) class number; (2) author or book number; (3) call number; (4) author's name, inverted; (5) author's date of birth; (6) title of book; (7) place of publication; (8) publisher; (9) date of publication; (10) collation; (11) bibliographical note; (12) descriptive note; (13) identifying number of book (International Standard Book Number); price at time of publication; (14) subject heading (the subject treated fully); (15) other subjects treated; (16) Library of Congress catalog card number; (17) Library of Congress classification and book number; (18) Dewey Decimal class number; (19) information on this card is available in machine-readable format (MARC means "machine-readable cataloging").

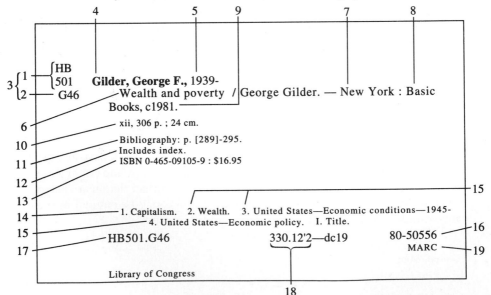

8. Subjects which are treated fully
9. Full name and usually the birth and death dates of the coauthor, translator, editor, or illustrator

It may give other pertinent information, such as a note concerning the contents or the pages on which a bibliography is located.

The author or main entry for a publication may be:

1. An individual
2. An individual who edits rather than writes the work
3. An institution or an organization
   a   Library of Congress
   b   Modern Language Association
4. A publication or a title
   a   *The American Scholar*
   b   *Whales Weep Not*

TITLE ENTRY

A title entry (Figure 5.2) is made for a publication which has a distinctive title. The title is typed at the top of the card in black, above the author's name. If the title is used as the main entry, the work will not have a title entry in the catalog.

FIGURE 5.2
Title entry.

PN 1992 .75 M36 Computers in video production

McQuillin, Lon B.
    Computers in video production / by Lon McQuillin. — White Plains, NY : Knowledge Industry Publications, c1986.
        x, 186 p. : ill. ; 29 cm. — (Video bookshelf)
        Bibliography: p. 167-170.
        Includes index.
        ISBN 0-86729-182-6 : $39.95

        1. Television—Production and direction—Data processing.   1. Title.   II. Series.

PN1992.75.M36   1986   791.43'0232—dc19   86-7314
                                                  AACR 2   MARC

Library of Congress

SUBJECT ENTRY

There is no set number of subject entries for each publication listed in the catalog; a subject card (Figure 5.3) is made for every subject which is discussed fully. A subject card differs from all other types of entries in that the subject is typed at the top of the card in red letters, or in black capital letters. No other kind of heading is typed in this manner. The remainder of the card is an exact duplicate of the main entry card.

Subject headings describe the contents of a work and therefore indicate to the reader its usefulness for a particular purpose. Subject headings in a given library catalog are uniform and are used consistently throughout the catalog. The subject headings used for one publication on a given subject will be used for *all* the publications in the library which deal fully with that same subject. A reader who is searching for material on folk music will find that all the works in the library in which this subject is discussed fully (works which are included in the catalog) are listed under the heading "folk music." They will be filed together in the catalog, alphabetically by author. A subject heading may be a word, a phrase, or a compound heading, inverted to emphasize the important words:

> Poetry
> Art in literature
> Authors, American

FIGURE 5.3
Subject entry.

```
                    MOGUL EMPIRE--HISTORY
    DS
    461         Hansen, Waldemar.
    .H33          The Peacock Throne : the drama of
    1981        Mogul India / Waldemar Hansen. -- Delhi
                : Motilal Banarsidass, 1981.
                    xi, 560 p. : ill. ; 25 cm.
                    Bibliography: p. 533-545.
                    First Indian reprint of the 1972 edition.
                    Includes index.

                    1. Mogul Empire--History.  2. India--
                History--1500-1765.  3. Taj Mahal--
                History.  4. Shahjahan, Emperor of
                India, ca. 1592-1666.  I. Title.


    FTS         02 Nov 81       7899974  FHMMsc
```

The subject heading may be determined by the form of the work (Engineering—Dictionaries), or by location (Education—U.S.), or it may be a location subdivided by subject (France—Social life and customs).

A knowledge and understanding of subject headings is essential to the efficient use of the catalog. If the student knows the author or title of a publication, finding it in the catalog is relatively simple, if the library has it. If, however, the assignment is to find material *on a subject*, the student must have an understanding of the nature of subject headings—how they are determined and how they are phrased—in order to know how to look for the topic in the catalog. For example, if the topic is contemporary American drama, the student will look in the catalog for American drama—20th century. If the topic is history of printing, the student will look for Printing—History.

Examples of other topics and their subject headings are:

Topic	*Subject heading*
Medieval art	Art, Medieval
Early American paintings	Paintings, American
History of art	Art, History
Writing for publication	Authorship
A dictionary of English literature	English literature—Dictionaries
Finding a job	Applications for positions
The American Revolution	U.S.—History—Revolution

Careful reading of the subject headings listed on each card will result in the discovery of related subjects under which material can be found.[10]

To ensure consistency in the subject headings used in the catalog, most libraries follow the headings used by the Library of Congress and listed in the publication *Library of Congress Subject Headings* (12th ed., 1989).[11] This volume is useful also to researchers because (1) it tells them under what headings a given subject may be found in the catalog; (2) it directs them to other headings under which material can be located and to other useful aspects of a subject. In some libraries, this volume is kept near the card catalog to be used by the public. Other sources which may be useful in deciding how to phrase a subject or which give subdivisions of a subject are indexes to encyclopedias and to periodicals and thesauri (which are lists of subject headings used in online searches).

[10] See Figures 5.3 and 5.6.

[11] *Library of Congress Subject Headings*, 12th ed., 2 vols. (Washington: LC, 1989). School libraries and some public libraries follow the *Sears List of Subject Headings*, 14th ed. (New York: Wilson, 1991), which is also based on the Library of Congress subject headings.

An understanding of subject headings (called "descriptors" in the field of computers) is essential to the successful use of any mechanized information retrieval system as well as to the use of the traditional library card catalog. Information is fed into the computer under given subject headings (descriptors) and retrieved by using the *same* subject headings. In general, a list of descriptors is referred to as a "thesaurus."

OTHER ENTRIES

If a publication has a joint author or an important editor, illustrator, or translator, an entry is made for each one. The name of such a person is typed above the author's name, in black. These cards are called "added entries."

Arrangement of Entries in the Card Catalog[12]

Rules for arranging entries in the catalog are adopted by each library. There are some variations, but in general these practices are followed:

1. Alphabetical arrangement is word-by-word rather than letter-by-letter.

Word-by-word	*Letter-by-letter*
New Guinea	Newcomer
New Hampshire	Newfoundland
New Mexico	New Guinea
New Orleans	New Hampshire
New products	Newman, John
New thought	New Mexico
New York	New Oreleans
Newcomer	Newport
Newfoundland	New products
Newman, John	News agencies
Newport	Newsboys
News agencies	News broadcasts
News broadcasts	Newsome, Mary
Newsboys	Newspapers

[12] In library catalogs in which cards are filed according to the *ALA Filing Rules* (1980), the arrangement of some of these entries will differ from the ones given here. The librarian will explain if necessary.

Newsome, Mary	New thought
Newspapers	Newton, Robert
Newton, Robert	New York

2. Definite and indefinite articles at the beginning of titles and other headings are ignored.

The academic library
Addition and subtraction
Airports
The All American team
An American Primer

3. Abbreviations are filed as if they were spelled out: "St." is filed as "Saint," "Mr." is filed as "Mister," and so on.

Mr. Mack	St. Augustine
Mrs. Miniver	St. Joan
Money and banking	Saint Nicholas
Mt. Olympus	School days
Mountie	Spelling bee

4. Names beginning with "Mc" are arranged as if they were spelled "Mac."

McHenry, William
machines
McNeill, Richard
mammals

5. Numbers are filed as if they were spelled out.

1984	20th century
Odyssey World Atlas	twins
100 Days	200 gold pieces
Origins	

6. Historical subheadings are filed in chronological order.

UNITED STATES—HISTORY—COLONIAL PERIOD
UNITED STATES—HISTORY—REVOLUTION
UNITED STATES—HISTORY—1789–1801

UNITED STATES—HISTORY—WAR OF 1812
UNITED STATES—HISTORY—1821–1823
UNITED STATES—HISTORY—CIVIL WAR

7. Works *by* a person are filed before works *about* that person.

Shaw, George Bernard, 1856–1950   (as author)
SHAW, GEORGE BERNARD, 1856–1950   (as subject)

An example of the simplest form of arranging catalog cards in a dictionary catalog, following these practices, is as follows:

The a cappella chorus book
Aaron, Daniel, editor
The Abbey Theater
Ability
Ability—Testing
Accent on teaching
Accents on opera
Education—History
Educational psychology
Literature
Literature—Dictionaries
Literature—History
McHenry, William
Machines
McNeill, Richard

Mr. Mack
Monetary fund
100 days
Only a rose
St. Augustine
School days
Shaw, George Bernard,
   1856–1950 (as author)
SHAW, GEORGE
   BERNARD,
   1856–1950 (as subject)
U.S.—History—Colonial
   period
U.S.—History—Revolution
U.S.—History—Civil War

Online and CD-ROM Catalogs

ONLINE CATALOGS[13]

In an ever-increasing number of academic libraries—as well as in other types of libraries—the catalog has ceased to be a relatively easy-to-use alphabetical file of printed cards and has become a highly sophisticated system of machine-readable information accessed from a computer terminal. Such systems are known as online catalogs. The online catalog, called OPAC (Online

[13] See pp. 56–57.

Public Access Catalog), may be online to a database containing all the cataloging information of a particular library only; it may also provide access to the collections of other libraries, e.g., a network of the libraries in a state or region such as all the college and university libraries, or all the research libraries; or it may provide access to materials other than cataloging information, such as periodicals or campus information. (See Figure 5.4.)

Online catalogs are not standardized at the present time. They differ in the steps employed in accessing information, in the search options available (author, title, subject, keyword, Boolean operators[14]), and in requirements regarding the use of a particular index or thesaurus. If online access is provided to several databases, one database may provide all the types of access mentioned above and others, and another database may be searched only by author and title, etc.

If the catalog search is by author or title (see Figure 5.5), the exact name of the author and the exact title must be given, if that is required. If the search is by subject (see Figure 5.6), the student must be aware that in most online catalogs subject headings have been taken from the *Library of Congress*

```
USF Main Menu                                              NERLUIS
                    Type h and press <ENTER> for help.


  1 University of South Florida          ARTICLES AND REPORTS:
                                         17* Applied Science/Technology 1988-
  3 Florida A&M University               18* Biological & Agricultural (1988-)
  4 FLoirda Atlantic University          19* Business (1988 to date)
  5 Florida International University     20* Business (1982 to 1987)
  6 Florida State University             21  ERIC <Education> (1988 to date)
  7 University of Central Florida        22  ERIC <Education> (1967 to 1987)
  8 University of Florida                23* General Academic (1988 to date)
  9 University of North Florida          24* General Academic (1982 to 1987)
 10 University of West Florida           25  Florida Times-Union


 12 Center for Research Libraries
 13 Santa Fe Community College
 14 SUS-Wide Author/Title Index          29  Return to previous menu
                                         30  Exit LUIS and sign off

 * Entries marked with an asterisk may require you to enter a patron ID. Type
 the number of your choice and press the ENTER key:
```

FIGURE 5.4
Union catalog information in LUIS. (University of South Florida LUIS information. LUIS is the NOTIS Systems, Inc. name for the online-public-access catalog supported by their NOTIS software. By permission from the Florida Center for Library Automation)

14 See p. 69.

```
                                                       Introduction
                                               UNIV OF SOUTH FLORIDA
-----------------------------------------------------------------------
         Welcome to the Library User Information Service -- LUIS!
           (Copyright 1985, State University System of Florida)

       Use the following command:           To search by:

                          A=            Authors
                          T=            All titles
                          TJ=           Journal/magazine/newspaper titles
                          S=            General subject headings
                          SM=           Medical subject headings
                          CL=           Library of Congress call numbers
                          K=            Keywords
                  or type  K  for the   Keyword input screen

                You may begin any search from any screen.
       Press <ENTER> for more information on search commands.
       Type NEWS and press <ENTER> for LUIS System News.
       Type MENU and press <ENTER> to select another database.
       Type START or STOP and press <ENTER> to begin or end your search session.

       NEXT COMMAND:
```

FIGURE 5.5
Example of user information from an online-public-access catalog; LUIS. (LUIS is the NOTIS Systems, Inc. name for the online-public-access catalog supported by their NOTIS software. By permission from the Florida Center for Library Automation)

Subject Headings, a copy of which will be near the terminal, and only those headings can be used to retrieve information by subject. If subject headings have been taken from a thesaurus, list, or index, only those headings can be used in a subject search.

Steps for retrieving catalog information must be followed exactly and in the order given. Means of access to the computer (turning it on) are different for each online catalog. The instruction may be: press a specific key, and then press enter; or type a word (e.g., menu), and then press enter; or press any key. Instructions for searching will be given on the screen. For example, if you are searching for an author and the instructions are "Press keys AU, type in the author's name, and press the Enter key, you will first type capital A, then type capital U, then type in the author's name, and then press "Enter." If the instructions are "Press keys a=, type in the author's name, and press the Enter key," you will first press the a key, then press the = key, then type in the author's name, then press Enter. The information for the author has been entered into the computer using a specific sequence, and it can be retrieved *only* in the same way. The instructions for subject, title, key word, and other searches will be similar to the instructions for author searches and must be followed exactly.

```
Search Request: S=RARE ANIMALS                              Long View
   BOOK - Record 83 of 110 Entries Found        UNIVERSITY OF SOUTH FLORIDA
  --------------------------------- Screen 1 of 1 ---------------------------
                                     ---
     Author:          Durrell, Gerald Malcolm, 1925-
     Title:           Golden bats and pink pigeons / Gerald Durrell.
     Published:       New York : Simon and Schuster,  c1977.
     Description:     190 p., <8> leaves of plates : ill.
     ISBN:            0671243721
     Subjects, General (type s=):
                      Rare animals--Mauritius.
                      Wild animal collecting--Mauritius.
  --------------------------------------------------------------------------
                                     --
    LOCATION:                   CALL NUMBER:       STATUS:
   1. TAMPA circulating         QL337.M37 D87      Not checked out
      collection


  --------------------------------------------------------------------------
                                     --
    COMMANDS:           BR Brief View      I  Index      MENU More databases
    E  Introduction     N  Next Record     G  Guide
    O  Other Options    P  Previous Record H  Help
```

FIGURE 5.6
*Subject search request. (University of South Florida LUIS record. LUIS is the NOTIS Systems,
Inc. name for the online-public-access catalog supported by their NOTIS software. By permission
from the Florida Center for Library Automation)*

In general, an item can be found in the online catalog by author, title, and subject. Additional search options may be allowed: key word, Boolean operators, and truncation.

Key word searching is very useful when the user does not know the exact name of the author, the exact title, or the subject heading used in the system. Key word searching enables the searcher to broaden or limit the search and allows linking of search terms using Boolean operators and, or, not, with, and ADJ:

And k= music and musicians (finds all entries with both words in the title)

Or   k= police or policemen (locates entries which include either word)

Not k= peace not war (searches for entries about peace but not war)

Adj k= southeast adj Asia (retrieves entries in which the word southeast appears in front of and next to the word Asia)

With k= advertising with music (locates entries in which both words are in the title or in the field being searched)

A search term can be shortened by using a truncation symbol (?, $, or other, depending on the online system being used). It retrieves other forms of the word, both singular and plural:

k= invest? (will retrieve invest, investors, investing, investment, investments)

Key word search options are provided for other materials, such as journals, in addition to author, title, and subject.

All search options follow a command: for example a = for a known author; t = for a known title; s = for a known subject; k = for a key word in a title, ka = for a key word from an author's name, and so on.

Information regarding use of the computer, the search options available, and illustrative examples are explained on the computer screen, in handouts provided by the library staff, and in manuals or directions posted at each terminal. Therefore, before beginning a search in any online catalog, read the instructions or explanations.

Even though the instructions vary from one online catalog to another, the same information is given about an item that is found on the traditional catalog card: author, title, place of publication, publisher, date, call number, subjects treated, number of pages, and descriptive notes, if any. The order of information will be different from that on the traditional card, and there may be other information on the screen, such as the number of titles the library has on the subject being searched, or by an author, whether the item is checked out, and if so, the date due. If the database includes other library catalogs, information about the library location of the item will be given. The display screen may list further steps you may want to take, such as asking for help, returning to the index, or ending the search.

Cataloging entries can be added to an online catalog at any time, and therefore it can be kept up to date. New databases may be added to the catalog system from time to time, and search options may be changed or new ones may be added. Instructions regarding these additions and changes are provided at the terminal.

Computer terminals may be placed throughout the library and in other buildings on the campus, making the library catalog more easily accessible. Access to the library catalog may be available from homes, offices, and dormitories if the proper equipment (a PC and a modem) is available.

CD-ROM CATALOGS[15]

CD-ROM, Compact Disk Read-Only Memory, is a plastic disk 4.72 inches in diameter (or larger) on which data are encoded by using a laser to

[15] See pp. 56–57, 69.

burn pits into the surface. When accessed at a terminal, the pits are read by a laser and reproduced on a computer screen. A disk has a storage capacity of 600,000 catalog cards.

The CD-ROM work station is made up of a special keyboard, a computer, a CD-ROM disk drive, a disk, and perhaps a printer. Cataloging information on the disk is reproduced from LC machine-readable records and from some original cataloging in machine-readable form, and gives the same bibliographical data that other catalogs give: author, title, subject headings, call number, illustration and bibliography notes, and pages. These items may appear on the screen in the form of a catalog card or in another format. The catalog record may provide additional information, such as the number of copies of the item the library owns; whether or not it is available; and the date it is due, if it has been checked out. The CD-ROM catalog offers various search options: author, title, subject, word, word in the title, browsing, and Boolean operators, depending on the system in use. Cataloging information is retrieved according to instructions provided at the CD-ROM work station or on the computer screen. *Instructions must be followed exactly.*

Information on the disk cannot be edited, erased, or added to. To update a CD-ROM catalog database, a new disk must be produced. CD-ROM cataloging was first introduced by BIBLIOFILE in 1984 and is used in many libraries.

PART

3

General Information Sources

6

Reference and Information Sources

The word "reference comes from the verb "refer," which means "to turn to for aid or information." Thus, any person or thing referred to for these purposes is a reference. A source consulted for aid or information on a topic, a theme, an event, a person, a date, a place, or a word is a reference source. In this sense, the entire library is a reference collection, because it was selected, organized, and arranged for study and reference.

In any library there are some sources which are consulted more frequently than others for certain kinds of information; there are books which, because of their organization and arrangement, lend themselves to quick and easy use; and there are other publications which were planned and written to be *referred to* for pieces of information rather than to be read completely. In most libraries these kinds of materials are brought together in one room or area and constitute what is called the "reference collection," the "reference room," or the "reference department." The use of these materials is restricted to the library. Questions may be answered completely from the resources in the reference collection, or a given source may only indicate other books and materials which the information seeker must consult to secure the full answer to a question. The other sources may be in another part of the library or in another library.

The reference collection, room, or department is not a separate library within itself but is only one of the parts of the total library that students will use in their search for material.

Characteristics of Reference Sources

Reference sources are organized for quick and easy use, either in an alphabetical or chronological arrangement or by the use of detailed indexes and numerous cross references.

Each kind of reference source is designed to do specific things. Theoretically, a given reference source does the specific things it is planned to do better than any other reference source can do them; thus it should be consulted *first* for the kind of information it covers, even though other reference sources may include some of the same information. For example, a dictionary or an encyclopedia may give information about a geographical location, but a gazetteer, which is designed for the sole purpose of providing information about geographical names and places, is the first place to look for information concerning a geographical location.

There are two types of reference sources: (1) those which contain the needed information, such as dictionaries, encyclopedias, handbooks, biographical dictionaries, atlases, and gazetteers; and (2) those which tell the user where the information can be found, such as indexes and bibliographies.

Reference materials are of two classes: general and specialized. The latter are referred to in this text as "subject" reference materials.

Using reference sources effectively and advantageously depends on knowing what they are, the kinds that are available, the types of questions each kind will answer, and how each one is arranged.

GENERAL REFERENCE SOURCES

General reference sources are broad in scope, not limited to any single subject, but useful for all, or at least for many, subject areas. They include dictionaries, encyclopedias, indexes, yearbooks, handbooks, almanacs, biographical dictionaries, directories, atlases, gazetteers, and bibliographies. Most of these sources are in print form at the present time. Some are also on CD-ROM, and others are in databases, online from a computer terminal. The number of sources in electronic formats increases daily.

The kinds of general reference and information sources, the purposes they serve, and examples of each kind are listed below:

1. A dictionary provides information about words—meaning, derivation, spelling, pronunciation, syllabication, usage, and current status.
   a *Webster's Third New International Dictionary of the English Language*
   b *The Oxford English Dictionary on CD-ROM*
2. An encyclopedia is concerned with subjects. It gives an overview of a topic, including definition, description, background, and bibliographical references.
   a *Encyclopedia Americana*
   b *The New Encyclopaedia Britannica*
   c *The New Grolier Multimedia Encyclopedia*
3. An index points out where information can be found. There are indexes to articles that appear in periodicals and there are indexes to articles,

essays, poems, and other writings that appear in collected works.

    a   Reader's Guide to Periodical Literature
    b   Essay and General Literature Index

4. A yearbook, often called an annual, presents the events of the past year in brief, concise form.

    a   The Annual Register of World Events
    b   Britannica Book of the Year

5. A handbook, literally a small book which can be held conveniently in the hand, provides miscellaneous items of information. It may also be called a miscellany, a manual, or a companion.

    a   Robert's Rules of Order
    b   Famous First Facts

6. An almanac, originally a projection of the coming year—days, months, holidays, and weather forecasts—is the name now given to a collection of miscellaneous facts and statistical information.

    a   The World Almanac and Book of Facts
    b   Whitaker's Almanack

7. A biographical dictionary is a collection of sketches of varying lengths about the lives of individuals, arranged alphabetically by surname.

    a   Who's Who
    b   Dictionary of American Biography

8. A directory lists the names and addresses of persons, organizations, or institutions. It may provide other pertinent information, such as the purposes, the dues, and the officers of the organizations.

    a   American Library Directory
    b   The Foundation Directory

9. An atlas is a volume of maps, plates, or charts, with or without explanatory text.

    a   National Atlas of the United States of America
    b   National Geographic Atlas of the World

10. A gazetteer is a volume that provides geographical information and data about places. It does not define geographical terms.

    a   Chambers World Gazetteer
    b   Webster's New Geographical Dictionary

11. A bibliography is a list of books and other materials which have some relationship to each other. The materials listed are described as to author, title, publisher, price, and number of pages. In some bibliographics, the materials are evaluated.

    a   Books in Print
    b   The Public Library Catalog

12. Periodical publications—newspapers, magazines, and journals—provide news or material of current interest in a particular field or at a particular time.

    a   *The New York Times*
    b   *National Geographic Magazine*
    c   *College English*
13. Abstract journals give digests or summaries of periodical articles and other literature.
    a   *Chemical Abstracts*
    b   *Psychological Abstracts*

    Nonbook Reference Sources include pamphlets, clippings, audio, visual, audiovisual materials, disks, databases, and microforms. They are discussed in Chapter 14 and throughout the text. Electronic sources are integrated with other sources in the same area.

SUBJECT REFERENCE SOURCES

Subject reference sources are those in which the material is devoted to a specific subject area, such as literature, art, or history. In most subject fields, there are the same kinds of reference sources as there are in the general field. Subject reference materials are discussed in Chapters 16 to 24.

Determining the Usefulness of a Reference Source

The usefulness of a reference source for a particular purpose may be determined by answering some basic questions.

1. Are those who produced the subject matter—the editorial staff as listed on the title page or in the preliminary pages—specialists in their fields, as indicated by the academic or other positions they hold?
2. Is the usefulness of the subject matter of the reference source under consideration affected by time, and if so, is this source out of date?
3. Is it arranged for quick and easy use, with adequate index and cross references?
4. Does it provide text alone, or does it include useful illustrative material as well?
5. How is the material treated? Is it
    a   Simple for the nonspecialist?
    b   Technical for the expert?
    c   Scholarly for the scholar?
6. Is there any indication of bias in the treatment of material?
7. Does the source provide bibliographies, and are they up to date?
8. Is the print clear and legible?

9. What kinds of questions will it answer:
 a Factual?
 b Statistical
 c Historical?
 d Current information?
10. What subject areas are emphasized?
 a Science?
 b Literature?
 c Social Sciences?
11. If it is an electronic source, is the information easily accessible by author, title, subject, key word, or other?

Choosing a Reference Source

In choosing a reference source to answer a given question most effectively, it is necessary to understand the nature of the question and to know the usefulness of the various reference sources in answering given questions. First analyze the question; then decide which reference source or sources provide the kinds of information required.

1. What kind of information is needed to answer the question:
 a A definition of terms?
 b Statistical information?
 c An exhaustive explanation or discussion?
 d A brief summary?
2. In what subject area does the question belong:
 a History, economics, geography?
 b An area touching several subject fields?
3. What factors affect the question:
 a Date?
 b Location?
 c Economic conditions?
 d Historical events?
4. What kind of reference source is needed:
 a A general dictionary or subject dictionary for definitions or terminology?
 b An encyclopedia for an overview or a summary?
 c A periodical article or a newspaper article for current information?
 d A yearbook for statistics?
 e An atlas or gazetteer for geographical information?
 f An audiovisual or other nonbook source (tape, film, picture)?
 g A combination of several reference sources?

Using Reference Sources

Use of any reference source is easier and more efficient if the user under-
stands its distinguishing features. These features are explained in the preliminary pages and include:

1. Plan followed in the organization and presentation of materials:
   a   Alphabetical, word-by-word or letter-by-letter[1]
   b   Chronological
   c   Topical, with detailed indexes giving page numbers or some other
       kind of numerical reference, such as the number of a poem in an
       anthology or the number of an entry
2. Symbols and abbreviations used in the text
3. Diacritical markings or phonetic transcriptions used to indicate pronunciation
4. Kinds of indexes it has
5. If it is an electronic source, the various search options that are available.

In Chapters 7 to 15, each kind of general reference source is discussed,
with emphasis on its usefulness for a particular purpose.

[1] See p. 64.

CHAPTER

7

Dictionaries¹

The earliest dictionaries were those in which the meanings of the words of one language were given in the words of another. Among the clay tablets recovered from the ruins of the Sumerian civilization are dictionaries which give Sumerian words with their Semitic-Assyrian meanings. The word "dictionarius," meaning "a collection of words," was first used in the English language about 1225 as the title of a collection of Latin terms. Several Latin-English dictionaries, as well as English and other modern language dictionaries, appeared before the end of the sixteenth century. In the seventeenth century, the name "dictionary" was gradually given to works explaining English words in English.

The first general and comprehensive dictionary of the English language was the *Universal Etymological English Dictionary* by Nathan Bailey, published in 1721, which gave pronunciation and authority for pronunciation but only very brief definitions.

Samuel Johnson's *Dictionary of the English Language*, which appeared in 1755, was designed to list all "good" words in the language with their "proper" meanings. There were many quotations to illustrate the uses of words, and these illustrative quotations have been repeated by makers of dictionaries since that time. Johnson's *Dictionary* was used in England and America until 1828, when it was superseded by Noah Webster's *American Dictionary of the English Language*. *Webster's Third New International Dictionary of the English Language*, which we use today, is the successor to the 1828 work.

The next important English dictionary was *A New English Dictionary on Historical Principles*. James Murray, as editor, began the task of publishing

¹ Dictionaries are included in Part Three, General Information Sources, because they cover words in all areas. See also Chapter 20, Language (Philology).

this scholarly ten-volume work in 1878. It was not completed until 1928. Reissued in 1933, with some corrections and additions, as *The Oxford English Dictionary* (often abbreviated OED), it is an example of the application of the historical method to words, giving the origin, meaning, and historical development of English words in general use now or at any time since 1150.

Characteristics of Dictionaries

Following the pattern established by the distinguished *American Dictionary of the English Language* and *The Oxford English Dictionary*, the dictionary today is, first of all, a collection of words in which each word is treated as to pronunciation, derivation, usage, meaning, and syllabication. In addition, the dictionary may give synonyms, antonyms, illustrative quotations, maps and plates, biographical facts, and geographical and historical information. Thus a dictionary may be a combination of wordbook, gazetteer, biographical dictionary, and encyclopedia.

Because most dictionaries are arranged alphabetically for convenience of reference, the word "dictionary" has come to mean any alphabetical arrangement of words or topics. A collection of items of information in a special subject area, arranged in alphabetical order, is often called a dictionary. There are dictionaries of psychology, education, philosophy, music, mathematics, and many other subjects, as well as dictionaries of dates, events, battles, plants, and sports. In fact, dictionaries of subjects and of things surpass in number those of words or language.

When only a few words, a small part of those belonging to a subject, are given, or when these words are only partially explained, the work is a "vocabulary." When it is a list of explanations of technical words and expressions in some particular subject or book, it is a "glossary."

Determining the Usefulness of a Dictionary

The primary purpose of any dictionary is to answer questions about words. The usefulness of a dictionary is determined by the way in which it answers them.

In judging the usefulness of a dictionary for a given purpose, consider these points:

1. What part of the language does the dictionary include? Does it cover slang, dialect, obsolete, and technical words, as well as standard words?

2. What period of the language does it cover?

3. Is usage indicated?

4. Are plurals, verb tenses, and participles spelled out?

5. Is syllabication indicated?

6. In what way is pronunciation shown? If diacritical marks are used, are they explained?

7. Are the definitions clear?

8. Are the definitions given in order of historical or current usage?

9. Is the etymology of the word given?

10. Is illustrative material—quotations, maps, pictures, charts—used? If so, is it appropriate and helpful?

11. Does it give synonyms and antonyms, and are they explained?

12. Are abbreviations and symbols explained?

13. Is encyclopedic information—that is, geographical, biographical, and historical facts and like material—included?

14. Is the dictionary easy to use?

Many of the questions listed above will be answered as one uses the various dictionaries; other answers will be found in the preface and introduction of each dictionary.

Kinds of Dictionaries

Dictionaries can be divided into (1) general word dictionaries, which provide overall information such as pronunciation, derivation, syllabication, and meaning, about the words of a language; (2) dictionaries that have to do with certain aspects of language, such as etymology, synonyms and antonyms, slang, colloquialisms, dialect, and usage; and (3) dictionaries concerned with a specific subject area.

General word dictionaries are (1) unabridged—that is, complete, covering all the words of a language; (2) abridged—that is, reduced in content but retaining the features of the unabridged work; or (3) general-purpose desk dictionaries, which are not abridgments of a work but which include only a selection of the words of a language. There are both English-language and foreign-language general dictionaries.

Dictionaries concerned with certain specific aspects of language are discussed in Chapter 20, Language (Philology).

Dictionaries in the subject fields are included in Chapters 17 to 24.

Representative Dictionaries[2]

GENERAL WORD DICTIONARIES—*UNABRIDGED*

Murray, James Augustus Henry, et al., eds. *The Oxford English Dictionary*. Being a corrected reissue, with an introduction, supplement, and bibliography, of *A New English Dictionary on Historical Principles*. 12 vols. and supplement. London: Oxford UP, 1933. Presents the historical development of each word introduced into the English language since 1150, giving the date it was introduced and the uses which have survived; each meaning illustrated with a quotation from literature; gives pronunciation, etymology, inflectional forms, and synonyms.

A Supplement to the Oxford English Dictionary. Ed. R. W. Burchfield. 4 vols. Oxford: Clarendon, 1972–1986. The four-volume *Supplement* incorporates the material in the 1933 *Supplement* and contains all words that came into common use in English during the publication of the *OED*, 1884–1928, and words which have come into use from 1928 to the present. It aims to record the vocabulary of the twentieth century, including literary, scientific, technical, legal, and other professional terminology, and popular, colloquial, and modern slang expressions.

The Oxford English Dictionary. 2d ed. Ed. J. A. Simpson and E. S. C. Weiner. 20 vols. Oxford: Clarendon, 1989. Defines more than half a million words, including the new entries in the supplements and 5000 additional new words; for each word, gives date it entered the language, meanings (illustrated with a quotation), pronunciation, etymology, inflectional forms, and synonyms; has 2.4 million quotations, some of them from recent sources. Pronunciation is based on the International Phonetic Alphabet.

The Oxford English Dictionary, Second Edition, on Compact Disc. New York: Oxford UP, 1992. The complete 20-volume second edition of *The Oxford English Dictionary* on one compact disk defines over half a million words; allows browsing and direct access to quotations, definitions, etymology, etc.; search by headword, date, phrase, punctuation, etymology, quotations, date of quotations, author, or word of quotation. Provides User's Guide and User's Manual. IBM PC and compatibles.

The Random House Dictionary of the English Language. 2d ed. Unabridged. New York: Random, 1988. Based on current usage, reflects changes and growth in the language in all fields; many definitions are given dates; illustrative phrases are given for some definitions; encyclopedic information includes biographical and geographical names, titles of literary

---

[2] See also Chapter 20, Language (Philology). For dictionaries currently available on CD-ROM, see *CD-ROMs in Print* or a similar source.

works, a world atlas, and four foreign language dictionaries: French, Spanish, Italian, and German; has more than 2,000 illustrations.

Webster's Third New International Dictionary of the English Language. Springfield: Merriam, 1981. Covers current vocabulary of standard written and spoken English; earliest meaning given first; single-phrase definitions are based on examples of usage; provides a simplified pronunciation key, etymologies, synonyms, illustrations; quotations from contemporary sources; has more than 460,000 entries; 200,000 examples of usage. *12,000 Words: A Supplement to Webster's Third New International Dictionary.* Springfield: Merriam, 1987. Gives meanings that have become established in the language since *Webster's Third* was published in 1966.

GENERAL WORD DICTIONARIES—DESK TYPE

Abridged

Merriam-Webster's Collegiate Dictionary. 10th ed. Springfield: Merriam-Webster, 1993. The latest in the Collegiate series, and based on Webster's *Third New International Dictionary*, aims to present the English language as it is written and spoken today; provides clear definitions and pronunciation, detailed etymologies, illustrative quotations, guidance in usage, pictorial illustrations, and synonyms; gives explanatory notes, an essay on the English language, a guide to pronunciation, and a number of appendixes; includes new words and meanings reflecting changes in our society.

The Random House College Dictionary. Rev. ed. New York: Random, 1988. Based on the unabridged *Random House Dictionary of the English Language;* contains more than 150,000 entries in one alphabet; includes many of the latest technical and slang words, general words, idioms, synonyms and antonyms, geographical and biographical information; gives usage labels; has pictures and maps.

Other desk dictionaries

American Heritage Dictionary of the English Language. 3d ed. Boston: Houghton, 1992. Contains 200,000 entries and 3000 illustrations; includes new words from business, science, technology; gives clear definitions; includes guides to punctuation and grammar and notes on preferred usage.

Chambers English Dictionary. 7th ed. New York: Cambridge UP, 1988. A dictionary of international English with 170,000 entries, includes literary, scientific and technical, popular, and archaic words.

The Merriam-Webster Online Dictionary. Crompton: Newsmedia, 1992. Defines over 65,000 words; includes foreign words and phrases with English translation; search inflected forms, tables, charts and maps, words, and phrases. IBM and IBM compatibles.

Oxford American Dictionary. Comp. Eugene Ehrlich and others. New York: Oxford UP, 1980. Compiled by American editors, has a selected vocabulary of 35,000 entries—words and phrases likely to be found in everyday life, including slang, informal words, technical words, idioms, and new words from the 1970s; gives brief concise definitions with the most current meaning first; offers guidance on correct usage; does not give etymologies; uses a simple system of pronunciation.

Random House Webster's College Dictionary. New York: Random, 1991. Based on the unabridged *Random House Dictionary*, has over 180,000 words, including new words and newly coined words.

Webster's New World Dictionary. 3d college ed. Englewood Cliffs: Prentice, 1988. Has 170,000 entries, including new words; gives new meanings and etymologies of American place names; has many words of American origin, includes scientific and technical terminology, slang, and colloquial expressions in one alphabet. Definitions are given in historical order; biographical and geographical information are in the text. Available on CD-ROM.

FOREIGN-LANGUAGE DICTIONARIES—*BILINGUAL*[3]

French

Harrap's New Standard French and English Dictionary. Ed. J. E. Mansion. Rev. and ed. by R. P. L. Ledesert and Margaret Ledesert. 4 vols. New York: Scribner's, 1973. Includes scientific and technical terms; gives examples of usage.

Harrap's New Collegiate French and English Dictionary. London: Harrap, 1982.

New Cassell's French Dictionary: French-English, English-French. Completely rev. by Denis Gerard and others. New York: Funk & Wagnalls, 1973. Includes new words in science, art, and commerce; gives pronunciation and translation of phrases and expressions; omits obsolete terms.

German

Cassell's German Dictionary: German-English, English-German. Ed. Harold T. Betteridge. London: Cassell, 1982. Includes technical words and geographical and proper names; reflects current usage.

---

[3] See Robert Lewis Collison, *Dictionaries of Foreign Languages*, 2d ed. (New York: Hafner, 1971). "A bibliographical guide to both general and technical dictionaries with historical and explanatory notes and references" (subtitle); includes dictionaries of the chief foreign languages; discusses specific dictionaries.

Greek

Greek-English Lexicon. H. G. Liddell, and Robert Scott, comps. 9th ed. rev. and aug. by Sir Henry Stuart Jones and others. Oxford: Oxford UP, 1940. *Supplement.* Ed. by E. A. Barber. 1968. The standard English-Greek lexicon, updated by scholars in many countries; includes scientific and technical terms.

Italian

The Cambridge Italian Dictionary. Comp. Barbara Reynolds. 2 vols. Cambridge: Cambridge UP, 1962. Vol. I: Italian-English; Vol. II: English-Italian. Designed for English-speaking users but also useful for Italians; presents Italian and English vocabulary, usage, and idioms; translation rather than definition of words and phrases; attention is given to specialized terms in arts, sciences, technology, industry, philosophy, etc.; illustrative phrases are used to clarify meaning.

Cassell's Italian Dictionary: Italian-English, English-Italian. Piero Rebora, and others, comps. London: Cassell, 1969. A general dictionary of the Italian language; includes colloquialisms and new words as well as obsolete words and words found in the classics.

Latin

Cassell's New Latin Dictionary: Latin-English, English-Latin. Ed. D. P. Simpson. Completely rev. New York: Funk & Wagnalls, 1960. Useful for beginning students.

Russian

The Oxford English-Russian Dictionary. P. S. Falla. Oxford: Clarendon P, 1984. For English-speaking users at the university or similar level; has some technical terms.

The Oxford Russian-English Dictionary. Wheeler, Marcus. 2d ed. Oxford: Clarendon, 1984. A general-purpose dictionary of Russian as it is written and spoken; designed for English-speaking users. Companion to *The Oxford English-Russian Dictionary.*

Spanish

Appleton's New Cuyas English-Spanish and Spanish-English Dictionary. Ed. Artūro Cúyas. 5th ed., rev. and enl. by Lewis E. Brett (Part I) and Helen S. Eaton (Part II). 2 vols. New York: Appleton, 1972. Includes idioms and specialized terms; gives particular emphasis to usage in the United States and Latin America and to scientific and technological terms; gives pronunciation, definitions, parts of speech.

The New Revised Velázquez Spanish and English Dictionary. New York: New Century, 1985. Spanish-English; English-Spanish; has thousands of new terms and idiomatic expressions of general use replacing those no longer in common usage; has many encyclopedic features, such as geographical terms, abbreviations, proper names, monetary units.

CHAPTER

8

Encyclopedias

Since ancient times, it has been the aim and desire of encyclopedia makers to bring together into one work *all* human knowledge.

The first encyclopedias were works of a single author, designed to summarize the knowledge and thinking of the time. Aristotle produced a large number of encyclopedic treatises. The *Historia Naturalis* of Pliny the Elder, dating from A.D. 77, has been called the first encyclopedia because of its method of compilation. It is the oldest encyclopedia in existence.[1]

In general, the encyclopedias of the Middle Ages were devoted to one or another of the sciences; but Isadore, Bishop of Seville, attempted to cover every branch of knowledge in his work *The Etymologiae*, which is sometimes called the "Encyclopedia of the Middle Ages."

In 1630 the first modern encyclopedia (the first work to be given the title "encyclopedia") was published in Switzerland by Johann Heinrich Alsted. French contributions to encyclopedia-making in the seventeenth century were the *Grand Dictionnaire* of Louis Moréri and the *Dictionnaire Historique et Critique* of Pierre Bayle.

English encyclopedias began with the two-volume *Cyclopaedia* of Ephraim Chambers in 1728, which became the model for all encyclopedias that followed. Translated into French, it provided the working basis for *L'Encyclopédie du XVIIIᵉ Siècle*, which was edited by Diderot and d'Alembert from 1751 to 1772, with all the savants of France as members of the editorial staff.

---

[1] Translated into English by Philemon Holland in 1601, the *Historia Naturalis* was the standard authority for many centuries on the subjects it included: physics, geography, ethnology, physiology, zoology, botany, medical information, minerals, and art. Forty-three editions were published before 1536.

The *Encyclopaedia Britannica* was first published in Edinburgh in 1771 in three volumes as a dictionary of the arts and sciences. The next edition, in ten volumes, added history and biography. Other and larger editions followed, including the scholarly ninth and eleventh editions. In 1920 it was acquired by Sears, Roebuck and Company, which gave it to the University of Chicago in 1943. It has been published since that time by Encyclopaedia Britannica, Inc., which was organized for that purpose.[2]

Encyclopedia editing in the United States began with the publication of the *Encyclopedia Americana* in 1829. The *New International Encyclopedia*, which introduced the journalistic style into encyclopedia writing, appeared in 1884.

By derivation, "encyclopedia" means "instruction in the circle of arts and sciences"—considered by the Greeks to be essential to a liberal education. Today, as it has from the beginning, the encyclopedia purports to be a repository of information on all branches of knowledge, presenting the basic general principles and the most essential details of each of the arts and sciences. It gives an overview of each subject, with definition, description, explanation, history, current status, statistics, and bibliography. It is organized, usually in alphabetical arrangement, for rapid and easy access. Most encyclopedias have an index volume. Use of the index enables the researcher to find small items in long articles.

Some encyclopedias are written for scholars and educated adults, some are addressed to the general public, and others are designed for young people and children. In each of these encyclopedias, the basic factual material may be the same; they differ in style of writing, in amount of additional material included, and in manner of presentation.[3]

Choosing and Using an Encyclopedia

Encyclopedias are of two types:

1. The dictionary type treats subjects under many specific alphabetically arranged headings.
2. The monographic type presents its subjects under large headings with many subdivisions. The monographic encyclopedia may be arranged

[2] See Herman Kogan, *The Great E. B.: the Story of the Encyclopaedia Britannica* (Chicago: U of Chicago P, 1958) 257–258.

[3] The name "encyclopedia" is given also to a work designed to present information on all phases of one particular branch of knowledge. This kind of encyclopedia is usually referred to as a "subject encyclopedia" as distinguished from a "general encyclopedia," which covers all branches of knowledge. Subject encyclopedias are included in Chapters 17 to 24.

alphabetically or by broad topic. In either case, a detailed index and many cross references are needed to locate topics within long articles.

Encyclopedias are evaluated on the basis of certain criteria:

1. Authoritativeness
   a Is the publisher well known and reputable?
   b Is the work dependable, as evidenced by an editorial staff of specialists in each field of knowledge?
2. Purpose
   a For whom is the work intended?
      (i) Scholars?
      (ii) The general public?
      (iii) Young people or children?
         (a) Is it planned to supplement a curriculum?
         (b) Is it written on grade or age levels?
3. Scope
   a Is it comprehensive in coverage?
   b Is it limited to one branch of knowledge?
4. Up-to-dateness
   a Is it a new work?
   b Is is based on an old edition of the same title or of another title?
   c Is the material in the articles, including statistics, maps, and charts, out of date?
   d Are the bibliographies adequate and up to date?
      (i) Are they references for further reading on the subject?
      (ii) Are they the sources used in writing the articles?
      (iii) Do they follow each article, or are they collected into a single volume?
5. Strong points
   a What subject areas are emphasized?
   b What features are superior to those in other encyclopedias?
6. Physical makeup
   a Does the physical makeup—that is, the size of the volumes, the kind of paper, the type, the headings, and the lettering on the spine—add to the ease of use?
   b Is the illustrative material adequate and suitable to the text?

Some of these questions can be answered by reading the preliminary pages in each encyclopedia; others will be answered as the student uses the several encyclopedias.

Using an Encyclopedia

In using an encyclopedia for the first time, try to determine:

1. Organization of the material
   a Are there short articles on small subjects?
   b Are there long articles on large, general subjects?
2. Arrangement
   a Is is alphabetical letter-by-letter or word-by-word?[4]
   b Is it arranged by broad topics?
3. Kind of index provided
   a Is there a detailed index, which points out small subjects within the long articles?
   b Is there an index to each volume or a single index for the entire work?
4. Kinds of aids to the reader
   a Is pronunciation indicated? If so, what system is followed?
   b Are cross references provided?
   c Are abbreviations and symbols explained?

The outstanding features of the general encyclopedias listed below are given in the annotations.

Representative Encyclopedias[5]

GENERAL ENCYCLOPEDIAS

Academic American Encyclopedia. 21 vols. Danbury: Grolier, 1992. An up-to-date reference work; aims to provide quick access to information on a wide range of subjects for high school and college students and adults; major emphasis is on science and technology, the arts and humanities, and biography; articles are short; there are many illustrations—75 percent in color—and maps; Vol. 21 is the index. Computer-produced, the entire contents are in machine-readable form. Online through several vendors; on tape, and on CD-ROM.

The Canadian Encyclopedia. 2d ed. 4 vols. Edmonton: Hurtig, 1988. A national encyclopedia, it covers all aspects of Canadian life; treats subjects from

[4] See p. 64.

[5] Increasingly, encyclopedias are becoming available in electronic formats. It is not possible to list all of them in this text. Consult information sources such as *CD-ROMs in Print*, periodical and newspaper literature, and review media for new titles which are available in CD-ROM or online to a database.

the Canadian viewpoint; includes topics in art, literature, science, technology, politics, religion, and popular events.

Collier's Encyclopedia. 24 vols. New York: Macmillan, 1993. Emphasizes current subjects; aims to cover every major area of knowledge; contains articles on the latest developments in the social sciences, science and technology, the arts and humanities; makes extensive use of maps and other illustrations—many in color. Vol. 24 includes the index, bibliographies on more than 120 broad subjects, and study guides to a number of selected topics.

The Concise Columbia Encyclopedia. 2d ed. New York: Columbia UP, 1989. Covers current topics as well as past events; has about 150,000 entries; identifies and describes places, persons, events, ideas, etc.; is a ready reference source.

Crystal, David, ed. *The Cambridge Encyclopedia.* New York: Cambridge UP, 1990. International in coverage; has 25,000 entries; covers topical, biographical, and geographical information; has more than 600 illustrations and maps, some in color; a ready reference section provides 7,000 additional entries, including charts on space travels, computer science, humanities, and social sciences; useful for quick reference.

The Encyclopedia Americana. 30 vols. Danbury: Grolier, 1993. A scholarly work which includes short articles on small subjects, as well as long articles; comprehensive in scope and depth of material; provides extensive coverage of science and technology; offers articles in the field of medicine and health, politics, environment, population origins; includes biographies; has many illustrations and maps; bibliographies follow articles.

Information Finder™ by World Book. Elk Grove: World Book, 1990. Based on the *World Book Encyclopedia*, contains over 17,000 articles, 1700 tables, 150,000 index entries from *World Book Index*, and 139,000 entries from the *World Book Dictionary*. Search by topic, keyword, and Boolean operators (and, or, not, etc.); screen displays an outline of the article and the text of the article; operates on IBM and IBM compatibles and on standard CD-ROM equipment.

The New Encyclopaedia Britannica. Ed. Philip W. Goetz. 15th ed, rev. 32 vols. Chicago: Encyclopaedia Britannica, 1993. The greatly revised *Encyclopaedia Britannica* is made up of the 1-vol. *Propaedia*, the 12-vol. *Micropaedia*, the 17-vol. *Macropaedia*, and a 2-vol. *Index*. The *Propaedia* is an outline of knowledge and a guide to the set; articles in the *Micropaedia* range in length from 300 words to 3,000 words. The *Macropaedia* contains essay articles averaging over 30,000 words each. The *Index* gives access to the *Propaedia*, the *Micropaedia*, and the *Macropaedia*. The *Index* is available on one compact disc. There are many illustrations, many in color, and maps. Available online from NEXIS.

The New Grolier Multimedia Encyclopedia. Danbury: Grolier, 1992. Contains all 21 volumes of the *Academic American Encyclopedia* on a single disk; offers text, color photographs, illustrations, sound and motion sequences; is up to date through the Persian Gulf War and the dissolution of the Soviet Union; access is by title, subject, keyword, and Boolean operators. Available on IBM PC and compatibles. Motion video feature only on DOS and Macintosh versions; animation on Macintosh and Windows/MPC versions.

The New Randon House Encyclopedia. 3d ed. New York: Random, 1990. Divided into two parts: the *Colorpedia* and the *Alphapedia*. The *Colorpedia* presents human knowledge in text and illustrations; 876 full-color spreads, each beginning with a lengthy essay keyed to the illustrations, transmits information by words and pictures as a unit. The *Alphapedia* is a traditional ready reference volume with entries ranging in length from one sentence to one column. Cross references are made to the *Colorpedia*. Other kinds of information include a bibliography, illustrations of national flags, and a 130-page atlas by Rand McNally.

The Randon House Encyclopedia: Electronic Edition. Based on the 3d ed, has more than 20,000 entries. Allows both browsing and precise searching; use of the accompanying manual is essential.

The World Book Encyclopedia. 22 vols. Chicago: World Book, 1993. Provides up-to-date and easy-to-read information in all areas of knowledge; vocabulary used in a given article is geared to the grade level of the article; many long articles begin with simple concepts and reading level and build to more advanced concepts and reading levels; illustrations—more than half in color—are combined with text; new areas of interest are covered (energy, the economy, computers, music, sports, minority groups, new nations); features reading lists, reading and study guides, and guidance in conducting research; provides maps. *World Book Year Book* and the 2-vol. *World Book Dictionary* add to the usefulness of the *World Book Encyclopedia.* See also *Information Finder by World Book,* page 93.

FOREIGN ENCYCLOPEDIAS

Brockhaus Enzyklopädie in zwanzig Bänden. 19th ed. Vol. 1–24. Wiesbaden: Brockhaus, 1986. New edition of a standard work; has many new entries; provides long articles on countries and continents.

Enciclopedia Italiana di Scienze, Lettere ed Arti. 35 vols. Rome: Instituto della Enciclopedia Italiana, 1929–1937. Provides long articles, many bibliographies, illustrations of all kinds, and biographies; illustrations for travel and art subjects are most notable. Vol. 36: *Indici.* 1939. Appendixes I–III cover 1938–1960. 10-year supplements.

Enciclopedia Universal Ilustrada Europeo-Americana. 70 vols. with a 10-vol. supplement and a 1-vol. appendix. Barcelona: Epasa, 1905–1933. *Suplemento Anual*. 1934–. Comprehensive in coverage; gives Spanish and Spanish-American biography and geographical names.

Encyclopaedia Universalis. 3d ed. 30 vols. Paris: Encyclopaedia Universalis, 1990. Divided into three parts: the encyclopedia proper (vols. 1–23), a summary of human knowledge with long and short articles (3 vols. unnumbered), and a thesaurus or analytical index to the encyclopedia (4 vols. unnumbered). The encyclopedia gives long, comprehensive articles with bibliographies; includes biographical sketches of important figures; has many illustrations, maps, and charts. Annual *Supplement*. 1974–.

La Grande Encyclopédie. 20 vols. and index volume. Paris: Larousse, 1971–1978. Emphasizes twentieth century with special attention given to recent developments in the sciences; offers both long and short articles. Supplement, 1985, covers 1977–1982.

Great Soviet Encyclopedia: A Translation of the Third Edition. 31 vols. and index. New York: Macmillan, 1974–1982. A volume-by-volume translation of the 3d ed. of *Bol'shaia Sovetskaia Entsiklopediia*; general in scope but concentrates on the Soviet Union; more than 100,000 articles give comprehensive treatment of Soviet life, including history, peoples, science, technology, economic life, military affairs, institutions, culture, and philosophy—past to present; includes current and past biography; a cumulative index is published after every five volumes. *Index*, 1983.

9

Indexes

The word "index" comes from the Latin *indicare*, "to point out." Thus an index does not provide the information sought; it *indicates* where it can be found.

The index of a book points out the page or pages on which certain information can be found. The library catalog is an index to the materials in a library. Each catalog record indicates, by means of a call number, the location of a book or other kind of material. It may give the pages on which certain material can be found in a given book; for example, Bibliography: pp. 210–212.

In addition to library catalogs and the indexes of books, three other kinds of indexes[1] are needed by the student who seeks material on a particular subject: (1) indexes to literature appearing in periodicals, (2) indexes to materials appearing in newspapers, and (3) indexes to literature appearing in collections or anthologies.

Periodicals

Periodicals appeared in the sixteenth century soon after the invention of printing. They began as pamphlets, grew into a series of related pamphlets,

---

[1] Some libraries compile indexes to special collections or special types of materials to supplement the published indexes, e.g., archival materials, pamphlets, and some nonbook materials. Libraries also have thesauri to be used with certain abstract journals and to gain access to a data base.

and by the seventeenth century had taken on the characteristics of our modern periodicals. Throughout the eighteenth century, the word "periodical" was used chiefly as an adjective, e.g., "periodical literature," "periodical publication." By the end of that century "periodical" was applied to all regularly issued publications except newspapers and is used in that sense today.

Periodical literature can be divided into two classes, general and professional. A general periodical is not limited to one area of interest but touches many interest areas. Examples are *Time*, *The Saturday Evening Post*, and *The New Yorker*. A professional periodical—usually called a "professional journal"—consists of articles on subjects of concern to a particular branch of knowledge that are usually written by members of the profession. Examples are *Journal of Geography*, *American Journal of Psychology*, and *American Historical Review*.

Periodical publishing has grown until now more than 75,000 titles, including general-interest magazines, trade journals, vocational and recreational periodicals, and professional journals, are published in the United States and Canada.[2] A certain number of issues, usually covering six months or a year, constitute a volume. Some magazines publish an index for each volume, but many others do not provide an index of any kind.

The search for information on any subject must include the examination of material that appears in periodical publications. The importance of this material cannot be overemphasized.

1. The most recent material on a subject, especially in the fields of science, technology, statistics, politics, and economics, will be found in periodicals.

2. Subjects too new, or even too obscure or too temporary, to be covered by books are treated in periodicals.

3. The trend of interest or opinion at any given period is traced easily in periodical literature. The current issues give contemporary information, and the old issues give a record of past ideas, problems, and accomplishments.

4. Books, or parts of books, often appear in periodicals before they are published as separate volumes.

5. Professional literature is supplemented by periodicals, which keep teachers, scientists, physicians, economists, lawyers, and members of other professions up to date.

---

[2] *The Standard Periodical Directory*, 15th ed. (New York: Oxbridge, 1992). See also *Ulrich's International Periodicals Directory*, 31st ed., New York: Bowker, 1992.

Periodical Indexes

It would not be possible to make use of the countless pieces of information in periodicals without the aid of indexes.[3] To aid the researcher in finding information in periodicals, there are indexes to periodical literature. The function of an index to periodical literature is to point out the location of the topics discussed in the periodicals covered by the index. In carrying out this function, the index lists not only the large, general subjects treated, but also the various subdivisions of each subject; it indicates where material can be found on each of the several aspects of a subject. For example, for purposes of indexing, the subject "Music" includes the following subdivisions:[4]

Music	Music, American
Music—Analysis	Music, Popular (songs, etc.)
Music—Criticism	Music and literature
Music—History and criticism	Music and science
Music—Performance	Music and society
Music—Rhythm	Music as a profession
Music—Scores	

This detailed breakdown of a subject and the innumerable cross references provided are valuable aids to the student who is trying to choose a subject for a research paper or who is trying to narrow and restrict a chosen subject.

Each of the indexes to periodical literature covers a group of periodicals of a certain kind—general, scientific, educational, business, and so on. The list of periodicals covered is provided in each issue of the index. Some indexes cover books, parts of books, reports, etc. An increasing number of indexes also provide abstracts of the articles indexed, and many indexes provide full text of articles. (See Figure 9.1.)

Periodical and other indexes are available in several formats: in print, on CD-ROM, online to a database, and on microform. It may be necessary to consult several indexes in order to locate the sources which can be of help in answering a question or in providing material for a research paper.

The location of a periodical article is given by volume, page, and date of issue. In general, each article is listed under author and subject, with com-

[3] Periodicals may be listed in the library catalog with a cross reference to a special file—called the serials file or the periodicals file—for complete information on the library's holdings. This file shows the volumes in the library; it is not an index to individual articles in periodicals. See Chapters 17 to 24 for indexes to periodicals in the subject fields. Not all periodicals are covered by the indexes to periodical literature.

[4] Entries from *Humanities Index*, June 1981. (*Humanities Index* Copyright © 1981 by the H. W. Wilson Company. Material reproduced by permission of the publisher.)

```
Search Request: S=ELECTRONIC MAIL                        Long View
CITATION - Record 146 of 337 Entries Found               ERIC (CIJE)
----------------------------+ Screen 1 of 3----------------------------
Authors:            Power, Claude
                    Brosnan, Tim
Title:              The Future Is Now!/ by Power, Claude; Brosnan, Tim
Pub. Date:          1992
Document no.:       EJ441860

FOUND IN:           Momentum; v23 n1 p42-43 Feb 1992

Availability:       UMI
Abstract:           Describes technological changes implemented by the
                    Diocese of San Jose, California, in the areas of
                    interschool communication via electronic mail;
                    collaboration with Apple Computer for training in
                    electronic mail; teacher training in basic computer
                    applications; facilities/equipment improvement; and
                    integration of technology throughout the
---------------------------------------------CONTINUED ON NEXT SCREEN---
COMMANDS:           BR Brief View    P  Previous Record  H  Help
E Introduction      F  Forward       I  Index               MENU More databases
O Other Options     N  Next Record   G  Guide

NEXT COMMAND·
```

FIGURE 9.1
Example of a subject search for a periodical article in an online-public-access catalog; LUIS.
(LUIS is the NOTIS Systems, Inc. name for the online-public-access catalog supported by their
NOTIS software. By permission from the Florida Center for Library Automation)

plete information under the author entry. Not all periodical indexes use both forms of listing. Some indexes include a title entry; others index by subject only, by key word, etc.

Some indexes point out only certain kinds of articles appearing in periodicals, such as book reviews (see Figure 9.2), bibliographies, or biographies.

CHOOSING AND USING A PERIODICAL INDEX[5]

In order to choose the right index in a search for material on a particular subject, the researcher should try to answer the following questions:

1. What is the nature of the subject?
   a Does it concern a topic or a person too new to be discussed in books?
   b It is a subject so limited in appeal that it would not receive treatment in a book?

[5] See Chapters 17 to 24 for examples of indexes in subject fields.

GENERAL INFORMATION SOURCES

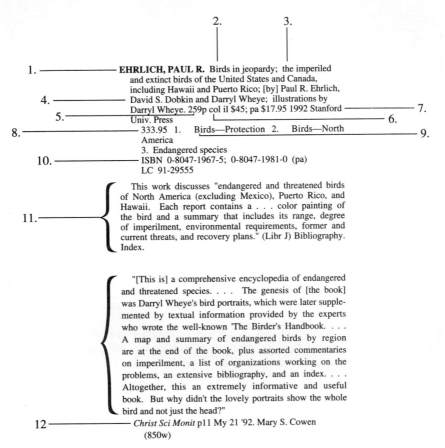

FIGURE 9.2

Explanation of an excerpt from *Book Review Digest:* (1) Author of the book that is reviewed. (2) Title of the book. (3) Subtitle of the book. (4) Coauthors of the book. (5) Number of pages in the book. (6) The book has color illustrations. (7) Date of publication and publisher. (8) Dewey Decimal class number. (9) Subjects treated in the book. (10) The identifying number of the book—the International Standard Book Number. (11) Excerpt from a review that appeared in *Library Journal.* (12) Excerpt from a review that appeared in *Christian Science Monitor*, page 11, May 21, 1992, written by Mary S. Cowen. The review has 850 words. (*Book Review Digest*, December 1992 issue. © by The H. W. Wilson Company. Material reproduced by permission of the publisher.)

c Is it a subject treated in a book but about which more recent information is needed?

d It is a topic which would be clarified by the discussions in one or more periodicals?

2. In what area does the subject belong?
   a Science
   b History
   c Literature
   d Education
   e General
3. Which of the periodical indexes covers the literature of the area in question
4. What years are involved, and which indexes cover those years?
5. Is an article from a general periodical, an article from a professional journal, or an article from each kind required?

In order to use a periodical index efficiently, the user should determine:

1. The format of the index: print, CD-ROM, online, other
2. The number and kinds of periodicals covered by the index and whether books or parts of books and other materials are included
3. The period of time covered by the index, when it began, and whether or not it is still being issued
4. The completeness of indexing of any periodical (all articles or only certain types of articles)
5. The fullness of information given—author, title page, date—as well as information about bibliographies and illustrations
6. The method of indexing: by subject, author, title, key word, or other
7. Whether it provides abstracts or full text
8. The search options available: author, title, subject, browse, key word, Boolean logic, controlled vocabulary
9. Frequency of issue: bimonthly, monthly, weekly, quarterly

EXAMPLES OF PERIODICAL INDEXES[6]

There are many indexing and abstracting services. Some indexes are published in more than one format, e.g., print and CD-ROM, print and online to a database, print and microfiche. Some are available in several formats. A library may have the print and the other editions as well. These versions may not be duplicates of each other: One may offer more or less than the other version.

Search options, help hints, and "how to use" information are provided in the preliminary pages of the print version; in a manual, a list of instructions,

---

[6] Indexes and abstracts in subject fields are found in the appropriate subject chapters.

or on-screen instructions for the computer version. Instructions for each index are different.[7] The instructions must be followed exactly in order to retrieve information.

Examples of some of the widely used indexes are given below. (See also Figures 9.1 and 9.5.) The format of each index is given in the brief annotation.

Biography Index. New York: Wilson, 1946–. Quarterly; annual permanent volumes. Gives birth and death dates and occupation or profession of each person listed; includes an index by profession; indexes biographical material in periodicals covered by The H. W. Wilson Company indexes and in current books of individual biography; international in coverage. In print; on CD-ROM, on tape, and online, 1984–.

Book Review Digest. New York: Wilson, 1905–. Monthly, except February and July; annual cumulations. Indexes reviews of current books appearing in ninety-five selected U. S., British, and Canadian periodicals; books are entered by author; information includes title, publisher, date of publication, and price of the book, citations to all reviews, and excerpts from some reviews; has a subject and title index. In print; on CD-ROM and online, 1983–. (See Figure 9.2.)

Book Review Index. Detroit: Gale, 1965–. Bimonthly. Indexes reviews appearing in more than 450 periodicals in several disciplines; excerpts are not given, only the source of the review. Title index in each issue. Print edition.

Canadian Periodical Index. Toronto: Information Globe, 1839–. Monthly. Indexes 370 Canadian magazines by author, title, and subject. In print; on CD-ROM.

Catholic Periodical and Literature Index. Haverford: Catholic Library Association, 1968–. Bimonthly. An author, title, and subject index to a selected list of Catholic periodicals published mainly in the United States, Canada, England, and Ireland; notes articles written from the Catholic point of view elsewhere. Indexes book, theater, and film reviews.

General Periodicals Index. Foster City: Information Access, 1985–. Monthly. This InfoTrac CD-ROM index[8] indexes and abstracts 1200 periodicals; it is issued in two editions. *Academic Library Edition* covers scholarly journals; the *Public Library Edition* is devoted to general interest magazines. *Expanded Academic Index*™ includes indexing of some 1500 journals, with abstracts for most titles, plus six months current coverage of *The New York Times*; subject areas include humanities, social sciences, and

---

[7] Print versions of Wilson indexes have approximately the same instructions.

[8] InfoTrac, Foster City: Information Access, is a group of 120 plus CD-ROM databases, including *Magazine Index*, *Magazine Index Plus*, *Newspaper Index*, *Business Index*, *General Periodicals Index*, *Academic Index*™, and *Expanded Academic Index*.

science and technology, education, health, women's studies, etc.

General Periodicals on Disc. Ann Arbor: UMI, 1990–. Monthly. Covers periodicals devoted to education, child care, health, and other topics; offers full text of the articles in *Periodical Abstracts on Disc*, which provides only abstracts from more than 900 general periodicals, e.g., *Time, U.S. News*, with photos, charts, maps, and graphs. Search from the index database.

Magazine Article Summaries Full Text Select. Birmingham: EBSCO, 1991–. Monthly. Offers 120,000 abstracts per year from 343 magazines; full text from 25 to 50 magazines, both scholarly and popular. Search by key word. On CD-ROM.

The Magazine Index. Foster City: Information Access, 1977–. Monthly. Indexes more than 400 popular magazines and professional journals. Each issue is on one reel of 16-mm Computer Output Microfilm; must be read with a COM reader; also available online through the DIALOG System.

Magazine Index Plus. Foster City: Information Access, 1990–. Monthly. Indexes some forty-three titles; gives brief annotations; full text coverage in microform is provided by the publisher; covers current affairs, consumer information, travel, arts, entertainment; includes *The New York Times*. On CD-ROM.

Readers' Guide Abstracts. New York: Wilson, 1984–. Monthly. Abstracts about 25,000 articles; online through WilsonLine; CD-ROM on WilsondDisc; in print, on CD-ROM, on tape, and online. (See Figure 9.3.)

FIGURE 9.3
Excerpt from Readers' Guide Abstracts:
(1) Subject. (2) Subdivision of the subject, that is, Automobiles—Air bags. (3) Title of the article on air bags. (4) Author of the article. (5) Title of the magazine in which the article can be found: Motor Trend: volume 44, pages 90–91, January 1992. (6) Abstract of the article. (*Readers' Guide Abstracts*, May 1992. © by The H.W. Wilson Company. Material reproduced by permission of the publisher.)

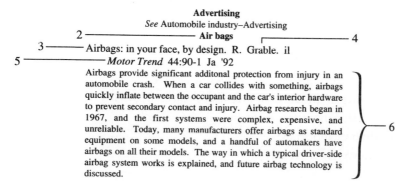

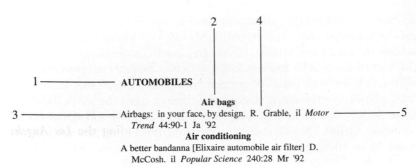

FIGURE 9.4
Excerpt from Readers' Guide to Periodical Literature: *(1) Subject. (2) Subdivision of subject: Automobiles—Air bags. (3) Title of the article on the subject "Automobiles—Air bags," (4) Author of the article. (5) Title of the magazine in which the article can be found,* Motor Trend: *volume 44, pages 90–91, January 1992. (Readers' Guide to Periodical Literature,* May 1992. © *1992 by The H. W. Wilson Company. Material reproduced by permission of the publisher.)*

Readers' Guide to Periodical Literature. New York: Wilson, 1900–. Eighteen issues per year. Indexes 240 periodicals of a general nature representing all important areas of contemporary interest; follows closely the publication date of the periodicals indexed; gives author and title of article, name, volume, date of periodical, and number of pages; indicates whether illustrations, bibliography, and maps are included in the article; book reviews appearing in the magazines indexed are listed in a separate section of the index. In print; on CD-ROM, on tape, and online, 1983–. (See Figure 9.4.)

NEWSPAPER INDEXES

The usefulness of a newspaper index for a particular purpose depends upon:

1. The number and kinds of newspapers indexed
2. The period of time covered
3. Completeness of indexing (all articles or selected articles)
4. The provision of abstracts of articles or selected articles
5. The fullness of information given
6. The method of indexing
7. The frequency of issue

8. The search options offered
9. Ease of use

There are many newspaper indexes and indexing and abstracting services. They may be in print, CD-ROM, online, wire, or other formats. Examples of useful indexes are given below.

Dialog on Disc: Newspapers. Palo Alto: Knight-Ridder, 1990–. Provides access to major newspapers with full-text service, including the *Los Angeles Times* and the *Detroit Free Press*.

Facts on File News Digest CD-ROM. New York: Facts on File, 1980–. Annual. Indexes the annual file of *Facts on File;* retrieves the full text of articles and/or list of index headings and abstracts. Search by key word, date, index topic, and Boolean logic.

Newspaper Abstracts on Disc. Ann Arbor: UMI, 1984–. Monthly. Indexes twenty five major regional and national newspapers, including *The New York Times, Atlanta Constitution* and *Atlanta Journal, Boston Globe, Chicago Tribune, Los Angeles Times, Wall Street Journal*, and *Washington Post*.

The National Newspaper Index. Foster City: Information Access, 1979–. Monthly. One of the InfoTrac group of CD-ROMs. Indexes *The New York Times, Wall Street Journal, Christian Science Monitor, Los Angeles Times* and *Washington Post*. Articles are available on microfiche.

Newsbank. New Canaan: Newsbank, 1970–. Monthly. Indexes newspapers of more than 450 cities; full text of articles on microfiche; covers all subject areas. Printed index; CD-ROM index available since 1982.

The Newsbank Electronic Index. New Canaan: Newsbank, 1986–. Provides access to over 900,000 articles on a range of subjects, e.g., business, current events, books, film, the arts television; to search, choose a database, e.g., *Newsbank* for issues or current events, and search by subject or by browsing the list of headings for that particular database. Full text articles are provided on microfiche by the publisher.

Proquest Newspapers. Ann Arbor: UMI, 1991–. Offers on CD-ROM full-text articles from the *Chicago Tribune, Christian Science Monitor, San Francisco Chronicle, Wall Street Journal*, and *Washington Post;* text only.

The New York Times Index. New York: New York Times, 1913–. Semi-monthly; annual cumulation. Gives exact reference to date, page, and column; summaries of articles may answer question without reference to the paper itself. Indexes book reviews. Print edition; online via NEXIS.

The Times Index. Reading, England: Research Publications, 1906–. Monthly. Compiled from the final editions of *The Times, The Sunday Times and Magazine, The Times Literary Supplement, The Times Educational Supplement*, and *The Times Higher Education Supplement*. Gives day of month, page, and column. Includes book reviews; gives brief abstracts.

Literature in Collections

The original use of "anthology" to mean a volume containing only the "flower" of literature has been extended to mean any collection of extracts from the writings of various authors—often on one subject or of one kind, such as a collection of poems, short stories, essays, plays, speeches, or quotations.

Volumes of collected writings, including those called "readings," constitute an important part of any well-chosen library collection. Some of these collected works are analyzed in the library catalog. Most of them contain so many selections that it is not possible to include all of them in the library catalog.

FIGURE 9.5

Excerpt from Essay and General Literature Index: *(1) Subject. (2) Author of the essay "Television/sound." (3) Title of the essay. (4) Title of the collection in which the essay "Television/sound" is located. (5) Editor of the collection* Studies in Entertainment *in which the essay "Television/sound" is located on pages 39–54. (6) Another subject relating to television broadcasting. (7) A cross reference from the subject "Television news," which is not used, to "Television broadcasting of news," which is used.* (Essay and General Literature Index, June 1987 issue, Copyright © 1987 by The H. W. Wilson Company. Material reproduced by permission of the publisher.)

1 ——— **Television broadcasting** ⟋—3   ⟋———— 4
2 ————— Altman. R. Television/sound. (*In* Studies
      in entertainment; ed. by T. Modleski p39-54) ├—5
         Mellencamp, P. Situation comedy,
      feminism, and Freud: discourses of Gracie
      and Lucy. (*In* Studies in entertainment; ed.
      by T. Modleski p80-95)
6 ——— **Television broadcasting of news**
         Morse, M. The television news personality
      and credibility: reflections on the news in
      transition. (*In* Studies in entertainment; ed.
      by T. Modleski p55-79)
      Television comedy programs *See* Comedy
      programs
      Television journalism *See* Television broad-
      casting of news
      Television news *See* Television broadcasting
      of news   ⟍————————7

Indexes to Literature in Collections

Indexes to literature in collections follow the general pattern of indexes to periodicals and newspapers, but they cover books only. There are indexes to general literature in collections—that is, essays, articles, and speeches covering a variety of subjects. An example of this kind of index is the *Essay and General Literature Index* (Figure 9.5). There are indexes to collections of poetry, stories, and plays. Examples are *Granger's Index to Poetry*, the *Short Story Index*, and the *Play Index*. Indexing is by author, subject, and title, and the location reference includes the name of the compiler of the anthology, the title of the anthology, and the page or pages on which the essay, poem, story, or play can be found.

Indexes to poetry, short stories, and plays are discussed in Chapter 23, Literature. Examples of indexes to collections of literature which cover several subject areas are listed below.

Biography Index. New York: Wilson, 1946–. Indexes current books of individual and collective biography. In print, on CD-ROM, on tape, and online.

Essay and General Literature Index. New York: Wilson, 1934–. Indexes English-language collections of essays, articles, and speeches relating to all subject fields. In print, on CD-ROM, on tape, and online.

CHAPTER

❧ 10 ❧

Biographical Dictionaries

The word "biography," from the Greek *bios*, "life," and *graphein*, "to write," is that form of history which is applied to individuals rather than to nations or civilizations. It is the purpose of biography[1] to tell accurately the history of a person from birth to death in a manner that will reveal various aspects of character, personality, and philosophy.

Since ancient times, people have been interested in the lives of others, either from a desire to eulogize them, to learn from them, or to imitate them, or just from simple curiosity.

Toward the end of the first century after Christ, Plutarch wrote his *Parallel Lives*, the life histories of forty-six Greeks and Romans. The word "biography," however, did not appear in the English language until 1683, when John Dryden described this work of Plutarch's as the "history of particular men's lives." This meaning of "biography"—the history of the life of a person—has become established as a literary form.

Other literary forms contribute to biography but must be distinguished from it. They are:

1. Autobiography, the narration of a person's life by himself or herself
2. Memoirs, the history of a person's times as seen by the individual who writes them
3. Diary, a day-by-day account of the happenings and events in a person's life, recorded by that person

---

[1] Biography is a subject area; biographical dictionaries, which cover persons in many fields and are general in that sense, are included in general reference materials.

4. Letters, written communications of a personal nature (as distinguished from belles lettres, meaning literature), which may be intimate narratives, records of events, or expressions of the writer's thoughts and philosophy.

Biography may draw from these and other sources to present all the significant characteristics of the subject.

The outstanding example of individual biography in English—or in any language—is James Boswell's *Life of Samuel Johnson*, written in the eighteenth century. Since that time biography has become an increasingly important form of literature and occupies a prominent place in all library collections. The student who seeks material on a country, a civilization, or a period of history will do well to investigate the lives of outstanding persons who were a part of that country, civilization, or period of history.

Biography as a literary form differs in purpose, style, and content from simple biographical information about a person.

In the nineteenth century, there appeared in most European countries publications called "dictionaries of national biography," presenting biographical information about all important national figures. These collections of biographical articles were the forerunners of the modern biographical dictionary, a work which combines biography (factual information about the life of an individual) and dictionary (alphabetical arrangement).

The biographical dictionary, with biographical sketches arranged alphabetically by surname, does not qualify as true biography, since it does not present all aspects of an individual's life. However, the *Dictionary of National Biography* and the *Dictionary of American Biography* are outstanding for their scholarly and objective treatment of the persons included.

Biographical dictionaries are among the most frequently used books in the academic library (or in any library). Questions about notable people and about people in the news—their lives, interests, education, background, affiliations, position, and even addresses—come from faculty and students alike.

There are numerous sources of biographical information concerning individuals; these include encyclopedias, encyclopedia annuals, dictionaries, newspapers, and magazines. However, the reference sources which were written for the specific purpose of providing the kinds of biographical information mentioned above or indicating where it can be found are:

1. Biographical indexes, which point out books, periodicals, and other sources in which the information can be found
2. Biographical dictionaries, which contain the information sought

Kinds of Biographical Dictionaries[2]

Biographical dictionaries can be divided into three classes according to the nationality, the profession, and the dates of the persons included:

1. Universal—not limited to any state, country, or profession
    a Persons not living
    b Living persons and persons not living
    c Living persons
2. National or regional—limited in coverage to particular countries or regions but including persons from all the professions and occupations
    a Persons not living
    b Living persons and persons not living
    c Living persons
3. Professional or occupational—limited to persons in a specific profession or occupation
    a Universal
        (i)   Persons not living
        (ii) Living persons and persons not living
        (iii) Living persons
    b National or regional
        (i)   Persons not living
        (ii) Living persons and persons not living
        (iii) Living persons

Choosing a Biographical Dictionary

To determine which biographical dictionary will provide information on a particular person, it is helpful to know the scope and purpose of each biographical dictionary and to establish, if possible, the following facts about the person before beginning the search for information:

1. Dates of birth and (if not living) death
2. Nationality
3. Profession or occupation

---

[2] Some biographical dictionaries are called "directories," e.g., *Directory of American Scholars* (see p. 168). They provide biographical sketches of the persons included.

Sources which will aid in establishing these facts are:

1. Library catalog. If the individual has written a book, and if this book is listed in the catalog, dates of birth and death may be given following the person's name on the catalog card. The subject matter of the book or books by and about this person may indicate field or work, and the place of publication may provide a clue to nationality.
2. *Cumulative Book Index.* If the library catalog does not include any books by or about the person in question, the *Cumulative Book Index*, which is a world list of books in the English language, will list the books he or she has written in English.
3. *Biography Index.* This index to biographical articles appearing in books and magazines (excluding biographical dictionaries) gives the dates and the profession of all persons included. If the individual is not an American, nationality is given also.
4. Periodical indexes. Any periodical articles by or about the person on whom the student seeks information should be listed in one of the indexes to periodical literature. The periodicals in which the articles appear often include a brief statement about the author. The dates of publication of these articles may provide a clue to the time when the individual might have been included in a biographical dictionary or was in the current news. The subject matter of the articles will indicate field of interest, and the place of publication may suggest nationality. Indexes to periodical literature also list obituaries, which often provide full biographical information.
5. A book by the person in question. The title page may list the author's position, such as Professor of History, McGill University, or Professor of English, Duke University, immediately following his or her name. The location of the university may be a clue to the nationality of the person teaching there. The position held indicates profession.
6. A yearbook or a handbook may give the nationality and dates of an individual, and this information will tell the researcher which biographical dictionary is likely to provide information on the person.

The advantage gained by establishing the dates, the nationality, and the profession of a person before consulting any biographical dictionary will more than make up for the time spent in locating this information. For example, if the subject is an important contemporary American politician, the following biographical dictionaries will be eliminated from consideration immediately:

> *Dictionary of American Biography*
> *Dictionary of National Biography*
> *Appleton's Cyclopaedia of American Biography*

Among the biographical dictionaries which are possible sources of information about a living American politician are:

> *Who's Who in America*
> *Current Biography*
> *International Who's Who*

Living American scientists are covered in *American Men and Women of Science*, but not in *Dictionary of Scientific Biography*. For other biographical sources in the subject fields, see Chapters 17 to 24.

It is necessary to point out that in some cases none of the sources mentioned above—library catalog, periodical indexes, *Cumulative Book Index*, *Biography Index*, books by the individual or yearbooks—will provide dates, nationality, or profession. In such cases, locating biographical material about the individual becomes a tedious process of trial and error. Even when dates, nationality, and profession have been established, it is not always possible to find the subject in the biographical dictionary or dictionaries designed to cover the person's profession, nationality, and time of prominence. Information in the several biographical dictionaries is provided, for the most part, at the request of the publisher by the individuals included. The fact that a person is not included may mean that he or she failed to furnish the biographical information requested and that the publisher was unable to secure it from other sources. In such cases, it may be necessary to identify individuals by piecing together bits of information from the jackets of their books, from a few titles of periodical articles by or about them, or from the fact that they edit, or contribute to, professional journals.

Using a Biographical Dictionary

Before using any biographical dictionary the first time, it is helpful to read the preliminary pages to determine (1) whether the alphabetical arrangement is letter by letter or word by word; (2) what special features are included; and (3) what abbreviations and symbols are used. The method of selecting names to be included should be noted, as a test of the objectivity of the work.

Representative Biographical Dictionaries[3]

UNIVERSAL BIOGRAPHY

Living persons and persons not living

The McGraw-Hill Encyclopedia of World Biography. 12 vols. New York: McGraw, 1973. Includes persons living and not living; articles include basic biographical facts and commentary on the person's background and character, evaluation of the person's role in history, and a portrait whenever possible; Vol. XII contains historical maps, index, and study guides. 20th Century Supplements, Vol. 13–16, 1987–1989; Vol. 16 provides study guide.

Magnusson, Magnus, ed. *Cambridge Biographical Dictionary.* New York: Cambridge UP, 1990. Includes notable twentieth century persons in all areas: popular culture, music, sports, and others "likely to be looked up." Gives attention to women; is international in scope.

Smith, Jessie Carney. *Notable Black American Women.* Detroit: Gale, 1992. Provides essays on some 500 African-American women born between 1730 and 1958; represents many fields of endeavor.

Webster's New Biographical Dictionary. Springfield: Merriam, 1988. Lists names of 40,000 noteworthy persons with pronunciation and concise biographies; is not limited by period, race, religion, or occupation; includes table of heads of state and other high officials, historical and contemporary.

Living persons

Current Biography. New York: Wilson, 1940–. Monthly except December. *Current Biography Yearbook,* 1946–. Aims to cover all important contemporary figures in all fields; includes pronunciation for unusual names, photographs, and a bibliography of the sources used. Yearbooks contain indexes by names and professions. *Current Biography Cumulated Index, 1940–1990.* 1991.

International Who's Who. London: Europa, 1935–. Annual. Includes sketches of important people in the world today.

The New York Times Biographical Service: A Compilation of Current Biographical Information of General Interest. New York: New York Times, 1974. Monthly. Gives profiles of people in the news; contains from twenty to fifty articles each week reprinted from *The New York Times;* represents all

---

[3] See Chapters 17 to 24 for biographical dictionaries in subject fields.

sections of the country; some articles are obituaries; some are news items; others are interviews. Loose-leaf format.

NATIONAL OR REGIONAL BIOGRAPHY

Persons not living

Appleton's Cyclopaedia of American Biography. Rev. ed. 6 vols. New York: Appleton, 1887–1900. Includes all important persons identified with American history from its earliest beginnings; has lengthy articles and many portraits.

Concise Dictionary of National Biography. 3 vols. New York: Oxford UP, 1992. Provides shortened versions of the articles in the original set. *Comprehensive Index,* 1990.

Dictionary of American Biography. Published under the auspices of the American Council of Learned Societies. 21 vols. New York: Scribner's, 1927–1981. Provides scholarly, signed articles on person who influenced their time; gives bibliographic references for further information on the person; covers only persons not living. Vol. 21 is the first supplement; Supplements 2 to 7 bring the work to 1965. Now available in ten base volumes (A-Z) and Supplements 1 to 8. *Complete Index Guide,* 1990, indexes the entire work. *New Concise Dictionary of American Biography,* 4th ed., 1991.

Dictionary of Canadian Biography/Dictionnaire Biographique du Canada. Toronto: U of Toronto P, 1966–. (In progress.) Vol. I: 1000–1700; Vol. II: 1701–1740; Vol. III: 1741–1770; Vol. IV: 1771–1800; Vol. VI: 1821–1835; Vol. IX: 1861–1870; Vol. X: 1871–1880; Vol. XI: 1881–1890; Vol. XII: 1891–1900. Follows the scholarly tradition of the *Dictionary of National Biography;* arranged by period, each volume covering a given range of years; includes persons born and residing in Canada and persons from other countries who have made contributions to Canadian life.

Dictionary of National Biography. Ed. Leslie Stephen and Sidney Lee. 22 vols. London: Oxford UP, 1922. Eight 10-year *Supplements* cover the period 1901–1985. Provides full, accurate biographies of all notable inhabitants of Great Britain and the colonies (exclusive of living persons) from the earliest historical period to the present time; includes bibliographical references.

James, Edward T., ed. *Notable American Women 1607–1950: A Biographical Dictionary.* 3 vols. Cambridge: Belknap P of Harvard UP, 1971. Sponsored by Radcliffe College; covers 300 years of women's history in America; includes women who have achieved distinction in their own right; includes bibliographies. *Notable American Women, the Modern Period: A Biographical Dictionary*, ed. by Barbara Sicherman and others (Cambridge: Belknap P of Harvard UP, 1980), supplements *Notable American Women 1607–1950* and brings it to December 31, 1975.

Who Was Who. 8 vols. London: St. Martin's, 1991. Companion volume to *Who's Who;* contains biographies of persons in *Who's Who* who have died, with the date of the death added. These volumes cover the period 1897–1980. *Index*, 1981. *Who Was Who Cumulated Index, 1897–1980*, 1991.

Who Was Who in America. 8 vols. Chicago: Marquis, 1942–1985. Gives biographies of persons in *Who's Who in America* who have died, with date of death added. *Index*, 1985. Vol. 9, 1989. Also available online via DIALOG.

Who Was Who in America: Historical Volume 1607–1896. Chicago: Marquis, 1963. Supplements *Who Was Who in America.* Treats Americans and other outstanding figures in the early development of America.

Living persons and persons not living

Clark, Judith Freeman. *Almanac of American Women in the 20th Century.* Englewood Cliffs: Prentice, 1987. Covers significant issues and events marking women's achievements in recent United States history; has a chronology of events to 1987.

Encyclopedia of American Biography. Ed. John A. Garraty. New York: Harper, 1974. Presents about 1000 biographical accounts of persons living and not living; selection is based on their significance, achievement, and fame. Each sketch consists of a summary of the essential biographical data, followed by an interpretative essay evaluating the person's career; includes minorities and women who may have been omitted from other sources.

The National Cyclopedia of American Biography. 63 vols. Clifton: James T. White, 1881–1984. Based on original materials; provides detailed biographical articles about noteworthy Americans from the beginning of this nation to the present; in every field of activity; covers men and women who are distinguished locally a well as nationally. Index volume includes names of all subjects in all volumes and thousands of topical entries.

Webster's American Biographies. Ed. Charles Van Doren and Robert McHenry. Springfield: Merriam, 1979. Covers some 3000 persons, living and not living, who have made a significant contribution to American life; special attention is given to groups often neglected (Indians, western pioneers, and women); geographical indexes and careers and professions indexes are provided.

Living persons

Who's Who, New York: St. Martin's, 1849–. Annual. The first "who's who"; includes persons of distinction in all fields; covers Great Britain and the Commonwealth nations.

Who's Who among Black Americans. Ed. Iris Cloyd and William C. Martinez. 6th ed. Detroit: Gale, 1990. Gives biographical sketches of more than 18,000 living notable black American men and women in many fields, selected on the basis of significant achievement; has geographical and occupation indexes.

Who's Who in America. Chicago: Marquis, 1899–. Biennial. Includes persons of special prominence in every line of work and those who are selected arbitrarily because of their positions in government, religion, education, industry, and other fields. Since 1972–1973, in 2 vols. Supplement to 44th ed., 1987.

Who's Who in the World. 10th ed. Chicago: Marquis, 1992. Aims to identify important personalities of the world; contains more than 28,000 names from some 150 countries of persons who are "shaping today's world and tomorrow's future"; entries are chosen by members of the Marquis staff. Other useful biographies of the "who's who" type, which include eminent living persons from all professions, are:

> *Official Catholic Directory*
> *Who's Who in France*
> *Who's Who in Germany*
> *Who's Who in Italy*
> *Who's Who of American Women*
> *Who's Who in Canada*

In addition to those listed above, there are biographical dictionaries by section of a country and by profession, e.g., *Who's Who in the East*, *Who's Who in American Art*.

Professional and occupational biographical dictionaries are discussed in the chapters which treat each subject field.

Indexes to Biography[4]

In addition to the biographical dictionaries which provide the desired information, there are indexes which point out biographies in books and in periodical literature. Indexes to periodical literature, indexes to newspapers,

[4] See also Chapter 9, Indexes.

and indexes to collected works cover biographical articles. The following indexes include only biographical material. They point out where biographical articles or books can be found and give the titles and pages of books or the volumes, dates, and pages of periodicals.

Biography and Genealogy Master Index. 2d ed. Detroit: Gale, 1982–. Annual. Contains more than 7 million citations to biographical articles which have appeared in some 700 works of individual and collective biography; covers persons living and not living. In print and online via DIALOG.

Biography Index. New York: Wilson, 1947–. Quarterly; annual cumulations. Locates biographical materials in some 2700 periodicals indexed in Wilson indexes; also indexed are current books of individual and collective biography, autobiographies, diaries, collections of letters, memoirs, biographical material in nonbiographical works, and obituaries of national interest published in *The New York Times;* bibliographies, portraits, and other illustrations are noted if they are included in the indexed material; provides an index by professions and occupations. In print, online, tape, and CD-ROM.

CHAPTER

❧ 11 ❧

Atlases and Gazetteers[1]

Before they could write, and perhaps before they could speak, primitive people left landmarks (cairns) to show where they had been. The oldest known map is a Babylonian clay tablet dating from about 2300 B.C. There are many other clay tablets which show geographical locations.

The Greeks, using their knowledge of science, philosophy, mathematics, geography, and astronomy, succeeded in developing mapmaking (cartography) to a point not again attained until the sixteenth century. Greek geographers from the fifth century B.C. believed that the earth is a sphere. About A.D. 150, Claudius Ptolemy of Alexandria, perhaps the greatest single contributor in history to cartography and geography, compiled his eight-volume *Geographia*, the first scientific and comprehensive treatment of cartography. It contained, in addition to the text, twenty-eight maps and a list of all the principal places then known. The *Geographia* disappeared during the Middle Ages and was not found until the fifteenth century. Its rediscovery[2] helped make possible the voyages of Columbus, Magellan, Vasco da Gama, John Cabot, and others, thus hastening the era of discovery and exploration. In turn, the discoveries of these explorers greatly increased the demand for maps.

Important contributors to mapmaking during this period were Mercator, famous for his celestial and terrestrial globes and for his system of projection, and Ortelius, credited with the publication of the first modern atlas in 1570. Both were members of the Dutch school of cartography.

---

[1] Atlases and gazetteers belong in the subject field of geography. They are included here because of their general reference value.

[2] The *Geographia* had been preserved by the Arabs.

Atlases

A map is a representation, usually flat, of the earth's surface or a part of it or of the celestial sphere or a part of it.[3] An atlas is a collection of maps, usually bound together in one volume. The word "atlas" was first used in this sense by Mercator, from the figure of the mythological Atlas, which was often used as the frontispiece of early collections of maps. It has come to mean any volume containing not only maps, but also plates, engravings, charts, and tables, with or without descriptive text. It is sometimes used as the name of a volume in which subjects are presented in tabular form.

While it is generally recognized that atlases are essential in studying history,[4] geography, and other branches of the social sciences, it is becoming increasingly apparent that many atlases are valuable also as general reference sources because of the descriptive materials they contain in addition to maps. Today, maps are necessary companions to the daily newspaper and radio and television news commentary, verifying names, places, and events in the news and presenting them in proper geographical relationship to other names, places, and events.

There are many sources of maps. Most of the general encyclopedias include maps either in a separate volume or as illustrative materials within the text; encyclopedia annuals include up-to-date maps; many handbooks, almanacs, newspapers, and periodicals also contain maps. However, the atlas is the reference source designed primarily to provide maps.

Atlases vary in quality, and they also vary according to the country of publication. For example, an atlas of the world which is published in America will include more or larger maps of America than one published in France. The latter will include larger maps of France.

CHOOSING AN ATLAS[5]

To be able to choose an atlas to answer a given question, it is necessary to know certain things about each atlas.

1. Scope
   a Is it worldwide in coverage, or is it limited to one or more regions?
   b Does it include all kinds of maps, political, topographical, thematic, relief, etc., or only one kind of map?
   c Does it provide descriptive material about the various geographical locations?

---

[3] *Webster's New Collegiate Dictionary* (Springfield, Mass.: Merriam, 1960), p. 513.

[4] A historical atlas is made up of maps which delineate past events or periods of history; it is not a collection of old maps.

[5] For examples of atlases in subject fields, see Chapters 17 to 24.

2. Place of publication as an indication of emphasis
3. Date of publication as an indication of up-to-dateness
4. Kind of index
    a Is there one comprehensive index for the entire volume, or are there separate indexes for each map or section of maps?
    b Is the index a separate volume, or is it part of the atlas?
    c Does it indicate pronunciation?
    d Is the reference to the location on a given map clear and definite?
5. Quality and content of the maps
    a Is the scale indicated clearly?
    b Are the symbols distinct and easily read?
    c Are the projections in keeping with the purpose of the map?
    d Is the lettering clear and legible?
    e Is the coloring varied and well differentiated?
    f Is the legend clearly explained?
    g Are the names of countries given in the language of each country or in translation?

Gazetteers

A gazetteer gives information about geographical places; it does not define them. In addition to geographic location, it gives historical, statistical, cultural, and other relevant facts about these places. It may also indicate pronunciation. Because they provide a variety of factual material about places, gazetteers are important reference sources. Recent editions describe a place as it is now; old editions give historical information about it. The economic growth or decline of a town or city, as indicated by data on population, number of industries, schools, and so on, will often be shown by the brief facts given in gazetteers over a period of years.

In using a gazetteer, it is important to note the copyright date as an indication of how recent the material is; the system of pronunciation and the abbreviations used; the arrangement of the material; and any additional material, such as maps and tables, which may be included in appendixes.

Useful Atlases and Gazetteers

ATLASES

Bartholomew, John W., ed. *The Times Atlas of the World.* Vol. I: *The World, Australasia & East Asia.* Vol. II: *South-west Asia & Russia.* Vol. III.

Northern Europe. Vol. IV: *Southern Europe & Africa*, Vol. V: *The Americas*, Midcentury Edition. London: The Times, 1955–1959. Each volume has its own index-gazetteer; provides inset maps of many cities; is outstanding for the beauty and accuracy of maps.

The Times Index Gazetteer of the World (1965) lists in 1 vol. the place names separately indexed in the 5 vols. of the Midcentury Edition.

Britannica Atlas. Chicago: Encyclopaedia Britannica, 1991. The text is in five languages: English, French, Spanish, Portuguese, German; has physical and thematic maps, plates, and tables.

Electromap World Atlas. Fayetteville: Electronoplane, 1989. Combines atlas and information; topographic and thematic color maps. CD-ROM.

Goode's World Atlas. 18th ed. Chicago: Rand, 1991. Includes physical and political maps, special maps relating to climate, temperature, major cities, regions, the ocean floor, etc.

Hammond Atlas of the World. Maplewood: Hammond, 1992. Notable for attractive format, up-to-date coverage of recent changes in the Soviet Union, Czechoslovakia, and Yugoslavia and for clarity of maps. Arranged by continent.

Hammond Gold Medallion World Atlas. Maplewood: Hammond, 1992. Places all the information about a continent, country, state, or province on consecutive pages; maps of various kinds plus all other relevant political, economic, and geographical data placed together.

Mason, Robert, and Mark T. Mattson. *Atlas of United States Environmental Issues.* New York: Macmillan, 1990. Surveys in text and maps the state of the environment throughout the United States, including specific natural disasters and problems such as conservation and pollution; treats the politics of environment.

Mattson, Catherine M., and Mark T. Mattson. *Contemporary Atlas of the United States.* New York: Macmillan, 1990. Presents basic information about the United States in color maps: climate, population physiography, government, environmental and social issues, agriculture, communication, family, etc.; uses charts and tables also.

National Geographic Atlas of the World. 6th ed. Washington: National Geographic Soc., 1990. Up to date through the invasion of Kuwait (August 1990); includes physical and thematic maps of each continent, spacecraft and satellite maps, earth maps of each continent and of the states of the United States; gives information about climate, resources, environment, agriculture, population of major cities (1990); shows Unified Germany.

The New International Atlas. Chicago: Rand, 1990. Offers political, physical, urban area, strategic, and geographic area maps of the countries of the world; gives population tables for all countries and principal cities; presents the world in broad view and also in detail; includes maps and charts on such topics as population distribution, energy production and consumption, and climate; has a glossary and abbreviations of geographical terms which appear on the maps; does not define terms; place names are in the language of the country.

The New Oxford Atlas. 3d ed. Prepared by the Cartographic Department of the Oxford University Press. London: Oxford UP, 1978. Includes general reference, thematic, and relief maps; covers oceans, temperature, climate, rainfall, land use, vegetation, and population data.

Peters Atlas of the World. New York: Harper, 1990. Shows global data on climate, population, vegetation, health, social issues, nature, etc. on 246 thematic maps in color; uses Peters projection, equal-area maps, techniques of imaging, and computer technology.

The Prentice-Hall Great International Atlas. Englewood Cliffs: Prentice, 1981. Gives full map coverage to the countries of the world; contains historical, cultural, scientific, and geographical information on every part of the world; extensive use of colored illustrations and color in maps.

Rand McNally Cosmopolitan World Atlas. Chicago: Rand, 1992. Shows changes in Western Europe—Unified Germany—and in the Baltic area; uses maps and text; 1990 census figures are used for the United States; includes maps of the world and special regions (polar region's oceans, etc.); regional maps, each state of the United States.

Rand McNally Premier World Atlas. Chicago: Rand, 1992. Covers space, the planets, special regions, mountains, lakes, rivers, all countries of the world, and population; includes United States highway maps; gives explanation of map projection.

The Times Atlas of World Exploration. Ed. Felipe Fernandez Armento. New York: HarperCollins, 1991. Gives the state of knowledge of various regions from early times to about 1500; relates the activities of the European explorers of the Age of Discovery; has color illustrations, antique maps, biographical information, and an index of place names.

The Times Atlas of the World. 9th ed. New York: Times Books, 1992. Gives physical-political maps for regions, nations, and localities of the earth; has thematic maps for world physiography, oceanography, climatology, vegetation, population; includes air routes.

U. S. Dept. of the Interior, Geological Survey. *The National Atlas of the United States of America.* Washington: GPO, 1970. The official national atlas of the United States; has 765 maps and an index which identifies more than 41,000 place names; includes many thematic maps which present the physical, economic, social, and historical features of the country; includes six plastic overlays correlated with the thematic and special maps; divided between "General Reference Maps" and "Special Reference Maps."

GAZETTEERS

Munro, David, ed. *Cambridge World Gazetteer*. 5th ed. New York: Cambridge UP, 1988. "An A–Z of Geographical Information" (subtitle); gives depth of detail in more than 20,000 entries, covering location, chief physical features, and industries; gives current version of place names that have changed in recent years; has a 120-page atlas of Bartholomew maps.

Paxton, John, ed. *The Statesman's Year-Book World Gazetteer*. 4th ed. New York: St. Martin's 1991. Gives information on the countries of the world: place names, locations, brief descriptions, recent history, population figures, industry, culture, and commerce; defines more than 700 geographical terms.

Webster's New Geographical Dictionary. 5th ed. Springfield: Merriam, 1988. Provides geographical, economic, and historical information about countries, cities, regions, and natural features of the world; gives pronunciations; includes maps.

CHAPTER

❧ 12 ❧

Yearbooks and Handbooks[1]

Every library has a number of books for quick reference which provide brief information on a multitude of subjects. Among these "ready-reference" works are yearbooks and handbooks.

A yearbook is a publication which is issued annually for the purpose of giving current information in narrative, statistical, or directory form. There are several types of yearbooks:

1. Encyclopedia annuals, issued by the major encyclopedia publishers as a means of keeping the encyclopedia up to date, are comprehensive in coverage and give a summary of all the major events of the preceding year.
2. Yearbooks, which treat several subject areas, include social, political, educational, cultural, and other information.
3. Almanacs, which were originally calendars of months and days with special dates and anniversaries, forecasts of the weather, and astronomical calculations, are now collections of miscellaneous facts and statistics.
4. Directories, which list persons or organizations in alphabetical or classified arrangement, include addresses and affiliations for individuals and officers and other data for organizations. Not all directories are issued annually.

A handbook (literally, a small book which can be held in the hand) is a volume which treats broad subjects in brief fashion. It may include odd bits

---

[1] See also yearbooks and handbooks in each of the subject fields.

of information about a variety of topics. Among the most useful types of handbooks are:

1. Manuals, which give instruction on, or serve as guides to, occupations, hobbies, art forms, trades, etc. Example: *Robert's Rules of Order*.
2. Miscellanies, which include bits of unusual and hard-to-find information on many subjects. Example: *Famous First Facts*.
3. Companions, which explain and interpret various aspects of a subject. Example: *The Oxford Companion to Ships & the Sea*.
4. Digests, which present in condensed form information that is classified and arranged under proper headings or titles; examples are digests of laws, digests of articles from periodicals, or digests of the plots of novels, short stories, dramas, or poems.[2] Example: *Masterplots*.

Selection and Use of a Yearbook or Handbook

Each yearbook or handbook is designed to provide certain kinds of information for the purpose of answering specific kinds of questions. Therefore, before attempting to choose a yearbook or a handbook, the student should examine the question to be answered:

1. Does it require statistical information?
2. Is it a directory-type question?
3. Is it a "trend" question?
4. Does it come under the heading of miscellany?

In order to use a yearbook or a handbook quickly and satisfactorily, it is necessary to understand:

1. Organization and arrangement of material
   a Is it organized into chapters or into broad general subjects, and does it have a detailed table of contents, a comprehensive index, or both?
   b Is it broken down into small topics, arranged alphabetically?
   c Does it have tables only, or does it give both text and tables?
2. Kinds of material included
   a Is it statistical? If it is, does it give the source for the statistics presented?
   b Does it give instructions and directions?

---

[2] See also pp. 243–245.

    c Is it a collection of miscellaneous information?
3. Scope
    a Does it cover all countries and all subjects?
    b Is it limited to one country and to a selected number of subjects?
4. Period covered
    a Is it one year? Two years?
    b If it is a handbook, is it revised often?
5. Special aids to the reader
    a Does it provide bibliographical references for further reading?
    b Does it provide cross references?
    c Is the illustrative material—charts, tables, maps, pictures—appropriate and adequate?
6. Kinds of questions it will answer
    a Will it answer factual and statistical questions?
    b Will it provide "trend" and background information?

Representative Yearbooks and Handbooks

YEARBOOKS

Encyclopedia annuals

Americana Annual. New York: Grolier, 1923–. Covers events of the previous year; features a brief chronological listing of events.

Britannica Book of the Year. Chicago: Encyclopedia Britannica, 1938–. Gives a calendar of events, many short articles under specific titles, statistics, and bibliography.

Collier's Year Book. New York: Collier, 1938–. Surveys the events of the year; is especially strong in sports and chronology.

Other yearbooks and annuals

Europa Yearbook. 2 vols. London: Europa, 1959–. Covers some 1500 international organizations and all countries; provides information about the press, political parties, trade, industry, television, statistics, education, and religion.

The Statesman's Yearbook. London: Macmillan, 1864–. Covers government, area, population, education, religion, social welfare, money, industry, defense, international relations, energy, economic conditions, trade, communications, and other information about the countries of the world; arranged alphabetically by country.

ALMANACS

Canadian Almanac and Directory. Toronto: Copp Clark, 1848–. Annual. Gives statistical and other information for Canada on miscellaneous subjects, including geography, history, education, law, sports, and religion.

Information Please Almanac, Atlas & Yearbook. Boston: Houghton, 1947–. Annual. Has a topical arrangement and subject index; covers people and places, facts, figures, news, views—past and present; emphasizes sports.

Whitaker, Joseph. *Almanack*. London: Whitaker, 1868–. Annual. Gives complete statistical information regarding government finances, population, and commerce for various nations in the world, with emphasis on Great Britain and the United States; contains material relating to astronomical and other phenomena; includes maps.

The World Almanac and Book of Facts. New York: Pharos, 1868–. Annual. Gives comprehensive coverage of factual material of all kinds; index is in the front of the book.

DIRECTORIES

The Foundation Directory. 14th ed. New York: Foundation Center, 1992. Arranged by state; lists foundations by types, geographical distribution, and economic factors; gives grant application information.

HANDBOOKS

Dreyfuss, Henry. *Symbol Sourcebook: An Authoritative Guide to International Graphic Symbols*. New York: McGraw, 1972. Covers more than 6000 symbols used internationally in business, industry, the sciences, and all fields; arranged by broad subject.

Kane, Joseph Nathan. *Famous First Facts*. 4th ed. New York: Wilson, 1981. Covers first happenings: events, discoveries, and inventions in the United States; has index by year, day, subject, personal names, and geographical location. *Supplement to the 4th ed.*, 1985, brings it up to date through Reagan.

Mossman, Jennifer, ed. *Holidays and Anniversaries of the World*. 2nd ed. Detroit: Gale, 1990. Covers every month and day of the year: anniversaries, fast days, feast days, Holy days, historical dates, important birthdays, sports events, etc.

The New York Public Library Book of How and Where to Look It Up. New York: Prentice, 1991. Gives both directory and bibliographical information; covers reference books, picture sources, special collections, electronic databases, and types of reference sources; explains how to do research in each area; has annotated entries.

The Oxford Companion to Ships & the Sea. Ed. Peter Kemp. London: Oxford UP, 1976. Covers a wide range of topics (terms related to the sea, names and kinds of ships, seafaring history, authors and artists of the sea, pirates, and fictional and mythological characters); has photographs, line drawings, and diagrams.

Post, Elizabeth, ed. *Emily Post's Etiquette*. 15th ed. New York: Harper, 1992. Gives attention to modern changes in etiquette as well as to traditional manners; offers charts and tables, samples invitations, etc.

Robert's Rules of Order. New rev. ed. A new and enlarged ed. by Sarah Corbin Robert. Glenview: Scott Foresman, 1981. A guide for parliamentary procedure; provides new material.

Smith, Whitney. *Flags and Arms Across the World*. New York. McGraw, 1980. Provides information on the flags of 174 countries, including a color illustration of the official flag; the presidential flag; the coat of arms or seal; and the date of official adoption.

Webster's New World Secretarial Handbook. New rev. ed. New York: Simon, 1981. Gives guidelines for typing, word processing, taking dictation, form and structure of business letters, grammar and usage, abbreviations, and office equipment; has a glossary of business terms.

CHAPTER
❧ 13 ❧

Bibliographies

The word "bibliography," deriving from two Greek words—*biblion*, "book," and *graphein*, "to write"—was used in postclassical Greece in the sense of "the writing of books." The scribes who copied books were the first bibliographers. This meaning was in use as late as 1761, as is indicated by the definition of the word "bibliographer" in Fenning's *English Dictionary* of that date as "one who copies books."

The transition from meaning the writing *of* books to meaning writing *about* books dates from the eighteenth century; the latter meaning is in use today.

In the sense of "writing about books," the terms "bibliography" has several uses:

1. It is the systematic description of groups of books, manuscripts, and other publications as to authorship, title, edition, and imprint, and their enumeration and arrangement into lists for purposes of information.[1]
2. It is the name given to a list of books, manuscripts, and other publications, systematically described and arranged, which have some relationship to each other. Thus, there are several kinds of bibliographies:
   a General—not limited to one author, subject, country, or period of time
   b Author—listing the works by and about one author
   c Subject—restricted to one subject or to one subject field
   d National or regional—including material relating to one country or to one region

---

[1] See pp. 275–282

    e Trade—directed to the book trade and supplying information needed in buying and selling books
3. It is the science of books, that branch of learning concerned with the historical and technical examination of written works, in which books and manuscripts are examined to discover or verify their origin, dates, number and order of pages, authorship, and textual material.

A bibliography may be complete, including *all* works of a particular kind, or it may be selective, containing only some of the works. It may be descriptive, having only a brief descriptive note (annotation); it may be evaluative, that is, with critical comment; or it may be both descriptive and evaluative. There are bibliographies of forms other than books, such as periodicals, newspapers, and nonbook materials, and bibliographies of types of material, such as book reviews, biographical materials, and bibliographies.

Bibliographies may be found in individual books, in periodical articles, and in encyclopedias and other reference books, or they may be separate books. There are bibliographies both of a general nature and in specific subject fields to aid the researcher in the quest for material.

The printed catalogs of individual and of national libraries such as the Library of Congress are forms of bibliographies. They are photographic reproductions of the cards in the card catalog of the libraries they represent. Some printed catalogs are union catalogs—that is, lists of the combined holdings of several or many libraries. Union catalogs and lists indicate by means of symbols the libraries which hold a given title and enable researchers to know where they can borrow a copy if their library does not have it or where they can secure a photocopy of a desired piece of material. There are union catalogs (lists) of books, periodical publications, nonbook materials, and combinations of these.

Bibliographies are useful sources in any search for material on a subject.

1. They locate material on the subject in question.
2. They provide a means of verifying such items as author's name, complete title of work, place of publication, publisher, date of publication, edition, number of pages, and price.
3. If they are annotated, they indicate the scope of the work and the manner in which the subject is treated; if the annotation is critical and evaluative, it comments upon the usefulness of the publication.
4. They point out material, including parts of books, which cannot be analyzed in the catalog.
5. They group works according to form, location, and period.

Bibliographies in subject fields are discussed in Chapters 17 to 24.

Representative Bibliographies

GENERAL BIBLIOGRAPHIES

The Bibliographic Index. New York: Wilson, 1938–. Three times a year; annual cumulation. A subject list of bibliographies; includes those published as books and pamphlets and those which appear in the more than 800 periodicals indexed in the Wilson indexes, both in English and in foreign languages. Lists bibliographies that name fifty or more citations. Available in print, online, on tape, and on CD-ROM from WilsonLine and WilsonDisc.

UNION CATALOGS

Library of Congress Catalogs: National Union Catalog. Washington: LC, 1956–. Nine monthly issues; quarterly and five-year cumulations. A list by author of materials held by some 1500 North American libraries; contains reproductions of cards for books, pamphlets, maps, atlases, and periodicals in many languages; locations for some titles are given. Since 1983, issued only in microfiche. Also available online and on CD-ROM.

Library of Congress Catalogs: Subject Catalog 1950–. Washington: LC, 1955–. Three quarterly issues with annual and five-year cumulations. A subject catalog of 1945 and later works represented by Library of Congress printed cards; includes books cataloged by members of the National Union Catalog arrangement; after 1956 a location in at least one library is given. Formerly *Library of Congress Catalog Books: Subjects.* Available on microfiche

BIBLIOGRAPHIES OF PERIODICAL PUBLICATIONS

Katz, Bill, and Linda Sternberger Katz. *Magazines for Libraries.* 7th ed. New York: Bowker, 1992. Provides an annotated list of magazines for the general reader and for school, junior college, college, university, and public libraries; includes more than 66,000 titles; gives complete bibliographical information; indicates whether available in editions other than print.

The Standard Periodical Directory. 15th ed. New York: Oxbridge, 1992. Lists 75,000 periodical publications in the United States and Canada, including consumer and special interest magazines, newsletters, house organs, directories, government publications, bulletins, yearbooks, and religious and association publications.

Ulrich's International Periodicals Directory 1992–93. 31st ed. New York: Bowker, 1992. Arranged by subject, lists some 120,000 periodicals covering

542 subjects; gives detailed information regarding content, sponsorship, frequency, language of text, etc.; lists serials available online, on CD-ROM, and on microfiche. *Ulrich's Plus:* CD-ROM; *Ulrich's on Microfiche 1992-93; Ulrich's Online:* through DIALOG, BRS, ESA-IRS.

Union List of Serials in Libraries of the United States and Canada. 3d ed. 5 vols. Ed. Edna Brown Titus. New York: Wilson, 1965. Lists more than 150,000 serial titles in 956 libraries—periodicals, proceedings, annual reports—which began publication before December 31, 1949; arranged by title; indicates by symbols the libraries which have copies of each title. Supplemented by *New Serial Titles, A Union List of Serials Commencing Publication after December 31, 1949.* Washington: LC, 1953–. Monthly with annual cumulations; beginning 1969, has eight monthly issues, quarterly issues, and annual and five- or ten-year cumulations.

SELECTIVE AND EVALUATIVE BIBLIOGRAPHIES

Reader's Adviser: A Layman's Guide to Literature 13th ed. 6 vols. New York: Bowker, 1986–1988. Lists and annotates the "best" books in nearly every field of human knowledge from antiquity to the present. Vol. I: *The Best in American and British Fiction, Poetry, Essays, Literary Biography, Bibliography, and Reference.* Ed. Fred Kaplan, 1986. Vol. II: *The Best in American and British Drama and World Literature in English Translation.* Ed. Maurice Charney, 1986. Vol. III: *The Best in General Reference Literature of the World, the Social Sciences, History, and the Arts.* Ed. Paula Kaufman, 1986. Vol. IV: *The Best in the Literature of Philosophy and World Religions.* Ed. William L. Reese, 1988. Vol. V: *The Best in the Literature of Science, Technology and Medicine.* Ed. Paul T. Durbin, 1988. Vol. VI: *Index to Volumes 1–5.* 1988.

Sheehy, Eugene P., comp. *Guide to Reference Books.* 10th ed. Chicago: ALA, 1986. Lists and annotates some 14,000 titles; reference materials are divided into five major areas with subdivisions by subject, specific kind of work, country, or all three; annotations are evaluative; emphasis is on sources for scholarly research, but some popular titles are included. *Supplement,* 1992. Ed. Robert Balay.

The Standard Catalog Series. New York: Wilson, 1991. Includes *Children Catalog,* 16th ed., 1991; *The Senior High School Library Catalog,* 14th ed., 1992; *The Junior High School Library Catalog,* 6th ed., 1990; *The Public Library Catalog,* 9th ed., 1989; and *Fiction Catalog,* 12th ed., 1991. Each catalog provides annotated lists of books for the type of library or material covered; each is kept up to date by annual supplements.

Walford, A. J., ed. *Guide to Reference Material.* 3 vols. London: Library Assoc., 1977–1982. Vol. I: *Science and Technology,* 4th ed., 1980. Vol. II: *Social and Historical Sciences, Philosophy and Religion,* 4th ed., 1982. Vol. III: *Generalities, Languages, the Arts and Literature,* 4th ed., 1987. Each title lists significant reference sources published in recent years in the subject areas included; international in scope with some emphasis on British publications.

Wynar, Bohdan A., ed. *American Reference Books Annual*. Littleton: Libraries Unlimited, 1970–. Annual. Provides a record of the reference books published and distributed in the United States during the preceding year; gives signed, critical, and comparative reviews; ARBA covers every subject area of general and specific interest; gives citations to additional reviews in major journals.

TRADE BIBLIOGRAPHIES

Books in Print. 8 vols. New York: Bowker, 1992. Lists available books by author and title; gives complete publishing information; lists more than 950,000 books of all kinds in print in the United States. *Books in Print Supplement*, 3 vols., is published annually in the spring; *Books in Print* is available in print form, online through DIALOG and other vendors, on CD-ROM disk, and on microfiche.

Books in Print with Book Reviews Plus. Bimonthly update. CD-ROM version offering, in addition to *Books in Print*, 160,000 current book reviews. Search by topic, author, title, publisher, ISBN, publication date, grade level.

Cumulative Book Index. New York: Wilson, 1898–. Monthly, except August; bound annual cumulations. An author-title-subject international list of books published in the English language; gives author's full name, complete title, edition, series, number of pages, publisher, date of publication, price, Library of Congress card number and ISBN number; continues the *U.S. Catalog*, 4th ed. (1928), which lists books in print on January 1, 1928. Online from WilsonLine; on CD-ROM from Wilson-Disc.

Forthcoming Books. New York: Bowker, 1966–. Bimonthly. Lists by author and title all books scheduled for publication in the coming five-month period. In addition to print, is available online, on CD-ROM, and on microfiche.

Paperbound Books in Print. 6 vols. New York: Bowker, 1955–. Semiannually in April and October. More than 275,000 paperbacks in print are listed by author, title, and subject with information for locating and ordering. Print, online, CD-ROM, microfiche versions.

Subject Guide to Books in Print. 5 vols. New York: Bowker, 1957–. Annual. Lists, according to the subject headings established by the Library of Congress, more than 500,000 nonfiction titles under some 63,000 subject headings; gives author, title, publisher, current price, and year of publication. Kept up to date by *Books in Print Supplement*. Available in print, on CD-ROM, online, and on microfiche.

Nonbook Information Sources

In addition to books, magazines, and newspapers, which have been discussed in the preceding chapters, the library provides other kinds of information sources for the student who is seeking the answer to a question, aid in solving or clarifying a problem, or illustrative material in any of the several subject fields. Since these materials are not always listed in the main catalog, it is important that users of the library know what they are, how they are organized and arranged, and the rules which govern their use. (Figure 14.1 shows some catalog cards for nonbook materials.)

Among these sources are (1) pamphlets and clippings; (2) audio, visual, and audiovisual materials; (3) microfilm, microcards, microfiche, and other microforms; (4) automated information sources, and (5) other electronic sources.

Pamphlets and Clippings

A pamphlet is a publication which deals with only one subject and consists of a few pages stitched together and enclosed in paper covers. Pamphlets cover topics of current importance in any subject field and appear more frequently in subject areas which are constantly changing.

When they are first published, pamphlets are excellent sources of recent information or opinion on a subject. Parts of books may appear first as pamphlets, and writings which have never been published in book form are often found in pamphlet form.

When pamphlets become out of date as current information, they serve as valuable historical sources because they indicate the trend of interest and opinion at a particular time.

Video
629.45
E39

The Eagle has landed : the flight of Apollo 11. ₁Videorecording₁ /
United States National Aeronautics and Space Administration.
— Washington : NASA : distributed by National Audiovisual
Center, 1979.

1 cassette, 29 min. : sd., col. : 3/4 in.

Transparency
611.2
H85

Human respiratory system. ₁Transparency₁ • —
Burlington, N.C. : Carolina Biological
Supply Co., c1970.
2 transparencies : 1 b&w. 1 col. : 26x30 cm.

Film
574.50979
L544

Life in the desert—the American Southwest. ₁Motion picture₁ /
Encyclopaedia Britannica Educational Corporation ; made by
Allied Films Artist. — ₁2d ed.₁ — Chicago : The Corp. 1978.

1 reel. 11 min. : sd., col. : 16 mm. & guide.

Microfilm
330.1
C94p

Cropsey, Joseph.
Polity and economy; an interpretation
of the principles of Adam Smith. Ann
Arbor, University Microfilms, 1952.

Multi-media
307.094436
P39

The People of Paris ₁kit₁ / Charles L.
Mitsakos, general editor; Edith West,
consultant. — Newton, Mass. ; Selective
Educational Equipment, c1976.
7 books and booklets. 3 maps. toy

Phonodisc
M22
C516

Chopin, Fryderyk Franciszek, 1810–1849.
₁Preludes, piano₁ ₁Sound recording₁
Preludes. Vox STPL 512.650. ₁196-?₁
1 disc. 33¹/3 rpm. stereo. 12 in.

Walter Klien, piano.
Program notes by C. Stanley on container.
Title from container.
CONTENTS: 24 preludes, op. 28.—Prelude in C# minor, op. 45.—
Prelude in A♭ major.

1. Piano music.   I. Klien, Walter.

[M22]   76–761709

Library of Congress   76   R

FIGURE 14.1
Sample catalog records for nonbook materials.

Pamphlets are organized for use in several ways:

1. Some are classified, cataloged, and shelved in the general collection.
2. Some are listed in the library catalog but are arranged in a filing cabinet.
3. Others may be filed in a cabinet designated as the "pamphlet file," arranged alphabetically by subject or numerically if part of a series. In this case, there is usually a separate catalog or listing of the available pamphlets on or near the filing cabinet.

Clippings which have been taken from newspapers, magazines, brochures, and other sources are useful for current events and for providing information on subjects too brief to be treated in pamphlets or books.

Clippings may be mounted on cardboard or placed in folders. In general they are kept in a filing cabinet called the "vertical file" and are arranged alphabetically by subject. As a rule, they are not listed in the library catalog.

Audiovisual Materials

Included in the broad field of audiovisual materials are pictures (clipped from newspapers and magazines), postcards, reproductions of art masterpieces, slides, filmstrips, motion picture films, charts, graphs, maps, models, phonograph records, tape and wire recordings, sheet music, transparencies, programmed books, kits, cassettes, videorecordings, and the equipment needed for their use.

There are audiovisual materials in all subject fields. They are essential in art and music appreciation courses and in language courses; they will enhance the study of drama, literature, and history; they are useful in all the social sciences and in the pure and applied sciences.

Originally, audiovisual materials were used for recreational purposes and to supplement textbook teaching, and they are still used for these purposes. But in some courses, and for some purposes, the audiovisual medium is the course, as in a course on films or television.

Audiovisual materials are no longer considered extra or additional; they are now a significant part of all areas of learning. The student seeking information on a subject or the answer to a question may find that a film, filmstrip, slide, videotape, transparency, or other nonbook form will provide the information needed more satisfactorily than a printed source. In any search for material on a subject, nonbook forms should be included.

Many academic libraries, especially community college libraries, have production facilities, including darkrooms, where teachers and students can make their own audiovisual materials. Students can use these facilities to make slides, films, prints, tapes, transparencies, or other audiovisual materials to illustrate, clarify, and support oral and written reports.

Audiovisual materials may be listed in the library catalog, or they may be kept in separate files in special rooms or areas, with a catalog or listing for each kind of material. In general, these types of materials are kept together according to kind (films, filmstrips, tapes, and so on) and are arranged on shelves or in files according to subject classification.[1] A library may have a map file, a picture file, a room where films, slides, filmstrips and other audiovisual materials are kept and projected, and booths for listening to phonograph and tape recordings.

Audiovisual materials are entered in the catalog, as other materials are, under author, title, subject, and under other appropriate headings, such as illustrator, producers, and so on. They are described on the catalog record by author, title, imprint, and subject matter, and by their peculiar features, such as form, running time, whether sound or silent, color or black and white, and size (see Figure 14.1).

Regulations governing the use of audiovisual materials and equipment vary greatly. In some libraries, certain kinds of materials are circulated while others must be used in specified areas or rooms of the library. Other regulations govern the use of production facilities.

Microforms

"Microform" is the name given to any microphotographically produced printed matter. A number of forms and production methods have been developed. Kinds of microforms include microfilm, microprint, microcards, and microfiche.

Microfilm may be 16-mm or 35-mm roll or cartridge film. It is one of the principal forms for reproducing information. Developed as a means of saving space by microcopying back issues of newspapers and magazines, it is used also to reproduce books, reports, government publications, dissertations, and other kinds of printed material.

A microfilm is a film which carries a photographic record, on a reduced scale, of printed material. The rate of reduction determines the number of pages of printed material which it can contain. Depending on the rate of reduction, a microfilm may have 207 frames (reduced 42 times), 269 frames (48 times), or more. Each frame can carry up to 100 lines of print. (See pp. 58–59 for a discussion of the Computer Output Microfilm catalog.)

A microfiche is a 4- by 6-inch film card which contains rows of micro-images of pages, cards, or other printed material. The reduction ratio—low,

---

[1] The Dewey Decimal Classification System or the Library of Congress Classification System may be used, or new classification systems may be devised for each kind of material. In some cases, materials may be numbered in the order they were received and shelved by that number.

medium, or high—determines the number of pages, cards, or other material on a fiche. A conventional fiche contains up to 98 pages of text.

In a microbook fiche, which is a photographic reproduction of printed material on a small transparent film card at very great reductions, each page is reduced photographically from 55 to 90 times, depending on the page size. Up to 1000 page images can be reproduced on a single fiche.

Microprint is a microphotograph of printed material reproduced in printed form on 6- by 9-inch cards or sheets, containing up to 100 pages of text. Images are placed on the sheet in rows.

A microcard is a microscopic photographic reproduction of printed material on standard-size 3- by 5-inch library catalog cards. A microcard contains up to eighty pages of printed material, and images are placed on the card in rows. Microfilm might be compared to the negative of a picture taken by a camera, microcard and microprint to the final snapshot. Increasingly, the microcard is giving way to microfiche.

Microforms are now used for numerous purposes; e.g.: (1) to preserve information which has been printed on poor-quality, perishable paper; (2) to duplicate material quickly and inexpensively; (3) to protect valuable information against loss; (4) to restore out-of-print books to in-print status; (5) to enable libraries in the United States to secure materials from foreign libraries; (6) to store very small images for production of full-size copy on demand; and (7) to store and retrieve bits of data from large data bases.

Among the kinds of materials which are available in microfilm, microcard, microprint, or microfiche are: periodicals, newspapers, reports of research, out-of-print books, rare books, new books, government publications, theses, dissertations, manuscripts, library card catalogs, records and reports of business and industry, archival materials, and telephone books.

All microforms must be read with the aid of a device which will enlarge the microphotographic image. Microcards, microprint, and microfiche are read left to right, beginning with the top line. Many devices have been designed ranging from hand viewers to large tabletop models. They are not always easy to use, and many devices do not produce an easily read image on the screen.

A reader-printer is available in many libraries. The reader-printer prints the image which is produced on the reading machine screen on a sheet of paper in print that is easily read without the aid of any device. In a sense, the reader-printer returns the microform to its original state.

Microforms are useful to any person who is looking for information on a subject. Because of the many kinds of material—on almost every subject—which are issued in one or another of the microforms, the student must learn about them and how and when to use them.

In some libraries, catalog cards for microforms are filed with other cards in the library catalog with a form or location included in the call number (see

Figure 14.1). Microforms are shelved in a separate area, usually in card catalog drawers or in other file drawers.

Some libraries have a special room, called "Microforms," "Microtext Reading Room," or the like, in which microforms are housed and reading machines are located. Light is controlled to provide good contrast for images on the reading-machine screens. A catalog or list of microforms is placed in or near this room.

Determining the Usefulness of Nonbook Information Sources

These questions can be asked in evaluating any nonbook source:

1. Are those who produced the material specialists in their fields?
2. Is the usefulness of the subject matter presented affected by time, and, if so, is this source out of date?
3. Is the quality of reproduction acceptable, or does it detract from the content?
4. Is the material presented clearly?
5. Is the material presented without bias?
6. What purposes will it serve:
    a Will it answer a question completely?
    b Will it supplement another source?
    c Will it illustrate and clarify a topic?
    d Will it give current information if it is needed?
7. What subject areas are emphasized?

Automated Information Sources[2]

THE ELECTRONIC DIGITAL COMPUTER

The computer was first used in libraries to assist with routine operations such a circulation, personnel records, acquisition of materials, and inventories. Since the success of the Library of Congress Machine-Readable Cataloging program (MARC) in the mid 1960s, computers have assumed an increasingly important role in the bibliographic functions of the library—cataloging and indexing of materials.

---

[2] See Chapter 5, Library Catalogs, for a discussion of online and CD-ROM catalogs.

Computers are now an essential part of a library. They are used in cataloging, circulation, acquisitions, management, compiling lists, word processing, desktop publishing, electronic communications, etc.

For the library user, the most important function the computer performs is in the area of computerized cataloging and in the access the computer provides to various databases. In addition to the library's catalog, the OPAC (Online Public Access Catalog) may provide access to a union catalog made up of the cataloging records of several or many libraries; it may also provide access to other types of materials, such as journal articles, contents of books, and campus, community, or other information.

New materials may be added to the OPAC from time to time, and search options may be changed or added. The full text of an item retrieved may be printed at the terminal immediately. If not, and if the library does not have the printed source, the document may be obtained by electronic mail, facsimile transmission, express mail, or from another library on interlibrary loan.

Information regarding means of access to the types of materials covered by the computer is given in instruction sheets or in instructions on the screen of the computer. Search options may vary with each type of material accessed by the computer, e.g., steps in searching a periodical file may differ from the search options for the book file. If it is a union catalog, one catalog may be searched by author, title, subject, or keyword; another may add to these options browsing or Boolean logic.[3] Still others may require the use of a controlled vocabulary, such as a thesaurus or index. Users must follow the instructions *exactly*. Misspelling of words, using the wrong word or term, punctuation errors, etc., will result in failure to receive anything except a message that the command is not in the database.

The computer alone is not an information source, as a dictionary or an encyclopedia is. The computer provides access to a printed source or sources of information, e.g., to the contents of the library catalog or to a union catalog,[4] to the contents of a group of periodicals, newspapers, or reference sources. The sources are in a database that has been developed from print sources and to which the computer has online access.

DATABASES

A database contains machine-readable records for the purpose of information storage and retrieval. Commercial database service was launched by DIALOG in 1972. The first databases were:

---

[3] See p. 142.
[4] See pp. 67, 130.

1. Bibliographic, providing descriptive information about a given source: author, title, publisher, price, etc.
2. Citations, giving the location of an article, the journal in which it appears—date, volume, and pages—with or without an abstract
3. Directory-type, providing names, addresses, and other information about persons or organizations
4. Statistical, providing statistics about various subjects
5. Legal, giving citations to and information about laws, court cases, etc.

In addition to these, there are now many new databases, some of which include several types of information and offer full text, abstracts, and illustrative material. The number of databases grew from 301 in 1975 to more than 7500 in 1991.[5]

Some major vendors of abstracting and indexing services are DIALOG, ORBIT SEARCH SERVICE, and OHIO COLLEGE LIBRARY CENTER (OCLC). OCLC offers cataloging information only.

Examples of reference sources which are online from a database are: *Psychological Abstracts, The New York Times,* and *McGraw-Hill Encyclopedia of Science and Technology.* These sources are available in print form also. The online version may offer more or less information than the print source; it may be updated more frequently.

NETWORKS

Most academic institutions are linked to each other by one or more data communication networks. There are local networks which include libraries in a given area; there are regional networks; and there are international networks, such as INTERNET, made up of the catalogs and information databases of more than 250 academic libraries in ten countries. INTERNET also allows access to other databases and computing resources.

Many users of this text have grown up in the computer age; some own or have access to a personal computer; others may own a portable computer—a laptop, a handheld, or a pocket-sized notebook—or whatever the latest model may be. In some colleges, a computer may be a required piece of equipment, just as textbooks are. Compact disks are everyday items; electronic bulletin boards, facsimile transmission (FAX), security systems of various kinds, videos, audiocassettes, and the equipment for their use are not new to today's students. What may be new to them is the fact that all of these are part of today's library offerings.

---

[5] Kathleen Young Maraccio, *Computer-Readable Databases: A Directory and Data Sourcebook,* 5th ed. (Detroit: Gale, 1992) xiii.

Having used a PC or other computer for games, word processing, or in computer-assisted instruction, the student may be less afraid of the OPAC in the academic library and have less difficulty in operating it. What will be difficult for the student is learning how to locate, in a database of millions of records, the items needed for a particular research topic and how to select, analyze, and synthesize the information retrieved.

CD-ROMs

In 1984, there was only one optical disk (CD-ROM), InfoTrac. By 1992, there were more than 3000 CD-ROMs available for purchase by libraries and individuals.[6] The number of CD-ROMs is increasing daily.

A CD-ROM is a plastic disk, 4.72 inches in diameter, on which can be stored up to 250,000 pages of text.[7] Information which has been encoded on a disk by using a laser to burn pits in the surface of the disk can be read by a laser and reproduced on a computer screen. The information on the disk cannot be edited, erased, or added to; new disks must be issued to update the master disk.

A CD-ROM workstation is a self-contained system and consists of a computer, a special keyboard, a CD-ROM drive, a floppy disc, and a printer. There are several kinds of CD-ROMs:

> CD-ROM, Compact Disk Read-Only Memory, the most widely used in academic libraries
>
> CD-I, Compact Disk Interactive, a multimedia disk containing digitized text, images, sound, motion, graphics; rapidly gaining in use
>
> CD-WORM, Compact Disk Write-Once-Read-Many Times; not in general use

The text on a CD-ROM is usually from one or more printed sources, e.g., *Readers' Guide to Periodical Literature* is a printed source; it is also on CD-ROM.

There are several ways of searching a CD-ROM database for information, varying with each CD-ROM. The search options available include author, title, subject, keyword, browsing, and Boolean logic.[8] A CD-ROM may have a controlled vocabulary, that is, search terms may be contained in a printed thesaurus, index, list, or in an index that appears on the screen and applies only to that CD-ROM.

---

[6] Norman Desmaris, ed., *CD-ROMs in Print* (Westport, Meckler, 1992) xv.

[7] The disk may be larger or smaller. The larger the disk, the more information can be stored.

[8] See pp. 69–70.

There is no standardization in CD-ROMs. Each one is different from all others and is accessed in a different way, although some of the same options may be used. Instructions for operating the system and for searching it are given in a manual or an instruction sheet at the terminal (work station) and on the screen. If additional information is needed, a reference librarian will give assistance. All instructions for operating and searching the database must be followed *exactly*. As in the case of a computer search, a misspelled word, an error in the required punctuation, a command not included in the instructions, or failure to consult the required thesaurus, list, or index will result in failure to retrieve information, frustration, and loss of time.

The most widely used CD-ROMs in libraries are bibliographic, providing information about and access to periodical and newspaper articles, including title of periodical or newspaper, title of article, volume, pages, date, and section, if it is a newspaper. Other CD-ROMs carry a complete reference source or sources, such as *The Academic American Encyclopedia* and *The Oxford English Dictionary*.

Lists of most widely used CD-ROMs in academic libraries include *Psyclit*, ERIC, ABI/INFORM, MLA, and *Dissertations Abstracts*. These and other CD-ROMs are discussed in appropriate chapters throughout the text.

Some major producers of CD-ROMs are: The H. W. Wilson Company, R. R. Bowker, Information Access Company, ERIC, Silver Platter, and the federal government.

Advantages and disadvantages of CD-ROMs

Advantages claimed for CD-ROMs are:

1. On one disk a CD-ROM provides access to more citations than the printed source offers, such as additional resources indexed, and may provide abstracts and/or full text of the items cited.
2. Information is accessible in one place, and the database can be searched by the student without a fee and, usually, without the help of a librarian as is the case with a computer search of a commercial database.
3. A CD-ROM search is faster than a manual search.
4. A CD-ROM is relatively easy to use.

Some disadvantages are:

1. Lack of standardization in the operation of a CD-ROM; users are forced to follow a different set of search instructions for each CD-ROM database.
2. Only one person at a time can use a CD-ROM unless there are multiple CD-ROMs in a network arrangement.

3. Searches are often slow and cumbersome.

4. The computer screen may not give a clear display.

5. Print and CD-ROM versions of a source are not always identical: both may have to be consulted.

Choosing and Using Automated Sources— Online and CD-ROM

In order to choose and use an automated or electronic source to find information on a given subject, the student should be aware of certain points:

1. The importance of subject headings and the sources which will aid in formulating them, e.g., the *Library of Congress Subject Headings*, which is used in most online catalogs, thesauri, and indexes

2. The commonly used access points—author, title, subject, keyword— and the special thesauri, lists, or indexes required by some databases

3. The types and purposes of databases available: bibliographic, citation, statistical, legal, encyclopedic, and when to search each kind

4. The fact that one tool may not adequately provide the information needed and that several sources may be required

5. The fact that an electronic format does not guarantee authenticity, so the user must evaluate the database as any other reference source is evaluated: on the basis of authoritativeness, scope, format, accuracy, recency

In order to use an electronic source efficiently, the student must have a well-formulated search plan or strategy. Important in any manual search for information, the search strategy becomes an essential ingredient of any database search. Begin your search for information with a well-defined problem, an understanding of subtopics and related words and terms that can be used to define and refine your topic, the kinds of information needed to develop the topic, and the types of reference sources that provide these kinds of information. This kind of preplanning will result in more efficient access to and retrieval of useful information, and a great saving of time.[9]

TRENDS

Computers and CD-ROMs are changing continually. Some relatively recent developments and uses, which may soon become commonplace or be superseded by more efficient and sophisticated devices are:

[9] See Chapter 25 for a detailed discussion of the search strategy.

1. Smaller, more powerful, and less expensive computers: pocket-sized and hand-held models and notebooks that can read hand-printed notes
2. Electronic journals
3. Full-text, full-image databases
4. Multimedia CD-ROMs
5. Multiple titles on a single disk: fiction, nonfiction, reference books
6. CD-ROMs on a dial-up basis: anyone with a modem and a PC can access a CD-ROM
7. Full-text database searching from any place with a telephone: home, dormitory, office
8. CD-ROM work stations for the visually handicapped: Braille printing for screen display; speech synthesized to read the information on the screen to the user
9. CD-ROM stations that allow users to search multiple databases
10. Networks of CD-ROMs

Reference Sources on Nonbook, Nonprint Materials

GENERAL

AV Market Place. New York: Bowker, 1979–. Annual. The complete business directory of audio, audiovisual, computer systems, film, video (subtitle), it lists more than 6300 companies that create, supply, or distribute AV equipment and services.

National Information Center for Educational Media. *NICEM Media Indexes.* Albuquerque: Access Innovations, 1967–. Includes databases covering a wide range of audiovisual materials: tapes, education films, educational videotapes, transparencies, 16mm educational films, etc. CD-ROM version; available online through DIALOG.

CD-ROM[10]

Armstrong, C. J. and J. A. Large. *CD-ROM Information Products: An Educational Guide and Directory.* Brookfield: Gower, 1990–. Lists by subject all identified CD-ROM titles: price, distribution, and address. Also on disk.

---

[10] See also reference sources in Chapter 21, Science and Technology.

Desmaris, Norman, ed. *CD-ROMs in Print 1992: An International Guide to CD-ROM, CDI, CDTV & Electronic Book Products.* Westport: Meckler, 1992. Lists some 3000 titles of commercially available optical disk products from around the world; covers all disciplines, reference and non-reference books; includes publisher, software, search methods, update frequency, and description of product.

Directory of Portable Databases. New York: Cuadra-Elsevier, 1990–. Lists 400 CD-ROM databases; about one-third of them are full text.

COMPUTERS

Dewey, Patrick. *Public Access Microcomputers.* 2d ed. Boston: Hall, 1991–. Provides information about library applications of microcomputers.

Schuyler, Michael. *Dial-In 1992: An Annual Guide to On-line Public Access Catalogs.* Westport: Meckler, 1991–. Expands the number of online catalogs from 150 in the 1991 volume to 250, representing over 175 million volumes in 47 states and Canadian provinces.

DATABASES

Marcaccio, Kathleen Young, et. al. *Computer-Readable Data Bases, A Directory and Data Sourcebook.* 8th ed. Detroit: Gale, 1992. Offers information about producers, vendors; gives profiles of databases; includes online, CD-ROM, disk; covers about 7637 databases and unique subfiles.

FILMS

National Information Center for Educational Media. *Film and Video Finder.* 3 vols. Albuquerque: NICEM, 1987–. Annual. Describes content, film or video format, audience level, date, running time, and source. Available on CD-ROM through Media Indexes; online, from DIALOG.

MICROFORMS

Guide to Microforms in Print: Author and Title. New York: Bowker, 1992–. Annual. Provides information about microforms from around the world: books, journals, newspapers, government publications, etc. *Subject Guide to Microforms in Print* gives subject access to all titles in *Guide to Microforms in Print: Author and Title.*

PAMPHLETS

Vertical File Index. New York: Wilson, 1935–. Covers selected government publications, charts, posters, maps, pamphlets, selected university publications, current tapes of public interest, etc.; gives vocational information, business, health, and travel; CD-ROM version offers coverage since 1985. Available through WilsonDisc.

TAPES

Audiocassette Finder. 2d ed. Albuquerque: NICEM, 1989. Locates more than 30,000 audiocassettes in all subject areas.

Words on Cassette: A Comprehensive Bibliography of Spoken-Word Audiocassettes. 7th ed. New Providence: Bowker, 1992–. Provides information on more than 50,000 tapes on more than 104 subjects, including reader's name, running time, price, and a summary of content. Available in print and tape formats.

TELEFACSIMILE (FAX)

Facsimile User's Directory. New York: Monitor, 1989–. Semiannual. Gives directory information about electronic mail systems and facsimile transmission in United States and Canada.

VIDEO

Bowker's Complete Video Directory. 2 vols. New York: Bowker, 1993. Vol. 1: *Entertainment;* Vol. 2: *Education/Special Interest*. Lists more than 75,000 videos in all formats: VHS, BETA, 3/4", Umatic, 8mm, and laserdisk.

The Video Source Book. 2 vols. Detroit: Gale, 1989–. Annual. Lists about 60,000 video programs on videotape and disk, including popular and educational titles.

PROFESSIONAL JOURNALS[11]

Data Base. New York: Association for Computing Machinery, 1969–.

Online. Weston: Online, 1982–. Bimonthly.

---

[11] See also *Ulrich's International Periodicals Directory*, 31st ed., and *Magazines for Libraries*, 7th ed., ed. by Bill Katz and Linda S. Katz.

CHAPTER

❧ 15 ❧

Government Publications

A government publication is a publication issued (or purchased) at public expense by authority of Congress or any other government office or institution—national, state, or local—for distribution to government officials or to the public. Documents which contain the records of government in their original form are placed in government archives. In published form, they are made available to libraries, organizations, and individuals, with some exceptions, e.g., classified materials.

At all levels of government—national, state, and municipal—some kinds of government publications are issued, but the chief source of government publications is the federal government. It is said that the United States government is the largest single publisher in the world. Each year the departments, offices, and agencies of the federal government prepare and issue tens of thousands of publications. The Government Printing Office operates twenty four bookstores around the country which carry a selection of titles. Any title currently on sale by the GPO can be ordered at these bookstores.

During the early years of our nation's history, printing was done by printers selected by Congress under a contract system. The publications of these contract printers were often poorly made and inadequately indexed, and sometimes they were not even identifiable as government publications. In 1846, Congress created a Joint Committee on Printing, composed of three members from each house, to bring about reforms in printing practices. In 1852, a Superintendent of Public Printing was appointed to supervise the work of the printers who were selected under the contract system. The establishment of a national printing plant was authorized by Congress in 1860, and the United States government began doing its own printing in 1861.

The United States Government Printing Office (GPO) is an independent body in the legislative branch of the government. The Public Printer, who is appointed by the President with the approval of the Senate, is responsible for its management. The Congressional Joint Committee on Printing has jurisdiction over the Government Printing Office in matters pertaining to the materials used in printing, wages of employees, and the efficient operation of the Office; it controls the arrangement and style of the *Congressional Record* and the *Congressional Directory*. The Superintendent of Documents (an office created in the Government Printing Office in 1895) is responsible for centralized distribution of government publications.

The Superintendent of Documents sells government publications to individuals, organizations, and institutions; distributes them to depository[1] libraries; compiles and distributes catalogs and lists; and provides information, on request, about government publications.

Individuals may obtain certain government publications free, when available, from members of Congress or from the issuing agency, or they may purchase them from the Superintendent of Documents. Free price lists are issued by certain agencies and lists of selected publications are available, free of charge, from the Superintendent of Documents.

Purpose and Kinds of Government Publications

Government publications grow out of the peculiar function of the governmental agencies which issue them and are a public record of the operation and activities of the government. They provide a means of keeping the public informed, so that each citizen can understand and make use of the services the government provides.

The contents of government publications are as varied as the departments, agencies, and bureaus which issue them, and they cover every subject area. They include annual reports, transcripts of congressional hearings, statistical analyses, manuals of instruction, recordings of proceedings, bibli-

---

[1] The distribution free of charge of federal government publications to designated libraries was authorized by act of Congress, February 5, 1859. The law provided for one depository library for each congressional district in the United States and for two depositories at large for each state. All state libraries and the libraries of land-grant colleges and universities were named federal depositories. Government publications in depository libraries are permanent and are available to the public, at least for reference use. The Depository Library Act of 1962 (Public Law 87-579) increased the total number of depository libraries to 792 and made available to them practically all government publications, including those not printed at the United States Government Printing Office. There are now more than 1370 federal depository libraries in the United States and its territories and possessions: Guam, the Canal Zone, Puerto Rico, and the Virgin Islands.

ographies, directories, speeches, rules and regulations, results of research, maps, atlases, nonbook materials, journals, and travel information.

They are printed or processed (that is, duplicated by photocopy or other process), and they appear in almost every form: loose-leaf, unbound and bound books, pamphlets, leaflets, newspapers, periodicals, maps, charts, multivolume reports, abstracts, motion pictures, filmstrips, posters, and catalogs of art reproductions; they are also available on CD-ROM or online to a database.

Usefulness of Government Publications

Government publications provide primary source material in many areas, especially in statistics, in government operations, and in certain areas of the sciences, such as the results of scientific and medical research or patent and copyright applications. They provide information which is not available from any other source. They are useful in most areas of study but are particularly useful in the study of history, the social sciences, education, personnel management, and the physical and biological sciences. Prepared by specialists who are in reality writing about their particular activities, they can be considered authoritative in the subjects they cover. They are up to date in that they present the latest information available to the agency which issues them. Many government publications provide bibliographies, which are useful for further study and research. In general, the publications are concise and readable.

Organization and Arrangement of Government Publications in Libraries

Library users are often confused by the great number of government publications and do not know how to select or locate them. There are several ways in which libraries organize and arrange them.

1. They may be classified, cataloged, and shelved like other library materials. This is usually the case if the library receives only a few titles. If government publications are treated like other library materials, they will be assigned a number from the classification system in use in the library and will be arranged on the shelves according to the call number. In this case, the reader will locate them by using the library catalog, just as any other kind of library material is located.

2. They may be classified and cataloged like other library materials but kept in a special file or section of shelves. If this is the case, the words "Gov. Doc." may be added to the call number.

3. They may be classified as "Government Documents" (or "Government Publications") and arranged alphabetically or numerically on shelves or in filing cabinets. Where this system is used, a listing, index, or catalog is kept nearby.

4. Some government publications in a given library may be classified and cataloged like other library materials, and others in the same library may be treated as government publications and kept in a separate place. The physical location will be included in the call number.

5. They may be treated as a separate collection, as they are in depository libraries, and arranged by the classification number of the issuing agency.

In general, the bibliographies or lists published by the Superintendent of Documents serve as an index to government publications when they are treated as a separate collection, as in a depository library. Instead of looking in the library catalog for a government publication, the students will consult a bibliography, such as the *Monthly Catalog* (Figure 15.1), in much the same manner as they would a periodical index. The bibliography will give the information needed to locate the item on the shelf. The location symbol is a combination of letters of the alphabet that designate the governmental agency that issued the publication, plus Arabic numerals that designate the individual office and the kind of publication (leaflet, bulletin, report, etc.), and letters and Arabic numerals that make up the number for that specific publication.

For example, the Defense Department is designated D, from the first distinctive letter in the title; the Secretary of Defense is designated D 1, and all annual reports are given the symbol .1. Thus the symbol for the annual report of the Secretary of Defense is D 1.1.

Every item in the symbol is important in locating a given publication in a library which uses this kind of organization. Every reference to the publication is important when ordering a publication from the Superintendent of Documents.

Examples of Superintendent of Documents classification numbers and the order in which they would appear on the shelf are:

D 1.2:	D 1.6/2:	D 1.16/3:	D 1.42:	D 7.2:
B 85/977-81	C 49	8	10	P 44/976

The bibliographies may provide descriptive and evaluative annotations for the publications listed and are useful in determining the kind of government publication to select for a particular problem.

1 ——— **NATIONAL INSTITUTE OF EDUCATION**
Education Dept.
Washington, DC 20208

ERIC documents may be ordered in microfiche or paper copy
from the ERIC Document Reproduction Service (EDRS). 3900
Wheeler Avenue, Alexandria, VA 22304. (800) 227-3742. To
obtain an order form, contact EDRS or consult any issue of
Resources in Education (RIE).

2 ——— **87-7262**

ED 1.310/2:253772 ———————————————— 3

4 ——— Marchilonis, Barbara A.

5 ——— Television technologies in combatting illiteracy : a monograph / written by Barbara A. Marchilonis and Herman Niehbur ; prepared for the National Adult Literacy Project. —[San
Francisco, Calif.?] : National Adult Literacy Project, Far West ⎤——6
Laboratory, [1985]   ⎦——8

7 ——— viii, 49 leaves ; 28 cm. Distributed to depository libraries in
microfiche. "January 1985." "Work ... was performed pursuant ——9
to Contract no. NIE-R-83-000-11 of the National Institute of

10——— Education"—P. [ii]. Bibliography: p. 45-49. ●Item 466-A-3 ——11
(microfiche) S/N ED253772 @ ERIC   ——12

13——— 1. Literacy. 2. Television in adult education. I. Niehbur,
Herman. II. National Adult Literacy Project (U.S.) III. National Institute of Education (U.S.) IV. Title. OCLC ——— 14
15208986

Subject Index

January — June 1987

15 ——— **Television in adult education**. ———————— 17

16 ———————Television technologies in/combatting illiteracy : a monograph / Marchilonbis, ——— 18
Barbara A. (ED 1.310/2:253772), 87-
7262 ——20
└——————— 19

FIGURE 15.1
Excerpt from Monthly Catalog of United States Government Publications, *May 1987,
p. 54, and the* Subject Index, *pp. 1–1150. (1) Government agency which issued the
publication. (2) Location in the* Monthly Catalog: *items are listed sequentially. (3) Education
Department classification number. (4) Author. (5) Title. (6) Place, publisher, date of publication. (7) Collation. (8) Depository information. (9) Explanatory note. (10) Publication has a
bibliography. (11) Item is available to depository libraries on microfiche. (12) It is an ERIC
publication; ED number. (13) Subject headings and added entry headings. (14) The number
assigned by OCLC to identify this record in the data base. (15) Heading in the subject index.
(16) Title. (17) The publication is a monograph (government publications are issued in many
formats). (18) Author. (19) Education Department classification number: call number. (20)
Location number—not the page number—in the* Monthly Catalog.

Reference Sources

In addition to the bibliographies and lists, there are reference works to aid the researcher in choosing government publications for particular purposes. Listed below are bibliographies and lists of government publications and other reference sources which are helpful in finding and using them.

BIBLIOGRAPHIES, GUIDES, AND INDEXES

Bailey, William C. *Guide to Popular U.S. Government Publications*. 2nd ed. Littleton: Libraries Unlimited, 1990. Lists and annotates some 2500 publications in 75 subject areas, such as energy conservation, careers, and health, of interest to the general reader.

Government Documents Catalog Service (GDCS): GPO on CD-ROM. Pomona: Autographics, 1986–. Index to all government documents catalogued by the GPO from June 1976–.

Morehead, Joe. *Introduction to United States Public Documents*. Library Science Text Series. Littleton: Libraries Unlimited, 1983. Gives an overview of the function, nature, and use of United States public documents; includes a discussion of the Government Printing Office, the Superintendent of Documents, micropublishing, computer-based bibliographical services, federal audiovisual information, and the depository library system; includes only publications of the federal government.

Schwarzkopf, LeRoy C., comp. *Government Reference Books: A Biennial Guide to U.S. Government Publications*. Littleton: Libraries Unlimited, 1972–. Biennial. Provides an annotated list of directories, bibliographies, indexes, dictionaries, catalogs, biographical dictionaries, handbooks, statistical works, and almanacs arranged by subject.

U.S. Library of Congress. Exchange and Gifts Division. *Monthly Checklist of State Publications*. Washington: GPO, 1910–. Arranged alphabetically by state; lists publications received by the Library of Congress; gives full bibliographic information and, in some cases, contents.

U.S. Superintendent of Documents. *Monthly Catalog of United States Government Publications*. Washington: GPO, 1895–. Provides complete bibliographical information about each document (author, title, issuing agency, date, etc.—see Figure 15.1). Includes sales information. Also available online from DIALOG. CD-ROM edition by Autographics, covers period 1976–. Also available on microfiche.

CONGRESSIONAL INFORMATION SOURCES

Congress A to Z. Washington: CQ, 1988. Explains the development of Congress, how it operates; describes significant events relating to Congress, and gives information about its past and present leaders.

Congressional Information Service. *Index to Publications of the United States Congress.* Washington: CIS, 1970–. Monthly, with quarterly cumulation; annual cumulation in three volumes in the *CIS/Annual.* Aims to provide access to all publications of the U.S. Congress except the *Congressional Record*; includes hearings, committee prints, reports, and other Congressional publications. In two parts; the *Index* section gives access by subject, author, and title; the *Abstract* section gives full title of the document and an abstract of most items indexed. Indexed items are available on microfiche; can be searched online through DIALOG; available on CD-ROM.

Congressional Quarterly Almanac. Washington: CQ 1945–. Covers the work of Congress; gives summaries of each bill introduced or passed; is divided into subject areas. Available online.

CQ Weekly Report. Washington: CQ, 1845–. Summarizes events of the past week; discusses Congressional activity of the past week.

U.S. Congress. *Official Congressional Directory for the Use of the United States Congress, 1809–.* Washington: GPO, 1809–. Biennial. Includes a variety of information about members of Congress, committees, other bodies of government, independent agencies, diplomatic representatives, and members of the press.

HANDBOOKS AND YEARBOOKS

The Book of the States. Lexington: Council of State Governments, 1935–. Biennial. Provides an authoritative source of information on the structure, working methods, financial and functional activities of state governments; gives a comprehensive listing of elected state officials and members of the legislatures; tables give information for each state; kept up to date by supplements.

Kane, Joseph Nathan. *Facts About the Presidents.* 6th ed. New York: Wilson, 1993. Provides facts, statistics, and miscellaneous information about each president from George Washington to Bill Clinton: life, background, family, tenure in office, etc. Includes bibliographical references.

———. *Facts About the States.* New York: Wilson, 1989. Covers each state in the United States, Puerto Rico, and Washington, D.C.; gives information about geography, climate, politics, government, education, culture, economy, industries, occupations, etc.

Municipal Year Book. Chicago: International City Managers' Association, 1934–. Annual. Gives information converning governmental units, personnel, finance, and activities of United States and Canadian cities; has a directory of chief officers of Canadian cities over 10,000 population and of mayors and clerks of United States cities over 2500.

United States Government Organization Manual. Washington: GPO, 1935–. Annual. The official organization handbook of the federal government, gives essential information regarding the executive, legislative, and judicial branches and the authority, organization, and functions of the agencies of these branches; includes directory-type information.

Yearbook of the United Nations. New York: UN, Department of Public Information, 1947–. Annual. Provides a comprehensive account of the activities of the United Nations and its related intergovernmental agencies.

STATISTICAL INFORMATION SOURCES

American Statistics Index. Washington: CIS, 1973–. Annual, monthly, and quarterly supplements. "A comprehensive guide and index to the statistical publications of the U.S. government" (subtitle); aims to provide access to all statistics produced by federal agencies. In two parts: *Index* section and *Abstract* section. Indexed by subject, names, and categories; a microfiche service provides most of the documents indexed; searchable online through DIALOG; on CD-ROM.

Historical Statistics of the United States, Colonial Times to 1970. 2 vols. Washington: GPO, 1975, 1979. Gives comparative statistics for the years covered.

United Nations Statistical Office. *Statistical Yearbook/Annuaire Statistique.* New York: UN, 1949–. Annual. Gives political, scientific, educational, and cultural data on the countries of the world.

U.S. Bureau of the Census. *County and City Data Book.* Washington: GPO, 1952–. Gives the latest census figures for each county and for the larger cities in the United States; covers many areas; is issued irregularly, at about five-year intervals.

U.S. Bureau of the Census. *Statistical Abstract of the United States.* Washington: GPO, 1878–. Annual. Summarizes statistics of political, industrial, economic, and social institutions and organizations in the United States; is the major source of statistical information about the United States. Additional publications can be found in other chapters.

PART

4

Information Sources in the Subject Fields

CHAPTER
❧ 16 ❧

Subject Information Sources

A general information source, which has many subject specialists on its editorial staff, provides much information on the different subject fields; however, since the aim of the general reference source is to give wide and unrestricted coverage, specialized treatment on any one subject is necessarily limited.

For those persons who require more than a general treatment of a specific subject, there are specialized reference sources in every subject area.

A subject reference source[1] can be defined as a publication in which items of information about one particular subject—literature, history, music, sports, education—are brought together from many sources and arranged so that individual items can be found quickly and easily.

Subject reference materials introduce the student (or nonspecialist) to the subject matter of the different branches of knowledge.

1. They provide specialized definitions and explanations for the words and phrases in a given field which are not found in general word dictionaries.
2. They trace the growth of important ideas in a subject area.
3. They provide an introduction to the development of the literature of the subject.
4. They give authoritative information on major questions and issues in a specialized area.
5. They explain and clarify concepts.
6. They locate, describe, and evaluate the literature of the field.
7. They provide facts which indicate trends, and they summarize the events of a given year in a given subject field.

---

[1] Nonbook sources are discussed in Chapter 14.

Subject information sources are adapted to the peculiar characteristics of the subject under consideration. For example, in music there are dictionaries of musical themes and musical scores; in art, catalogs of reproductions and auctions; and in science, handbooks of tables and formulas.

Kinds and Purposes of Subject Information Sources

The kinds of information sources in each subject field are the same as those in the general area, and they serve similar purposes for a given subject. Not all the reference materials listed below provide all types of information indicated.

1. Bibliographies and guides
   a   Point out the literature of the field in question
   b   Provide descriptive and evaluative information which the catalog record cannot include and point out materials in the library which are not listed in the catalog, such as periodical articles, parts of books, nonbook sources, and so on.
   c   Arrange works according to form: dictionaries, histories, encyclopedias, handbooks, indexes, and books of criticism (if the subject field is literature), and give instructions regarding their use

   Examples:
   Bibliography of American Literature
   A Reader's Guide to the Great Religions

2. Indexes
   a   Indicate where periodical articles on a subject can be found
   b   Indicate collections in which plays, short stories, essays and poems can be found
   c   Analyze books and parts of books

   Examples:
   Short Story Index
   Applied Science and Technology Index

3. Dictionaries
   a   Provide specialized definitions and explanations of terminology and concepts
   b   Help to establish terminology

c Serve as a guide to current as well as historical usage of words and phrases

d Give short, concise answers to questions

e May give chronology

f May give biographical information

g May give pronunciation

Examples:
Harper's Dictionary of Music
Electronics Dictionary

4. Encyclopedias

a Give a "summary treatment" of the different phases and aspects of a subject

b Explain historical backgrounds, trends, and the influence of events outside the subject area, such as the influence of social conditions on the literature of a period

c Trace the development of ideas in a subject field

Examples:
Encyclopedia of World Art
The Encyclopedia of Philosophy

5. Handbooks and manuals

a Identify references, allusions, dates, quotations, and characters in literature

b Summarize literary plots

c Provide statistics and useful bits of information

d Give instructions in specialized areas

Examples:
The Oxford Companion to American Literature
Halliwell's Film Guide

6. Yearbooks and annuals

a Summarize events of the past year, including research projects undertaken and completed

b Provide a source for hard-to-locate items of information

Examples:
Yearbook of Agriculture
Municipal Yearbook
McGraw-Hill Yearbook of Science and Technology

7. Collections (anthologies)
   a Bring together in one place selections or quotations from essays, poetry, drama, short stories, periodicals, and other forms of literature
   b Serve as source materials for courses in literature, history, education, psychology, and other subject fields

   Examples:
   The Oxford Dictionary of Quotations
   Documents of American History

8. Atlases and gazetteers
   a Provide geographical information in any subject area in maps, text, or both
   b Give overall picture emphasizing location of industries, products, literature

   Examples:
   Atlas of American History
   Oxford Bible Atlas

9. Biographical dictionaries
   a Provide concise information about important persons in a subject field: authors, scholars, scientists, educators
   b May include bibliographies and evaluations of an author's work

   Examples:
   World Authors, 1980–1985
   American Men and Women of Science

10. Reference histories give factual information, trends, and main facts of development, covering
    a Chronology
    b Interpretation of events
    c Biographical data
    d Bibliographical information

    Examples:
    The Oxford History of English Literature
    The Cambridge History of American Literature

11. Professional journals provide up-to-date articles, essays, book reviews, and other material relating specifically to the subject matter of a given branch of knowledge

Examples:
American Journal of Philosophy
Scientific American

12. An abstract is a brief digest or summary which gives the essential points of an article, pamphlet, book, monograph, or report. An abstract journal is a collection of such abstracts (in a particular field) with subject and author indexes. Usually an abstract of a work gives the researcher enough information to decide whether or not the entire work should be read. Abstract journals give bibliographical information regarding the works abstracted. Abstracts may be in the original language in which the work appeared, or they may be in translation.

Examples:
Psychological Abstracts
Science Abstracts

13. Nonbook information sources are available in all subject fields. They include audiovisual materials, disk and tape recordings, transparencies, multimedia kits, videorecordings, musical scores, microforms, and data bases. (See also Chapter 14 and Figure 14.1).
14. Government publications cover every subject area. These materials are discussed in Chapter 15.

The choice of an information source in a subject field, as in a general area, depends upon the nature of the question to be answered: (1) the kind of information required, (2) the subject area of which it is a part, and (3) the factors affecting the question, such as time and location.

Using Subject Information Sources[2]

Reference materials in the subject fields are entered in the library catalog under author or editor, title, and subject. Subject headings consist of the subject, subdivided by kind of material: for example, American literature—Bibliographies; Education—Yearbooks; English language—Dictionaires; Literature—Dictionaries.

Efficient use of subject sources is dependent upon an understanding of (1) the purposes of each kind of subject reference source, (2) the organization and the arrangement of the material, and (3) the distinguishing features. Before using a subject information source, one should examine the table of

[2] See also pp. 79–80.

contents and the preliminary pages which explain the purpose, the plan and arrangement, and any special features.

Since new sources and new editions of old ones are being published continually, it is necessary to consult the library catalog frequently in order to keep up to date on the subject materials in the library. The titles listed here are only suggestions, they represent but a small portion of the thousands that are available. Each reader will supplement them and, in time, replace them with new publications.

CHAPTER
❦ 17 ❦

Philosophy and Psychology

Philosophy

The first subject class in both the Dewey Decimal Classification System (100) and the Library of Congress Classification System (B) is philosophy. When there was infinitely less to learn than there is today, philosophy comprised all learning except technical rules and the practical arts. In medieval universities, it was the omnibus subject which covered the whole body of sciences and the liberal arts. Remnants of this comprehensive meaning are carried forward in the present in the highest academic degree, doctor of philosophy (Ph.D.), although increased specialization in the social sciences and humanities, as well as in the pure and applied sciences, has greatly narrowed the range of interest and inquiry of most "doctor of philosophy" students.

Derived from two Greek words—*philein*, "to love," and *sophia*, "wisdom"—"philosophy" has historically been thought of as both the seeking of wisdom and the wisdom sought. In this day of rapidly advancing science and technology, of wide-sweeping change, and of increasingly complex domestic and world problems which overlap and intertwine and thus require the most mature thought and judgment of generalists as was well as of specialists, philosophy is more often thought of as the quest for wisdom than as the wisdom for which search is made. Consequently, philosophy is seen as a mode and method of thought, as a continual invitation to those of serious concern to ask reasoned questions of life and to examine and criticize rationally the ends and purposes which men and women establish and the methods they pursue in their efforts to achieve those purposes. Today, no area of investigation is denied to scientific research; correspondingly, no presupposition, premise, prejudice, assumption, belief, or disbelief—in short, no area of action and thought—is "protected" from the disciplined, probing, analytical approach of philosophy.

In this concept of philosophy as the quest for wisdom, the central emphasis is on *values* (moral and ethical) and on the rational ways (logic) by which value judgments can and should be developed and criticized. Philosophy tries to locate, to understand, and to clarify the nature and importance of the issues and values at stake in situations of uncertainty, confusion, dispute, competition, and conflict. Philosophers who are true to the principles and procedures inherent in the philosophical method of inquiry are concerned about mature, serious, constructive, and hard-won matters. On the basis of facts and knowledge which they draw from wide-ranging fields of recorded and observable experience, philosophers offer for critical examination their own concepts, ideas, and propositions; and they seek to analyze rationally the concepts, ideas, and propositions set forth by others.

Consequently, since there is no such thing in a free society as an "established" philosophy—an accepted, authoritative credo of belief and action—but only philosophers and their philosophies, the basic literature of philosophy is the writings of past and present philosophers and critical commentaries on these writings.

Reference Sources in Philosophy

BIBLIOGRAPHIES AND INDEXES[1]

Bynagle, Hans E. *Philosophy: A Guide to the Reference Literature*. Littleton: Libraries Unlimited, 1986. Includes materials for many types of users: professionals, teachers, students, graduate and undergraduate. Illustrated.

DeGeorge, Richard T. *The Philosopher's Guide: To Sources, Research Tools, Professional Life, and Related Fields*. Lawrence: Regents Press of Kansas, 1980. Lists materials in philosophy and reference works in related disciplines; covers history of philosophy, individual philosophers, movements, and professional activities; useful for philosophy students and researchers.

The Philosopher's Index: An International Index to Philosophical Periodicals and Books. Bowling Green: Bowling Green U, 1967–. Quarterly. Indexes

[1] See also Chapter 9, Indexes, and Chapter 13, Bibliographies.

major American and British philosophical journals and books in philosophy; provides some abstracts.

Tice, Terence, and Slavens, Thomas P. *Research Guide to Philosophy*. Sources of Information in the Humanities, 3. Chicago: ALA, 1983. Provides material on the history of philosophy; various philosophies, such as logic; and reference sources with annotations.

DICTIONARIES AND ENCYCLOPEDIAS

Baldwin, James Mark, ed. *Dictionary of Philosophy and Psychology*. New ed. 3 vols. New York: Macmillan, 1925. Reprinted by Peter Smith, 1946. Out of date for modern developments, but still useful; covers the entire field. On microfiche, 1974.

Becker, Lawrence C., and Charlotte B. Becker, eds. *Encyclopedia of Ethics*. New York: Garland, 1992. Presents a broad variety of topics in moral philosophy and related areas; focuses on the English-speaking cultures, but others are given attention.

Bullock, Alan, and Oliver Stallybrass, eds. *The Harper Dictionary of Modern Thought*. New York: Harper, 1977. Covers twentieth-century words and phrases; defines words in their intellectual, historical, and cultural context.

Edwards, Paul, ed. *The Encyclopedia of Philosophy*. 8 vols. New York: Macmillan and Free Press, 1967. For specialists and nonspecialists; covers all of philosophy and related disciplines; treats topics at length and emphasizes individual thinkers; provides bibliographies and many cross references; contributors are from all parts of the world; Vol. 8 is the index. (Also available in four vols.)

Lacey, A. R. *A Dictionary of Philosophy*. Boston: Routledge, 1976. Published in paperback by Scribner's, 1976. Intended for students and nonspecialists; covers only western philosophy; defines terms; explains concepts; gives some biographies; entries are brief; some have bibliographies.

Reese, William L. *Dictionary of Philosophy and Religion: Eastern and Western Thought*. Atlantic Highlands: Humanities P, 1980. Delineates the ideas of a particular thinker or school of thought; explains various meanings of a term; lists principal writings of individual philosophers.

Weiner, Philip P., ed. *Dictionary of the History of Ideas: Studies of Selected Pivotal Ideas*. 4 vols. New York: Scribner's 1973. *Index*, 1974. A collection of long scholarly articles by an international group of experts; provides interdisciplinary coverage of many topics in the history of ideas, including philosophy, history, religion, science, mathematics, literature, the arts, and the social sciences; bibliographies are provided.

HANDBOOKS AND DIGESTS

Burr, John R., ed. *Handbook of World Philosophy: Contemporary Developments since 1945*. Westport: Greenwood P, 1980. Surveys recent philosophical trends throughout the world. Provides a selected bibliography and a directory of associations.

Magill, Frank N., ed. *Masterpieces of World Philosophy*. New York: Harper-Collins, 1990. Digests selections from the world's great philosophers; for each selection, gives the type of work, when it was first translated, and the principal ideas advanced.

Magill, Frank N. *World Philosophy: Essay-reviews of 225 Major Works*. 5 vols. Englewood Cliffs: Salem, 1982. Reviews important philosophical works from the 6th century B.C. to the present with commentary and bibliographical references. Major philosophers are represented by one work; chronologically arranged; has a glossary of terms.

BIOGRAPHICAL DICTIONARIES[2]

Directory of American Philosophers. Bowling Green: Bowling Green U, 1962–. Biennial. Companion volume to *International Directory of Philosophy and Philosophers*; gives a list of colleges and universities in the United States and Canada, with information about the philosophy department, if any; includes a list of societies, journals, and publishers of materials in this field.

Directory of American Scholars. 8th ed. Vol. IV: *Philosophy, Religion and Law*, Ed. Jaques Cattell Press. New York: Bowker, 1982. Devoted to United States and Canadian scholars; gives brief biographical information; provides a geographical index by state or province.

International Directory of Philosophy and Philosophers. 1st ed. Bowling Green: Philosophy Documentation Center, 1966–. Biennial. Serves as a worldwide guide to philosophy; provides survey essays on the history and character of philosophy in the various parts of the world; lists organizations, institutes, research centers, members of college and university philosophy faculties and of associations and societies.

Kersey, Ethel. *Women Philosophers: A Bio-Critical Sourcebook*. Westport: Greenwood, 1989. Gives information about some 160 women from ancient times to the present, including little known and obscure women philosophers: their nationality, field of specialization, and philosophical thought; each person's work is evaluated.

---

[2] See also Chapter 10, Biographical Dictionaries.

EXAMPLES OF PROFESSIONAL JOURNALS IN PHILOSOPHY[3]

The Journal of Philosophy. New York: Journal of Philosophy, Inc. Columbia U, 1904–. Monthly. Provides historical articles on philosophers or systems; includes notes and news.

Journal of the History of Philosophy. St. Louis: Washington U, Department of Philosophy, 1963–. Quarterly. Includes articles on the history of western philosophy, some in foreign languages; has book reviews.

The Philosophical Review. New York: Cornell U, 1892–. Quarterly. Publishes papers on problems of interest to contemporary philosophers; discusses philosophers and their ideas; gives book reviews.

Psychology

Psychology, from the Greek words *psyche*, meaning "mind" or "soul," and *logos*, meaning "law," has historically been the science that treats of the mind in any of its aspects—function, organization and structure, and effect on behavior. Once a part of philosophy and still a close companion, psychology developed and became a separate branch of learning within the past century. Class B of the Library of Congress Classification and 100 of the Dewey Decimal Classification include both philosophy and psychology.

In recent times, psychology has been thought of as the serious study of the activities of an organism rather than of the physiological functions. For example, the study of the functions of the brain is thought of as a physiological, rather than a psychological, theme. Thus the general theme of psychology is the study of the activities of the total organism (humans and lower animals) in its interrelations with its physical environment and with its social setting and influences.

Psychology is often referred to and identified in terms of a school or system—for example, behaviorist psychology or Gestalt psychology.

Perhaps the best and most comprehensive way in which to see modern psychology is through an acquaintance with some of its many subdivisions, which are determined by, and are named to describe, the kinds of problems studied. These kinds and fields of psychological study are so connected that one should not try to arrange them either chronologically or in order of their current importance. Some of the more important subdivisions of psychology are abnormal, analytic, animal, applied, experimental, genetic, motor, and

---

[3] See also *Ulrich's International Periodicals Directory*, 31st ed., and *Magazines for Libraries*, 7th ed., ed. Bill Katz and Linda S. Katz.

physiological. Other subdivisions of psychology are child, adolescent, adult, educational, social, and industrial. Related fields include psychiatry, psychoanalysis, psychotherapy, and psychopathology.

Representative Reference Sources in Psychology

BIBLIOGRAPHIES[4]

Harvard University. *The Harvard List of Books in Psychology*. 4th ed. Compiled and annotated by psychologists at Harvard University. Cambridge: Harvard UP, 1971. A guide to important titles in psychology; arranged by types of psychology: gives some evaluations.

INDEXES[5]

Council on Research in Bibliography. *Mental Health Book Review Index*. New York: Research Center for Mental Health, New York U, 1956–1972. Gives references to book reviews which appeared in some 200 journals, many of which are listed elsewhere; worldwide in coverage; useful especially for large and specialized libraries.
Index Medicus. (See p. 208.)

DICTIONARIES AND ENCYCLOPEDIAS

Corsini, Reymond J. *Encyclopedia of Psychology*. New York: Wiley, 1984. Treats concepts, theories, and terminology; includes biographies and bibliographical references; provides brief as well as in-depth coverage.
Eysenck, H. J., ed. *Encyclopedia of Psychology*. 3 vols. New York: Herder, 1972. International in coverage; treats all facets of psychology; gives definitions of terms, historical overview, discussion of research and scientific controversies, and descriptions of various schools of psychology and related disciplines; gives background and summary of leading international opinion on current issues; includes bibliographies.
Goldenson, Robert M., ed. *The Encyclopedia of Human Behavior: Psychology, Psychiatry, and Mental Health*. 2 vols. Garden City: Doubleday, 1970. Aims to cover all major phases of these areas: presents essential information for students and nonprofessionals; gives definitions, illustrative cases, and illustrations.

---

[4] See also Chapter 13, Bibliographies.
[5] See also Chapter 9, Indexes.

Harré, Rom, and Roger Lamb. *The Encyclopedic Dictionary of Psychology*. Cambridge: MIT, 1983. Gives an overview of psychology, definitions, and theories; treats many areas of contemporary psychology.

Sutherland, Stuart. *The International Dictionary of Psychology*. New York: Continuum, 1989. Defines technical terms, language, and phrases in psychology and from related fields.

BIOGRAPHICAL DICTIONARIES AND DIRECTORIES[6]

American Men and Women of Science: Social and Behavioral Sciences. 18th ed. Ed. Jaques Cattell Press. 8 vols. New York: Bowker, 1992. Provides a biographical profile of persons engaged in teaching or research in psychology; Vol. VIII is an index by location and discipline.

American Psychological Association. *Biographical Directory*. Washington: APA, 1970–. Triennial. Lists affiliated organizations; gives brief biographical information on members and background information on the association.

O'Connell, Agnes N., and Nancy Felipe Russo. *Women in Psychology: A Biobibliographical Sourcebook*. New York: Greenwood, 1990. Aims to present the diverse contributions women have made to psychology and sociology; gives brief biographical information about each one, list of works, and influence.

YEARBOOKS

Annual Review of Psychology. Palo Alto: Annual Reviews, 1950–. Gives interpretative and evaluative reviews by psychologists of many topics in contemporary psychology.

Buros, Oscar Krisen. *The Eigth Mental Measurements Yearbook*. 2 vols. Highland Park: Gryphon, 1978. Makes available bibliographies of critical reviews of tests published in English and bibliographies of references on the construction and use of tests and on books in the field.

EXAMPLES OF PROFESSIONAL AND ABSTRACT JOURNALS IN PSYCHOLOGY[7]

American Journal of Psychology. Urbana: U of Illinois P, 1887–. Quarterly. Publishes reports of original research; emphasis is on experimental psychology; includes some short notes and discussions; gives book reviews.

---

[6] See also Chapter 10, Biographical Dictionaries.

[7] See also *Ulrich's International Periodicals Directory*, 31st ed., and *Magazines for Libraries*, 7th ed., ed. Bill Katz and Linda S. Katz.

Journal of General Psychology. Provincetown: The Journal P, 1928–. Quarterly. Covers experimental, physiological, and comparative psychology.

Psychological Abstracts. Washington, APA, 1927–. Monthly. Contains non-evaluative summaries of the world's literature in psychology and related disciplines; includes abstracts from journals, books, technical reports, and other scientific publications; abstracts are arranged under sixteen major subject categories; has author and subject indexes. In print, online via DIALOG and other major vendors, and on CD-ROM.

The Psychological Review. Lancaster: APA, 1894–. Bimonthly. Presents articles of theoretical significance to any area of scientific endeavor in psychology.

Psychology Today. New York: Ziff-Davis, 1967–. Monthly. Presents current developments in American psychology for professionals and nonprofessionals; broad coverage.

PsycLit. Wellesley Hills: Silver Platter, 1990–. Monthly update. The CD-ROM version of *Psychological Abstracts* covers the years 1974 to the present; gives bibliographic citations to and abstracts of journal articles in psychology and related fields. Search by keywords from the alphabetical listing found in the database and by subject headings from the *Thesaurus of Psychology Index Terms*.

CHAPTER
❧ 18 ❧

Religion and Mythology

Religion

The story of books and libraries (Chapter 1) revealed that the earliest records of every civilization contain religious or moral works. Since the time of Cicero, who defined religion as "the worship of the gods," attempts have been made to define religion. Some definitions are:

Action or conduct indicating a belief in, reverence for, and desire to please, a divine ruling power; the exercise or practice of rites or observance implying this.[1]

Religion is a feeling of dependence upon the unseen powers which control our destiny, accompanied by a desire to come into friendly relations with them.[2]

A specific and institutionalized set of beliefs and practices generally agreed upon by a number of persons or sects.[3]

A cause, principle, or system of beliefs held to with ardor and faith.[4]

---

[1] *The Oxford English Dictionary*, VII, 1933, 310.

[2] George Thomas White Patrick, *Introduction to Philosophy*, rev. ed. (Boston: Hougton, 1935) 37.

[3] *The Random House College Dictionary*, rev. ed. (New York: Random, 1975). Copyright © 1982 by Random House, Inc.

[4] *Webster's New Collegiate Dictionary* (Springfield: Merriam, 1981) 969. By permission. From *Webster's New Collegiate Dictionary* © 1981 by G. & C. Merriam Co., Publishers of the Merriam-Webster ® Dictionary.

In Hebrew and Christian thought, religion is man's recognition of his relation to God and his expression of that relation in faith, worship, and conduct.[5]

There are many religions, and while there is no generally accepted definition of religion, religions have common characteristics, such as form or forms of worship; rites, rituals, and practices; a set of beliefs, rules or laws, or guiding principles; and sacred writings.

Religious literature is perhaps the largest subject class in extent and variety. There are the basic scriptures or writings of each religion or sect and commentaries on them, historical studies, devotional and inspirational works, rituals, informal literature, church doctrines, works of interpretation, ecclesiastical law, religious music, lives of the saints, lives of important persons in each religious group, statistical information, periodical literature, and many nonbook forms—audio, visual, and audiovisual materials.

Reference works in the field of religion, like all other reference sources, are compilations of factual information and are planned to answer specific questions about religions and the literature of the various religions and to aid in further study of a given area. These reference sources include bibliographies, guides, indexes, concordances, dictionaries, encyclopedias, books of quotations, collections of hymns, digests of religious literature, historical and Bible atlases, yearbooks, biographical dictionaries, and professional journals. (See Chapter 14 for types of nonbook sources.)

Representative Reference Sources in Religion

BIBLIOGRAPHIES, GUIDES, AND INDEXES[6]

Adams, Charles J., ed. *A Reader's Guide to the Great Religions.* 2d ed. New York: Free Press, 1977. A collection of bibliographic essays by authorities on the literature, history, and beliefs of the world's great religions; includes religions of the ancient world, Mexico, and South America; provides guidance on what to read.

Cornish, Graham, ed. *Religious Periodicals Directory.* Santa Barbara: ABC-Clio, 1986. Offers a wide range of periodicals in religion and related fields, such as history, anthropology, linguistics, art, and archaeology; worldwide in coverage.

Religion Index One: Periodicals, July–December 1977–. Chicago, ATA, 1978–. Semiannual. Formerly entitled *Religious Periodical Literature* (1949–1977);

---

[5] Madeleine S. Miller and J. Lane Miller, *Harper's Bible Dictionary*, 8th ed. (New York: Harper, 1973) 608.

[6] See also Chapter 9, Indexes, and Chapter 13, Bibliographies.

indexes 532 periodicals published in the United States and in foreign countries; has a subject index, an author index with abstracts, and a book review index.

CONCORDANCES

Cruden, Alexander, comp. *A Complete Concordance to the Holy Scriptures of the Old and New Testaments.* New ed. Westwood: Revell, n.d. Includes a concordance to the Apocrypha.

Morrison, Clinton. *An Analytical Concordance to the Revised Standard Version of the New Testament.* Philadelphia: Westminster, 1979. Lists and analyzes both the English and the original Greek words of the New Testament; English words and phrases of the *Revised Standard Version* are arranged alphabetically, each entry followed by a definition of the Greek original and the word in Greek in transliteration; uses of the word are listed in context, with identification of the book, chapter, and verse.

Nelson's Complete Concordance of the Revised Standard Version of the Bible. Compiled under the supervision of John W. Ellison. 2d ed. New York: Nelson, 1972. Gives context and location of each key word.

The New Strong's Exhaustive Concordance of the Bible. Nashville: Nelson, 1990. Indexes the contents of the King James Version; includes a *Dictionary of the Hebrew Bible* and a *Dictionary of the Greek Bible.*

Thompson, Newton Wayland, and Raymond Stock, comps. *Complete Concordance to the Bible (Douay Version).* St. Louis: Herder, 1945. Indexes the actual words of the Douay Roman Catholic version of the Bible.

DICTIONARIES

Abingdon Dictionary of Living Religions. Nashville: Abingdon, 1981. Presents the beliefs, practices, historical development and current status of the religions of the world today; covers sects, doctrines, movements, and sacred writings; major religions are given extensive coverage; includes illustrations, maps, and drawings, and some bibliographies. Useful for students and scholars.

Achteimer, Paul, ed. *Harper's Bible Dictionary.* New York: Harper, 1985. Covers archaeology, geography, persons, places, developments in theology, and religion; gives some pronunciation; illustrated.

The Anchor Bible Dictionary. 6 vols. Ed. David Noel Freedman, and others. New York: Doubleday, 1992. Provides articles about the Bible and relevant biblical topics, including historical and archaeological subjects. Illustrated.

Brandon, S. G. F., ed. *A Dictionary of Comparative Religion.* New York: Scribner's, 1970. Articles cover a wide variety of topics relating to the world's religions from prehistoric times to the present; aims to "treat the religions in proportion to their significance in the history of human culture" (Preface).

Butler, Trent C. *Holman Bible Dictionary*. Nashville: Holman, 1991. Defines terms, explains Bible subjects; gives an outline of each book of the Bible; provides illustrations, maps, and charts.

Childress, James F., and John McQuarrie. *The Westminster Dictionary of Christian Ethics*. Philadelphia: Westminster, 1986. Represents many points of view; includes contemporary issues; treats basic ethical concepts, biblical and theological; does not have biographical material.

Cross, F. L., and E. A. Livingstone, ed. *The Oxford Dictionary of the Christian Church*. 2d ed. London: Oxford UP, 1974. Covers historical developments, doctrine, and definitions of terms; includes biographies and provides bibliographies; gives attention to recent developments in the churches, movements, and personalities.

Gentz, William. *The Dictionary of Bible and Religion*. Nashville: Abingdon, 1986. Gives definitions and/or explanations of people, places, and events in the Bible and beliefs, practices, and organizations of religion. Jewish and Christian tradition receive more attention than other major religions. Illustrated.

The Interpreter's Dictionary of the Bible. 4 vols. Nashville: Abingdon, 1962. "An illustrated encyclopedia indentifying and explaining all proper names and significant terms and subjects in the Holy Scriptures, including the Apocrypha, with attention to archaeological discoveries and researches into the life and faith of ancient times" (subtitle). Serves the needs of students, scholars, teachers, preachers, and general readers. Supplementary volume, 1976.

Parrinder, Geoffrey. *A Dictionary of Non-Christian Religions*. Philadelphia: Westminster, 1971. Explains terminology, concepts, gods, and religious systems of all non-Christian religions; covers primitive and classical as well as contemporary religions; emphasis is on Hinduism, Buddhism, and Islam; provides drawings and photographs.

Reid, Daniel, et al., eds. *Dictionary of Christianity in America*. Downers Grove: Intervarsity, 1990. Discusses religious bodies, movements, individuals, organizations, rituals, events, denominations, and issues in the development, history, and practice of Christianity in America; emphasis is on the United States, but attention is also given to Canada and Latin America.

ENCYCLOPEDIAS

Eliade, Mircea. *The Encyclopedia of Religion*. 16 vols. New York: Macmillan, 1987. Discusses in detail worldwide religions of Judaism, Christianity,

Islam, and Buddhism—growth, development, beliefs, texts, doctrines, practices, leading figures, and current issues; other religions are treated, including ancient religions.

Encyclopaedia Judaica. 16 vols. New York: Macmillan, 1972. Presents all aspects of Jewish life and knowledge up to the present time; gives bibliographies for further reading; includes biographical articles. Yearbook, 1973–.

Fischer-Schreiber, Ingrid, et al., eds. *The Encyclopedia of Eastern Philosophy and Religion: Buddhism, Hinduism, Taoism, Zen.* Boston: Shambhala, 1989. Provides information on the basic terminology and doctrinal systems of "the four great wisdoms of the East" (Preface); includes historical and biographical information; intended for the general reader.

Glassé, Cyril. *The Concise Encyclopedia of Islam.* San Francisco: Harper, 1989. Provides information on the background, practices, observances, people, places, and texts of Islam; is illustrated.

Melton, J. Gordon. *Encyclopedia of American Religion.* 3d ed. Detroit: Gale, 1989. Describes religious bodies in North America: origin, development, and practices; includes 1588 churches, sects, cults, and societies through the 1980s.

The New Catholic Encyclopedia. Prepared by an editorial staff at the Catholic University of America. 15 vols. New York: McGraw, 1967. "An international work of reference on the teachings, history, organization, and activities of the Catholic Church and on all institutions, religions, philosophies, and scientific and cultural developments affecting the Catholic Church from the beginning to the present" (subtitle). Vol. XVI: *Supplement 1967–1974.* Ed. David Eggenberger, 1974.

Wigoder, Geoffrey, ed. *The New Standard Jewish Encyclopedia.* 7th ed. New York: Facts on File, 1992. Treats all aspects of Jewish life, including religious tradition, culture, people, and events.

BOOKS OF QUOTATIONS

Stevenson, Burton Egbert. *The Home Book of Bible Quotations.* New York: Harper, 1949. Based on the *King James Version* of the Bible; has a key-word concordance index arranged by subject.

DIGESTS

Magill, Frank N., ed. *Masterpieces of Catholic Literature in Summary Form.* New York: Harper, 1965. Presents, in the form of essay-reviews, a selection of Roman Catholic literature from earliest times to the present; includes books in the fields of philosophy, theology, and history.

————. *Masterpieces of Christian Literature in Summary Form*. 2 vols. New York: Harper, 1963. A selection of literature in essay-review form from the Protestant viewpoint.

HYMNS

Christ-Janer, Albert, et al., eds. *American Hymns Old and New*. New York: Columbia UP, 1980. Offers more than 600 American hymns from the British psalters of the seventeenth century to hymns of this century; traces influences on hymns; group hymns by denomination or type; includes forty new hymns written for this edition.

ATLASES

Al Faruqi, Isma'il R., and David E. Sopher, eds. *Historical Atlas of the Religions of the World*. New York: Macmillan, 1974. Historical and geographical approach to the world's religions; covers major religions or groups of religions—past and present—including American Indian religions, African religions, and such universal religions as Buddhism, Christianity, and Islam. Maps, bibliographies, and chronologies are provided; covers origin and distribution; locates shrines and temples.

May, Herbert Gordon, et al., eds. *Oxford Bible Atlas*. 3d ed. revised by John Day. London: Oxford UP, 1984. Covers physical geography, historical changes, and geographical name changes; maps are accompanied by explanatory text; includes articles on historical background of the region; gives archaeological data; has a gazetteer.

Pritchard, James B., ed. *The Harper Concise Atlas of the Bible*. New York: HarperCollins, 1991. Offers current knowledge of the history and geography of the Bible; uses maps, charts, and artwork.

YEARBOOKS AND HANDBOOKS

Each denomination has its own yearbook, which provides information regarding its organization, membership, officers, local officials, development, publications, and annual achievements; it may include articles on doctrine and questions regarding theology. Examples are *American Jewish Yearbook*, *Official Catholic Almanac*, and *The Episcopal Church Annual*. The titles listed below cover all denominations.

Handbook of American and Canadian Churches. Nashville: Abingdon, 1973–. Annual. Provides information on most of the established religious groups in the United States and Canada; gives brief historical description of the religious body, names and addresses of officers, organizations, periodicals, and statistics.

Mead, Frank Spencer. *Handbook of Denominations in the United States*. 8th ed. rev. by Samuel S. Hill. Nashville: Abingdon, 1985. Provides factual information on the history, organization, doctrines, and status of more than 250 religious bodies; includes statistical material, a glossary of terms, and bibliographies.

BIOGRAPHICAL DICTIONARIES[7]

Bowden, Henry Warner, ed. *Dictionary of American Religious Biography*. Westport: Greenwood, 1977. Presents 425 biographies of men and women (no longer living) who influenced American religious life; covers more than three centuries and includes religious leaders, reformers, philosophers, and members of minority groups; emphasis is on ordained clergy, but the laity is represented; gives essential biographical information and an evaluation of the person's contribution to religious history, a brief list of works by the biographee, and bibliographical references.

Directory of American Scholars. 8th ed. Vol. IV: *Philosophy, Religion and Law*, 1982. Covers persons active in the field of religion.

Who's Who in Religion. Chicago: Marquis, 1985. Covers current religious leaders; includes religious educators, church officials, and writers; emphasis is on large denominations, but small groups are included.

PROFESSIONAL JOURNALS IN RELIGION

Each denomination has its own journals. See *Ulrich's International Periodicals Directory*, 31st ed. and *Magazines for Libraries*. 7th ed., edited by Bill Katz and Linda S. Katz, for a comprehensive listing. The following titles are examples of general-coverage journals in the field of religion.

Church History. Wallingford: American Soc. of Church Hist., 1932–. Quarterly. Nondenominational; considers all aspects of church history; gives information on religion in the United States and abroad; includes book reviews.

Harvard Theological Review. Cambridge: Harvard UP, 1908–. Quarterly. Nondenominational; covers Bible studies, history and philosophy of religion, and theology.

History of Religions: An International Journal for Comparative Historical Studies. Chicago: U of Chicago P, 1961–. Quarterly. Devoted to the study of historical religious phenomena; one primary aim is the integration of results of the several disciplines of the science of religion.

---

[7] See also Chapter 10, Biographical Dictionaries.

Mythology

"Mythology" is a collective word, usually thought of by social anthropologists as including the stories and tales (myths) which describe the origin, nature, and adventures of the gods and goddesses of a people. In other words, myths are concerned with the supernatural and are especially associated with religious feasts, festivals, rites, and beliefs. For this reason, mythology is often classified by social scientists as a part of primitive religion. Both mythology and religion have their beginnings in prehistory.

Representative Reference Books in Mythology

INDEXES[8]

Art Index. (See p. 219.)

ENCYCLOPEDIAS AND HANDBOOKS

Cavendish, Richard, ed. *Mythology: An Illustrated Encyclopedia.* New York: Rizzoli, 1980. A survey of world mythology divided into six large geographical areas: Asia, the Middle East, the West, Africa, the Americas, the Pacific; brief text; more than 400 illustrations, many in color.

Cotterell, Arthur. *A Dictionary of World Mythology.* Rev. ed. New York: Oxford UP, 1986. Gives short articles on the chief mythologies of the world, divided by geographical area, with historical background of the mythologies represented; arranged according to the "seven great traditions of world mythology: West Asia, South and Central Asia, East Asia, Europe, America, Africa, and Oceania." Includes illustrations and bibliographies.

Frazer, Sir James, ed. *The Golden Bough: A Study in Magic and Religion.* 3d ed., rev. 12 vols. New York: St. Martin's, 1955. A comprehensive collection of information about primitive religions; traces many myths and rites to their prehistoric beginnings.

Gray, Louis Herbert, ed. *The Mythology of All Races, Greek and Roman.* 26th ed. 13 vols. Boston: Marshall Jones, 1958. Includes text and illustrations.

Grimal, Pierre, ed. *Larousse World Mythology.* New York: Putnam, 1965. Translated from two French works, *Mythologies de la Méditerranée au Gange* and *Mythologies des Steppes, des Iles et des Forêts.* Includes mythology

---

[8] See also Chapter 9, Indexes.

of every region in the world; has outstanding illustrations, many in color; a reference work for students of art, literature, history, theology, etc.

Shapiro, Max. S. *Mythologies of the World: A Concise Encyclopedia.* Garden City: Doubleday, 1979. Gives short definitions or explanations of gods, heroes, and others in about twenty mythologies from all parts of the world, including Africa and North America. Useful for quick reference.

Tripp, Edward, ed. *Crowell's Handbook of Classical Mythology.* New York: Crowell, 1970. Designed as a companion to reading, tells major myths of Greece and Rome in readable story form; includes personal and place names.

CHAPTER

❦ 19 ❦

The Social Sciences and Education

Social Sciences

The social sciences[1] comprise those branches of knowledge which have to do with the activities of the individual as a member of society, excluding history. Included in the social sciences class of the Dewey Decimal Classification System (300) are sociology, statistics, political science, economics, law, government, social welfare, education,[2] commerce, and customs and folklore. These areas are part of Library of Congress classes H, J, K, and L.

There are numerous reference sources devoted to the subject matter of the several social sciences. They include bibliographies, guides, indexes, dictionaries, encyclopedias, handbooks, yearbooks, biographical dictionaries, atlases, and professional journals.[3]

Representative Reference Sources in the Social Sciences

BIBLIOGRAPHIES AND GUIDES[4]

American Behavioral Scientist. *The ABS Guide to Recent Publications in the Social and Behavioral Sciences.* New York: ABS, 1965. Lists and annotates a selection of books, pamphlets, and articles from material cited in the

---

[1] The social sciences are not to be confused with "social studies," which are portions of the subject matter of the social sciences suitable for study in elementary and secondary schools and are developed into courses of study which place emphasis on social aims.

[2] Education as a subject field is discussed on pp. 192–196.

[3] See also Chapter 14, Nonbook Information Sources, and Chapter 15, Government Publications.

[4] See also Chapter 13, Bibliographies.

"New Studies Section" of the *American Behavioral Scientist* from 1957 to 1964. Supplemented by *Recent Publications in the Social and Behavioral Sciences.* 1966–. Annual.

Ballou, Patricia. *Women: A Bibliography.* 2d ed. Boston: Hall, 1986. Annotates books, pamphlets, essays, and journal articles about women.

Daniells, Lorna M. *Business Information Sources.* Rev. ed. Berkeley: U of California P, 1985. Annotates a selected list of basic reference works in business; covers sources on investments, statistics, management, real estate, insurance, etc. Gives examples of textbooks and books for people in business; includes collections of readings.

Fisher, Mary L. *The Negro in America: A Bibliography.* 2d ed., rev. and enl. Cambridge: Harvard UP, 1970. Lists titles on numerous subjects such as black theater, dance, art, music, and blacks in literature and the arts; includes books, journals, pamphlets, and government documents; gives references to language and idiom, black studies, etc.

Handbook of Latin American Studies. Gainesville: U of Florida P, 1936–. Annual. Various publishers. A critical bibliography of Latin American research; provides an annual record of important publications in the various disciplines; beginning with Vol. 26 (1964), the handbook is divided into two parts: (*Humanities*) and (*Social Sciences*), published in alternate years.

O'Brien, Jacqueline Wasserman, and Steven R. Wasserman. *Statistics Sources.* 15th ed. Detroit: Gale, 1992. Identifies primary sources of statistical data on more than 20,000 subjects; includes information about statistical sources for each country in the world.

Public Affairs Information Service. *Bulletin.* New York: PAIS, 1915–. Semimonthly. A subject index to current books, pamphlets, government publications, reports of public and private agencies, and periodicals relating to economic and social conditions, public administration, and international relations published in English throughout the world.

Tze-Chung, Li. *Social Sciences Reference Sources: A Practical Guide.* 2d ed. Westport: Greenwood, 1990. Lists types of reference sources available in the social sciences, with examples; brief annotations.

Webb, William H. *Sources of Information in the Social Sciences.* Chicago: ALA, 1986. Describes monographs, periodicals, and reference sources in history, psychology, social science, and education.

INDEXES[5]

ABI/INFORM. Louisville, UMI, 1971–. Monthly. Abstracted Business Information. Offers bibliographic citations and abstracts of more than 800

---

[5] See also Chapter 9, Indexes.

business and management journals; uses controlled vocabulary; search by subject, author's name, word, company name; does not have a print version. Available via DIALOG and other major vendors, and on CD-ROM. Offers some full-text documents.

Business Periodicals Index. New York: Wilson, 1958–. Monthly except August. Indexes, by title and subject, 335 English-language periodicals in business and related fields. Book reviews are arranged by author in a separate section of the index. Print edition, online, on tape, and on CD-ROM through WilsonLine and WilsonDisc.

Business Periodicals on Disc. Ann Arbor: UMI, 1987–. Provides digitally scanned full-text images from over 300 business and management periodicals.

Index to Legal Periodicals. New York: Wilson, 1908–. Monthly except September. Indexes articles in more than 570 legal journals, yearbooks, bar association organs, university publications, law reviews, and government publications originating in the United States, Canada, Puerto Rico, Great Britain, Ireland, Australia, and New Zealand. Other features include a "Table of Cases," a "Table of Statutes," and book reviews of current books. Print edition, online, on tape, and on CD-ROM.

PAIS on CD-ROM. New York: PAIS, 1987–. Quarterly update. Indexes literature on national and international economic, political, and social issues; covers international relations, education, environment, business, and finance; gives access to periodical articles, books, government documents, and statistical journals; also available online and in print.

Social Science Citation Index. Philadelphia: Inst. for Scientific Information, 1973–. Quarterly. Provides access to 1400 of the world's leading social science journals in fifty disciplines. Search by title, Boolean logic, author, citation, address, and journal.

Social Sciences Index. New York: Wilson, 1974–. Quarterly; annual cumulations. Indexes by author and subject 342 periodicals in the social sciences; book reviews are in a separate section. Print edition, online, on tape, and on CD-ROM.

Wilson Business Abstracts. New York: Wilson, 1990–. Monthly. Abstracts the 345 business journals indexed in *Business Periodicals Index.* Available online, on tape, and on CD-ROM.

DICTIONARIES

Ammer, Christine, and Dean Ammer. *Dictionary of Business and Economics.* Rev. and expanded ed. New York: Free Press, 1984. Covers terminology, people, associations, theory, and practical applications of economic theory in business.

Black's Law Dictionary. 6th ed. St. Paul: West, 1990. Defines terms and concepts; includes a guide to pronunciation, rules for admission to the bar, code of professional ethics, abbreviations.

Gould, Julius, and William L. Kolb, eds. *A Dictionary of the Social Sciences*. Compiled under the auspices of UNESCO. New York: Free Press, 1964. Defines and describes in essay form the key concepts most widely employed in the various social science disciplines with illustrative quotations from the literature; definitions are signed. Gives all major definitions of a term, including both common usages and "accepted scientific usages." Omits highly technical terms.

Greenwald, Douglas, et. al., eds. *McGraw-Hill Dictionary of Modern Economics*. 3d ed. New York: McGraw, 1983. Written for the nonspecialist; defines 1300 selected contemporary terms in economics; has some charts and tables; lists references to additional sources; identifies some 200 organizations and agencies connected with economics.

Jary, David, and Julia Jary, eds. *The HarperCollins Dictionary of Sociology*. New York: HarperCollins, 1991. Defines some 1800 terms and concepts in sociology and related areas; gives biographical information for prominent individuals.

Johnston, R. J., et. al., eds. *Dictionary of Human Geography*. 2d ed. New York: Free Press, 1986. Defines terms and concepts and provides lengthy articles on theories and topics relating to the relationship between human societies and their environments.

Pass, Christopher. *The HarperCollins Dictionary of Economics*. New York: HarperCollins, 1991. Defines terms; gives biographical information, uses graphs.

Pearce, Donald W. *The MIT Dictionary of Modern Economics*. 3d ed. Cambridge: MIT, 1986. Gives brief definitions of terminology in economics; for beginning students.

Plano, Jack C., and Milton Greenberg. *The American Political Dictionary*. 8th ed. New York: Holt, 1989. Provides an overview of important concepts, terms, court cases, statutes, and agencies; includes state and local governments.

Shafritz, Jay M. *The HarperCollins Dictionary of American Government and Politics*. New York: HarperCollins, 1992. Defines terms relating to U.S. government at every level; provides articles on influential people; defines terms in government and politics.

ENCYCLOPEDIAS

Borgatta, Edgar F., and Marie L. Borgatta. *Encyclopedia of Sociology*. 4 vols. New York: Macmillan, 1992. Covers every aspect of the field, including continuing concepts and newer concerns, such as terrorism, drug abuse, and homelessness; uses nontechnical language; is international in coverage; is illustrated.

Collier, Simon, et. al., eds. *The Cambridge Encyclopedia of Latin America and the Caribbean.* Cambridge: Cambridge UP, 1987. Covers numerous aspects, including history, people, economic problems, political events, culture, and physical environment; has many maps and photographs.

Greenwald, Douglas, ed. *Encyclopedia of Economics.* New York: McGraw, 1982. Covers the entire field of economics: terminology, economic thought, influences such as the industrial revolution, the great depression, the Federal Reserve, collective bargaining, political philosophies, etc.; does not include biographies; has lengthy bibliographies.

Harvard Encyclopedia of American Ethnic Groups. Ed. Stephan Thernstrom. Cambridge: Belknap P of Harvard UP, 1980. Each ethnic group is described in detail (social organization, origin, migration, settlement, culture, education, religion, and politics); includes native-born American ethnic groups, e.g. Indians, Eskimos; has a detailed table of contents but no index.

International Encyclopedia of the Social Sciences. 17 vols. New York: Macmillan and Free Press, 1967. Aims to "reflect and encourage the rapid development of the social sciences throughout the world" (Preface); represents the social sciences of the 1960s; emphasis is on the analytical and comparative aspects of each topic; contains some biographical articles, including living persons; selected bibliographies follow articles; Vol 17 is the index. Vol. 18: *Biographical Supplement*, 1980.

Klein, Barry T. *Reference Encyclopedia of the American Indian.* 6th ed. West Nyack: Todd, 1993. Gives information on associations, organizations, museums, education, government agencies, reservations, and tribal councils; includes directories, biographies, and bibliographies.

Kodansha Encyclopedia of Japan. 9 vols. Tokyo: Kodansha, 1983. Surveys Japanese life and culture; gives information on history, philosophy, literature, fine arts, business, politics, economics, technology, etc. *Supplement*, 1986.

Kurian, George Thomas, ed. *Encyclopedia of the Third World.* 4th ed. 3 vols. New York: Facts on File, 1992. Treats most of the nations of the world; gives a chronology of events for each country dating from the year of independence; covers political, cultural, economic, military, legal, and geographic aspects of each country.

Laszlo, Ervin, and others, eds. *World Encyclopedia of Peace.* 4 vols. New York: Pergamon, 1986. Covers theories and philosophies of peace, contemporary peace issues, outstanding peace theorists from ancient times to the present; provides information on worldwide peace organizations and peace treaties; includes a chronology of war since the Napoleonic period. Vol. IV is a bibliography of more than 1500 citations for further study.

Lawson, Edward, ed. *Encyclopedia of Human Rights*. New York: Taylor Francis, 1991. Covers national and international activities undertaken from 1945–1990 to protect human rights; gives the status of human rights in various countries; discusses concepts and issues relating to human freedoms, important developments, covenants, and national and international organizations.

Levy, Leonard W., et. al., eds. *Encyclopedia of the American Constitution*. 4 vols. New York: Macmillan, 1986. Designed as a general introduction to the Constitution, this scholarly work also celebrates the bicentennial of the United States Constitution; covers numerous aspects of the Constitution: history, development, concepts, individuals associated with it, and specific cases.

Levy, Leonard, Kenneth Karst, and John West, Jr. *Encyclopedia of the American Constitution, Supplement I*. New York: Macmillan, 1992. Updates the basic set, discussing significant recent constitutional cases; covers new issue and cases.

Low, W. A., and Vergil A. Clift. *Encyclopedia of Black America*. New York: McGraw, 1981. Aims to present the "totality of the past and present life and culture of Afro-Americans—their education, politics, history, family life, literature, art"; articles define, describe, and elaborate; includes some 1400 brief biographical articles; alphabetically arranged, illustrated.

O'Leary, Timothy J., and David Levinson, eds. *Encyclopedia of World Culture*. 10 vols. Boston: Hall, 1991–. A projected 10-volume work, it aims to provide information on cultures throughout the world: geography, languages, history, economy, politics, religion, family. The volumes will include North America (1991), Oceania (1992), South Asia, Europe and the Middle East, East and Southeast Asia, Soviet Union and China, South America, America and the Caribbean, and Africa. The tenth volume will provide a cumulative list of cultures and bibliography.

Porter, Glenn, ed. *Encyclopedia of American Economic History: Studies of the Principal Movements and Ideas*. New York: Scribner's, 1980. Aims to present American economic history as it was understood in the late 1970s; contains articles by historians and economists; covers such topics as technology, taxation, business cycles, institutions, social history, slavery, automobiles, prices, wages, women, immigration, and economic growth and thought.

Wilson, Charles, and William Ferris. *Encyclopedia of Southern Culture*. Chapel Hill: U of North Carolina P, 1989. Organized by themes, e.g., folk life, language, black life, social life, media, environment, music, sports, education, literature, history, etc.; covers aspects of southern life; focuses on the eleven states of the Confederacy, but other states and regions are given attention; thematic essays are followed by biographical sketches.

Worldmark Encyclopedia of the Nations. 7th ed. 5 vols. 1988. New York: Worldmark, 1984. Gives factual information in uniform format relating to topography, language, religion, and certain socioeconomic categories on countries which belong to the United Nations; Vol. I is devoted to the United Nations; remaining volumes are devoted to Africa, the Americas, Asia and Australasia, and Europe.

Worldmark Encyclopedia of the States. New York: Wiley, 1986. Gives detailed information about each state, the nation's capital, and the United States as a whole and its dependencies; covers government, population, education, agriculture, finance, social conditions, economic conditions, services provided, housing, the arts, sports, famous persons, industries, political parties, the press, and many other items in the same format for each state; has maps and tables.

HANDBOOKS[6]

Africa Contemporary Record, 1968-69–. Ed. Colin Legum. London: Rex Collings, 1969–. Annual. An annual survey and documents; divided into three parts—Part One: Essays on Current Issues; Part Two: A Country-by-Country Review (Legal, Political, Social, Military, Economic); Part Three: Documents.

Banks, Arthur S., ed. *Political Handbook of the World, 1991.* Binghampton: CSA, State U of New York P, 1991. Presents the status of governments and international organizations of the world—government and politics, foreign organizations, news media, etc.

Barone, Michael, and Grant Ujifusa, eds. *The Almanac of American Politics, 1992.* Washington, D.C.: National Journal, 1992. Biennial. Covers senators, representatives, governors, their records, states districts, election results; discusses economics, politics, and social conditions.

Carpenter, Allan. *Facts About the Cities.* New York: Wilson, 1992. Gives statistical information on major cities in America, Puerto Rico, Guam, and the Virgin Islands.

Davidson, Sidney, and R. Weil, eds. *Handbook of Modern Accounting.* 3d ed. New York: McGraw, 1983. Covers accounting as a whole—traditional

---

6 See also Chapter 12, Yearbooks and Handbooks.

problems and procedures and new techniques arising from computer applications.

Horton, Carrell Peterson, and Jessie Carney Smith. *Statistical Record of Black America*. Detroit: Gale, 1990–. Biennial. Contains statistical tables which give a record of black America in numerous areas, e.g., business and economics, education, family, government service, income, religion, sports, etc.; gives comparable data for whites, Hispanics, and Asian-Americans.

Inge, Thomas M., ed. *Handbook of American Popular Culture*. 2d ed., rev. and enl. 3 vols. Westport: Greenwood, 1989. Covers such popular culture areas as the automobile, pulp fiction, film, circus, television, the western movie, games and toys, and literature; for each area, includes a brief history, a critical guide to most useful sources, and a description of research centers and collections of primary and secondary materials.

Jessup, Deborah Hitchcock. *Guide to State Environmental Programs*. 2d ed. Washington: Bureau of National Affairs, 1990. Discusses environmental problems: air pollution control, hazardous waste, water resources protection and management, and laws; lists Federal agencies, state, and local directories.

Kane, Joseph Nathan. *Facts about the States*. New York: Wilson, 1989. Gives information about the fifty states, Puerto Rico, and Washington, D.C.; covers geography, history, politics, etc.; provides tables and bibliographies.

Lean, Geoffrey. *Atlas of the Environment*. New York: Prentice, 1990. Presents basic facts about the natural and human environments and what is happening to them; covers forests, wetlands, mountains, rivers; discusses pollution, wildlife, energy, food production, and health; uses text, maps, and charts.

Ploski, Harry A., and William James, eds. The *Negro Almanac*. 5th ed. Detroit: Gale, 1989. Covers history and biographical information; gives statistical charts and graphs; includes photographs and reproductions of art, chronologies, tables, and bibliographies.

Schmittroth, Linda, comp. *Statistical Record of Women Worldwide*. Detroit: Gale, 1991. Presents statistics of all aspects of women's interests: health, family, education, occupation, income, religion, sports, etc.

Sturtevant, William C., ed. *Handbook of North American Indians*. Washington, D.C.: Smithsonian Institution, 1978–. In progress. The aim of the projected twenty volumes is "to give an encyclopedic summary of what is known about the prehistory, history, and cultures of the aboriginal peoples of North America"; gives linguistic, ethnographic, historical, and archaeological information on each tribe. Vols. 4–11 and 15 are completed.

YEARBOOKS[7]

The Annual Register: A Record of World Events. London: Longman, 1958–. Annual. Discusses events of the year concerning every country, the UN, other international organizations; social and economic trends, major developments in all fields; has maps, statistical charts, and reprints of important documents.

Britain: An Official Handbook. London: Her Majesty's Stationery Office, 1948–. Annual. Gives a factual account of the administration and the national economy of the United Kingdom; describes activities of many of the national institutions both official and unofficial.

Canada Yearbook. Ottawa: Minister of Supply and Services, 1981–. Annual. Gives a review of economic, social, and political developments in Canada.

The Far East and Australasia. London: Europa, 1969–. Annual. Covers the region as a whole, then subdivisions, giving social, physical, and economic surveys on each area, information about government, political parties, education, religion, finance, trade, etc.; includes a "who's who" of the Far East and Australasia.

Keesing's Contemporary Archives: Record of World Events. London: Longman, 1983–. Monthly. Covers important events in all countries; includes text of speeches, documents, statistics, and obituaries; arranged in chronological, topical, and geographical sections.

Municipal Year Book. Chicago: International City Managers' Assoc., 1934–. Annual. Gives information concerning governmental units, personnel, finance, and activities of United States and Canadian cities; has a directory of chief officers of Canadian cities over 10,000 population and of mayors and clerks of United States cities over 2500.

South American Handbook. London: Trade and Travel, 1924–. Annual. Covers South and Central America, Mexico, and the West Indies; presents information about government, transportation, communication, natural resources.

Yearbook of the United Nations. New York: UN, Department of Public Information, 1947–. Annual. Provides a comprehensive account of the activities of the United Nations and its related intergovernmental agencies.

ATLASES

Allen, James Paul, and Eugene James Turner, eds. *We the People: An Atlas of American Ethnic Diversity*. New York: Macmillan, 1987. Provides information on the ethnic character of the population of the United States,

---

[7] See also Chapter 12, Yearbooks and Handbooks.

e.g., people of southern European origin, of African origin, western European origin, Asian and Pacific origin, etc.; intended for all persons interested in their ethnic background; points out differences in ethnic composition of the population of a given area; data based on 1980 census. Text, maps, charts, diagrams, and tables are used.

Shortridge, Barbara G. *Atlas of American Women.* New York: Macmillan, 1986. Provides information about the current status of women: where and how they live, age groups, employment, education, occupations, health, and other topics.

Ulack, Richard, and Gyvea Pavec. *Atlas of Southeast Asia.* New York: Macmillan, 1989. Covers political, economic, population, and other data current in the 1980s.

BIOGRAPHICAL DICTIONARIES[8]

American Men and Women of Science: Social and Behavioral Sciences. 18th ed. Jaques Cattell Press. New York: Bowker, 1992. Gives brief biographical sketches of some 125,000 social scientists actively engaged in teaching or research in economics, political science, psychology, and sociology.

Who's Who in American Politics. 13th ed. Comp. and ed. by Jaques Cattell Press. New York: Bowker, 1991. Covers important political figures and public servants in the United States on the national, state, and local levels from the president of the United States to local political figures about whom information is not easily available; entries are arranged geographically, with a separate name index.

EXAMPLES OF PROFESSIONAL JOURNALS IN THE SOCIAL SCIENCES[9]

American Academy of Political and Social Science. *Annals.* Newbury Park: Sage, 1890–. Bimonthly. Each issue is devoted to a selected topic of current social or political interest; articles present different aspects of the subject.

American Economic Review. Nashville: American Economic Association, 1911–. Quarterly. Reviews new books; has articles on such topics as wages, employment, marketing, inflation, and unemployment; provides bibliographical references.

American Journal of Economics and Sociology. New York: American Journal of Economics and Sociology, Inc. 1941–. Quarterly. Reports original re-

---

[8] See also Chapter 10, Biographical Dictionaries.

[9] See also *Ulrich's International Periodicals Directory*, 31st ed., and *Magazines for Libraries*, 7th ed., ed. Bill Katz and Linda S. Katz.

search; covers social aspects of economic institutions and economic aspects of social and political institutions.

American Political Science Review. Washington, D.C.: American Political Science Association, 1906–. Quarterly. Stresses theoretical rather than practical aspects of political science; has book reviews.

Journal of Economic History. New York: Economic History Association, New York U, 1941–. Quarterly. The journal of the Economic History Association; presents articles on economic history and related aspects of history or economics, taxation, investments, business, and industry.

Political Science Quarterly. New York: Academy of Political Science, 1886–. Quarterly. Covers the broad field of political science; has long articles and many book reviews.

Sociological Quarterly. Columbia: The Midwest Sociological Society, 1960–. Quarterly. Emphasizes trends in social thought, ideas, and contributions of individual sociologists; is the journal of the Midwest Sociological Society.

Education

The word "education" has several meanings, and it is necessary to make clear its meaning as a *subject field* before beginning a study of reference materials in this area. A brief statement of two of the several meanings of "education" will help to clarify its meaning as a branch of knowledge.

In the broad sense, education is the sum total of all the ways, both formal and informal, in which a person develops attitudes, abilities, and behavior patterns and acquires knowledge.

In another and less broad sense, education is the social process by which people are placed under the influence of an organized and controlled environment, such as a school, in the hope that they will attain more rapidly and effectively their fullest possible development as individuals and will learn how to live as competent citizens in their society. Elementary school, high school, and college are some of the stages in this controlled process.

Education as a subject field—that is, as a branch of knowledge—is the science which has to do with the principles and practices of teaching and learning. It is also the name given to that curriculum, in institutions of higher education, which consists of professional courses for the preparation of teachers, supervisors, and administrators. Included in these courses are philosophy and history of education (that is, education as a social process), psychology as applied to learning and teaching, curriculum, methods of teaching (how to teach), administration, and supervision.

The following reference sources are designed to answer, in the language of the educator, some of the numerous and specialized questions in this subject field.

Representative Reference Sources in Education

BIBLIOGRAPHIES, GUIDES, AND INDEXES[10]

The Education Index. New York: Wilson, 1929–. Monthly, except July and August. Indexes by author and subject some 330 education periodicals; monographs and yearbooks are also indexed; covers all aspects of education; book review citations are in a separate section of the index. Online and on tape from WilsonLine; on CD-ROM from WilsonDisc.

Current Journals in Education. (See p. 196.)

O'Brien, Nancy Patricia, and Emily Fabiano. *Core List of Books and Journals in Education.* Phoenix: Oryx, 1991. Offers a basic list of about 1000 titles in the English language covering educational research, special education, comparative education, educational administration, educational psychology, and other topics.

Resources in Education. (See p. 196).

Sparks, Linda, comp. *Institutions of Higher Education: An International Bibliography.* Westport: Greenwood, 1992. Provides information on the history of educational institutions worldwide; divided by country; United States is divided by state; cites books, dissertations, theses, and ERIC microfiche.

DICTIONARIES AND ENCYCLOPEDIAS

The Encyclopedia of Education. 10 vols. New York: Macmillian and Free Press, 1971. Intended for all persons concerned with education; gives an overview of education covering history, theory, research, philosophy, and structure of education; emphasizes American education.

Clark, Burton R., and Guy Neave, eds. *Encyclopedia of Higher Education.* 4 vols. Tarrytown: Pergamon, 1992. Describes 135 higher education systems and reviews the state of higher education internationally.

Dejnozka, Edward, ed. *American Educators' Encyclopedia.* Rev. ed. by Edward L. Kapel and David Kapel. Westport: Greenwood, 1991. Defines and explains names and terms frequently found in the literature of professional education in areas relating to administration and supervision, philosophy and history of education, and the subject areas; identifies important people in the field.

Good, Carter Victor, ed. *Dictionary of Education.* 3d ed. New York: McGraw, 1973. Defines and explains more than 30,000 professional terms in education and related fields.

Kurian, George Thomas, ed. *World Education Encyclopedia.* 3 vols. New York: Facts on File, 1986. A descriptive survey of national education systems:

---

[10] See also Chapter 9, Indexes, and Chapter 13, Bibliographies.

performance, growth, and legal, political, and social problems; offers graphs, charts, and a glossary.

Metzel, Harold E., ed. *Encyclopedia of Educational Research*. 6th ed. 4 vols. New York: Macmillan, 1992. Gives the status of research in all aspects of education and includes articles on methods of research and the characteristics of particular groups, such as the gifted and the retarded; covers computer-assisted instruction, bilingual education, aptitude measurement, etc.

Shafritz, Jay M., Richard P. Koeppe, and Elizabeth W. Soper. *The Facts on File Dictionary of Education*. New York: Facts on File, 1988. Defines words and terms peculiar to the field of education regarding theory, practice, concepts, law, institutions, literature, etc.

DIRECTORIES

American Universities and Colleges. 14th ed. Ed. the American Council on Education. Hawthorne: Walter de Gruyter, 1992. Gives detailed information about more than 1900 four-year accredited institutions of higher education in the United States: history, admission requirements, fees, educational programs, faculty, enrollment, library, officials, etc.

Cass, James, and Max Birnbaum. *Comparative Guide to American Colleges*. 13th ed. New York: Harper, 1987. Gives admission requirements, curricula, costs, scholarships, regulations; arranged alphabetically by name of the institution.

The College Blue Book. 23rd ed. 5 vols. New York: Macmillan, 1991. Gives narrative descriptions of more than 3200 colleges in the United States and Canada, covering cost, accreditation, enrollment, faculty, administration, curricula, faculty, scholarships, etc. More than 10,000 trade and business schools and community colleges are included. Available on CD-ROM, 1991–.

International Handbook of Universities. 11th rev. ed. Ed. International Association of Universities. Hawthorne: Walter de Gruyter, 1986. Describes in English institutions of higher education in over 100 countries outside the United States and British Commonwealth: administration, faculties, degrees, diplomas, fees, admission requirements.

Peterson's Annual Guides to Graduate Study. 5 vols. Princeton: Peterson's Guides, 1976–. Annual. Gives an overview of accredited institutions offering graduate work, with a profile of each institution: data on students and programs, housing, financial aid, fields of study, etc.; has separate listing by field of study and institutions offering it, e.g., Humanities and Social Sciences. *Peterson's Guide to Four-Year Colleges* and *Peterson's Guide to Two-Year Colleges* offer the same kinds of information.

HANDBOOKS AND YEARBOOKS

Commonwealth Universities Yearbook. 1914–. 4 vols. London: Association of
    Commonwealth Universities, 1914. Presents the essential facts about the
    history, facilities, organization, staff, and admission requirements of
    universities in the Commonwealth; arranged by countries.
World of Learning. 2 vols. London: Europa, 1947–. Annual. Arranged alpha-
    betically by country; gives information about educational, cultural, and
    scientific organizations all over the world.

BIOGRAPHICAL DICTIONARIES[11]

Directory of American Scholars. 8th ed. Ed. Jaques Cattell Press. New York:
    Bowker, 1982–83. Covers currently active scholars in the United States
    and Canada.

EXAMPLES OF PROFESSIONAL JOURNALS IN EDUCATION[12]

Educational Leadership. Alexandria: ASCD, 1943–. Monthly, October–May.
    Emphasizes curriculum; reports research data to the membership.
Journal of Higher Education. Columbus: Ohio State UP, 1930–. Monthly. A
    general magazine devoted to issues of interest to higher education; in-
    cludes book reviews.
Phi Delta Kappan. Bloomington: Phi Delta Kappa, 1918–. Monthly, Septem-
    ber–June. Aims to promote leadership in education at all levels.

ABSTRACT SOURCES

Dissertation Abstracts International. Ann Arbor: UMI, 1984–. Annual. Gives
    bibliographical citations to and abstracts of doctoral dissertations com-
    pleted at more than 500 North American universities and from many
    European universities. Search by keyword from the title or the abstract,
    author, title, year, and from the word index.
ERIC. Boston: Silver Platter, 1986–. Quarterly. The CD-ROM provides
    bibliographic citations and abstracts of journal articles and documents on
    educational and related subjects in the social sciences; has two sections:
    Current Index to Journals in Education, indexing about 750 journals, and
    Resources in Education indexing unpublished materials; covers 1966 to
    date; has controlled vocabulary; users must search by subject headings
    from *Thesaurus of ERIC Descriptors*, title words, or author's name.

[11] See also Chapter 10, Biographical Dictionaries.
[12] See also *Ulrich's International Periodicals Directory*, 31st ed., and *Magazines for Libraries*, 7th ed.,
ed. Bill Katz and Linda S. Katz.

Current Index to Journals in Education. Phoenix: Oryx, 1969–. Monthly. A monthly journal of abstracts of education-related articles from about 760 journals in the ERIC database.

Resources in Education, Vol. 1, No. 1, November 1966–. Washington: GPO, 1967–. Monthly. An abstract journal announcing recent report literature related to the field of education; made up of résumés and indexes numbered sequentially in the Document Section by ED number. The ED prefix identifies documents of educational significance selected by ERIC.[13] These journals are a part of the ERIC database.

The source of all subject headings used in the ERIC collection and in indexing *Current Index to Journals in Education* and *Resources in Education* is *The Thesaurus of ERIC Descriptors* (Phoenix: Oryx, 1980; Annual), which lists descriptors and synonyms or near synonyms.

---

[13] The Educational Resources Information Center (ERIC), a nationwide information network for acquiring, abstracting, indexing, storing, and disseminating significant research reports and projects in the field of education, was established in June 1966. Sixteen special clearinghouses acquire, evaluate, abstract, and index these report materials and the abstracts in *Resources in Education*. Reports are available in microfiche or paper-copy reproductions from the ERIC Document Reproduction Service. ERIC collections are found in every state and in more than sixty countries. The ERIC collection is usually housed in the area where microfilm and other microforms are kept. Each microfiche is filed in a drawer by its identifying ED number (ED 174744, ED 174745, etc.), which is given in the entry in *Resources in Education*. Microfiche must be read with a reader. The ERIC database of more than 700,000 abstracts is accessible in print form, online, and on CD-ROM. See Figure 9.1, page 99.

CHAPTER

❧ 20 ❧

Language (Philology)

Philology (by derivation, "love of learning" and "love of speech and discourse") is that branch of learning concerned with human speech and what it reveals about humans. The 400 class in the Dewey Decimal Classification is devoted to language; class P of the Library of Congress Classification includes language and linguistics.

Language as a subject was first studied because it was important in reading and in understanding literature, and emphasis was placed upon the study of Greek, Latin, and Hebrew, since most of the early writing was done in those languages. When the study of language, as such, emerged as a branch of learning during the nineteenth century, it was called "linguistics."

Linguistics, the scientific study of human speech, includes an investigation of the sound, form, and meaning of language and of the relations of one language to another.

The study of language as a branch of knowledge includes:

1. Morphology, the study of the historical development of speech patterns
2. Syntax, the study of the use and forms of the language and of the parts of speech and their various forms
3. Etymology, the study of the origin of words
4. Semantics, the historical and psychological study of the meaning and change of meaning of words

In the study of language and linguistics, dictionaries[1] are the major aids, both the general word dictionaries of a language and dictionaries which

---

[1] This chapter is concerned with specialized dictionaries of language. See Chapter 7 for a discussion of general word dictionaries.

provide more than a mere listing of words of a language and their several meanings. The latter include:

1. Dictionaries based on the historical development of words
2. Etymological dictionaries
3. Dictionaries of usage
4. Dictionaries of slang, dialect, and colloquialisms
5. Dictionaries of synonyms and antonyms

In addition to these kinds of dictionaries, there are specialized dictionaries which treat abbreviations, acronyms, eponyms, foreign words and phrases, and pronunciations.

Other types of reference sources useful in the study of language are bibliographies, indexes, general histories of language, biographical dictionaries, and nonbook sources, such as tapes and discs.

Useful Reference Sources in Language[2]

BIBLIOGRAPHIES, INDEXES, AND GUIDES[3]

Comrie, Bernard. *The World's Major Languages*. Oxford: Oxford UP, 1987. A guide to forty of the world's major languages; covers languages in general and language families.

De Miller, Anna L. *Linguistics: A Guide to the Reference Literature*. Englewood Cliffs: Prentice, 1991. Lists sources with brief annotations.

Modern Humanities Research Association. *Annual Bibliography of English Language and Literature*. Cambridge: Cambridge UP, 1921–. Annual. Includes books, periodical literature, pamphlets, and references to book reviews; the language section is arranged by subject.

Modern Language Association of America. *MLA International Bibliography of Books and Articles on the Modern Languages and Literatures*. 2 vols. New York: MLA, 1921–. Annual. Offers a classified list of books and articles on language, literature, linguistics, and folklore. Author index follows listings in first volume; second volume is a subject index.

MLA International Bibliography. Bronx: Wilson, 1988–. Quarterly. CD-ROM covers 1981–present; indexes books and journal articles on English and American literature, all modern European literature, literatures of Latin America, Africa, and Asia, folklore, language instruction, linguistics,

---

[2] See also Chapter 7, Dictionaries.
[3] See also Chapter 9, Indexes, and Chapter 13, Bibliographies.

film and television criticism. Search according to WilsonDisc: author, title, and subject options.

DICTIONARIES AND ENCYCLOPEDIAS

Barnouw, Erik, ed. *International Encyclopedia of Communications*. 4 vols. New York: Oxford UP, 1989. Discusses the history and social roles of media from clay tablets to communications satellites; treats influences on and contributions to the evolution of communication; social processes, psychological, sociological, and anthropological influences; uses maps, tables, and illustrations.

Bright, William, ed. *The International Encyclopedia of Linguistics*. 4 vols. New York: Oxford UP, 1991. Covers all branches of language; emphasizes the importance of interdisciplinary studies; treats syntax and semantics.

Collinge, N. E., ed. *An Encyclopaedia of Language*. New York: Routledge, 1990. Looks at all aspects of human language; treats most of what is now known about language.

Crystal, David, ed. *The Cambridge Encyclopedia of Language*. New York: Cambridge UP, 1987. Discusses the structure of language, dictionaries, recent popular ideas about grammar and meanings; includes information about languages of the world and communications; treats the many subfields of linguistics.

Pei, Mario. *Glossary of Linguistic Terminology*. New York: Columbia UP, 1966. Includes the historical, descriptive, and geolinguistic terminology, American and European, that has gained acceptance in the field.

DICTIONARIES OF CERTAIN ASPECTS OF LANGUAGE

Abbreviations and acronyms

Crowley, Ellen T., ed. *Acronyms, Initialisms, and Abbreviations Dictionary*. 17th ed. 3 vols. Detroit: Gale, 1992. Vol. 1 contains more than 200,000 entries ranging from the time of ancient Rome to the present day; all areas of knowledge are represented; humorous and slang acronyms are included. Vol. 2, *New Acronyms, Initialisms, and Abbreviations*, is the annual supplement. Vol. 3, *Reverse Acronyms, Initialisms, and Abbreviations Dictionary*, companion to Vol. 1, is arranged alphabetically by complete word or term; the acronym is the definition.

De Sola, Ralph, ed. *Abbreviations Dictionary*. 8th ed. New York: Elsevier, 1992. Defines and explains abbreviations, acronyms, anonyms and eponyms, contractions, geographical equivalents, historical and mythological characters, initials and nicknames, signs and symbols, slang, and short forms in all areas.

Etymology [4]

Barnhart, Robert K. *The Barnhart Dictionary of Etymology*. New York: Wilson, 1987. Gives information regarding derivation, changes of meanings, earliest dates of borrowing from another language, how a word entered the language and where; includes coined words.

Klein, Ernest. *A Comprehensive Etymological Dictionary of the English Language.* 2 vols. New York: Elsevier, 1966–1967. Treats the origin of words and the development of their meanings, thus illustrating the history of civilization and culture; includes many scientific and technical terms and personal and mythological names.

Onions, Charles Talbut, et al., eds. *The Oxford Dictionary of English Etymology*. New York: Oxford UP, 1966. Based on the *Oxford English Dictionary*, but brought up to date by recent research; includes some words of United States origin and some proper names; notable for its breadth of coverage, scholarship, and ease of use. *The Concise Oxford Dictionary of English Etymology*, ed. T. F. Hoad, 1986.

Foreign words and phrases

Guinagh, Kevin, comp. *Dictionary of Foreign Phrases and Abbreviations*. 3d ed. New York: Wilson, 1982. Aims to help students and nonspecialists understand foreign expressions, proverbs, mottoes, etc., which they frequently hear or read; covers phrases in law, philosophy, business, medicine, etc.

Pei, Mario, and Salvatore Ramondino. *Dictionary of Foreign Terms*. New York: Delacorte P, 1974. Explains foreign terms and phrases that English-speaking people encounter in reading or listening; original language, pronunciation, and definitions are given for each term; some usage labels are given.

Historical development of words

Craigie, William, and James R. Hulbert, eds. *A Dictionary of American English on Historical Principles*. 2d ed. 4 vols. Chicago: U of Chicago P, 1938–1944. Indicates words which originated in America or which are in greater use here than elsewhere and words which are important in the history of America; follows the plan of *The Oxford English Dictionary*.

A Dictionary of Canadianisms on Historical Principles. Produced by the Lexicographical Centre for Canadian English, U of Victoria, British Colum-

---

[4] In etymological dictionaries, definitions as such are not given. The meaning of the word is determined through the etymology.

bia. Scarborough, Ont.: Gage, 1967. Modeled after *The Oxford English Dictionary*; covers the period from the sixteenth century to the present; each entry is "substantiated" with dates and quotations from books, periodicals, and newspapers; includes regional, political, historical, and proper names; does not claim that all entries originated in Canada, but all are original or are closely related to Canada.

Matthews, Mitford N., ed. *A Dictionary of Americanisms on Historical Principles.* Chicago: U of Chicago P, 1956. Includes words which have been added to the English language in the United States from colonial times to the present. *Americanisms: A Dictionary of Selected Americanisms on Historical Principles*, 1966.

Morris, William, and Mary Morris, eds. *Dictionary of Word and Phrase Origins.* 3 vols. New York: Harper, 1962, 1967, 1971. Explains a variety of additions to the English language from many sources. *Morris Dictionary of Word and Phrase Origins*, 1977. To some extent an abridgment of the 3-vol. works by these authors.

Murray, James Augustus Henry, and others, eds. *The Oxford English Dictionary.* 12 vols. and Supplement. London: Oxford UP, 1933. Presents the historical development of each word which has entered the English language since 1150.

A Supplement to the Oxford English Dictionary.[5] Ed. R. W. Burchfield. 4 vols. Oxford: Clarendon P, 1972–1986. Incorporates the material in the 1933 *Supplement* and contains all words that came into common use in English during the publication of the OED, 1884–1928, and words which have come into use from 1928 to the present; aims to record the vocabulary of the twentieth century, including literary, scientific, and technical terminology; legal and other professional terminology; and popular, colloquial, and modern slang expressions.

Webster's Word Histories. Springfield: Merriam, 1989. Traces the history of some 1500 words: how they came into the language, their use in various periods, the changes in meaning at various times, the individuals who coined them or used them in different ways.

New words

Allen, R. E., ed. *The Concise Oxford Dictionary of Current English.* 8th ed. New York: Oxford UP, 1990. Includes contemporary English throughout the world; gives etymology, and usage labels; is illustrated.

Barnhart, Robert K., and Sol Steinmetz, with Clarence Barnhart. *Third Barnhart Dictionary of New English.* New York: Wilson, 1990. Treats some 12,000 new words and terms resulting from technological and

[5] See p. 84.

cultural advances of the past decade; gives pronunciation, illustrative quotations, etymology, usage, and date of first appearance.

Tulloch, Cara, comp. *The Oxford Dictionary of New Words: A Popular Guide to Words in the News.* New York: Oxford UP, 1991. Contains about 2000 new words and phrases in the news during the past decade, including some slang; includes words from many areas, e.g., science, technology, the arts, politics, the environment, etc.; gives origin, usage, events which made the word prominent, and illustrative examples.

Pronunciation

Erlich, Eugene, and Raymond Hand, Jr., eds. *NBC Handbook of Pronunciation.* 4th ed rev. New York: HarperCollins, 1991. Gives pronunciation only for more than 21,000 commonly used words and proper nouns.

Sign language

Sternberg, Martin L. A. *American Sign Language: A Comprehensive Dictionary.* New York: Harper, 1981. Has about 5000 word and phrase entries, with a description of each and an illustration of how it is conveyed in English.

Slang, dialect, colloquialisms, idioms and regionalisms

Berrey, Lester V., and Melvin Van Den Bark, eds. *The American Thesaurus of Slang.* 2d ed. New York: Crowell, 1953. A collection of colloquialisms, slang, and vulgarisms arranged according to the ideas which they express; has an alphabetical word index for ease of use.

Cassidy, Frederic G. *Dictionary of American Regional English.* Cambridge: Belknap P of Harvard UP, 1985–. The first of a projected five-volume work, aims to record English as it is spoken in the United States, covering regional usage, dialect, colloquialisms, and ethnic words; includes illustrative examples, definition, pronunciation, alternative forms, and places where the word is used; selected maps show where the word or term is used. Vol. I. A–C.

Cowie, A. P. and others. *Oxford Dictionary of Current Idiomatic English.* 2 vols. New York: Oxford UP, 1975–1983. Treats parts of speech, phrases, clauses, sentences, and idioms.

Green, Jonathan. *The Dictionary of Contemporary Slang.* New York: Stein & Day, 1985. Emphasis is on post-1945 words and terms, British and American; gives definitions, part of speech, country of origin, users of the word or term, including authors.

Partridge, Eric. *A Dictionary of Slang and Unconventional English.* 8th ed. Ed. Paul Beale. New York: Macmillan, 1984. "Colloquialisms and catchphrases, solecisms and catachreses, nicknames or vulgarisms" (Subtitle). Emphasis is on British English.

Weiner, Richard. *Webster's New World Dictionary of Media and Communications*. New York: Webster's, 1990. Defines words and terms used in fields of communication technology, journalism, graphic arts publishing, advertising, television, etc.; includes some jargon and slang.

Wentworth, Harold, and Stuart B. Flexner, comps. and eds. *Dictionary of American Slang*. 2d supplemented ed. New York: Crowell, 1975. Gives brief definition of each term, and multiple meanings if appropriate; notes the group which uses the term; gives synonyms and antonyms. *New Dictionary of American Slang*, ed. Robert L. Chapman (Harper, 1986), is a revised edition.

Synonyms and antonyms

Chapman, Robert L., ed. *Roget's International Thesaurus*. 5th ed. rev. and updated. New York: Harper, 1992. Offers more than 325,000 words and phrases in 1073 categories tells how words are used, including recent words; gives synonyms, antonyms, related words.

Webster's New Dictionary of Synonyms. Springfield: Merriam, 1978. "A dictionary of discriminated synonyms with analogous and contrasted words" (subtitle); has illustrative quotations from old and new authors.

Usage

Copperud, Roy H. *American Usage and Style: The Consensus*. New York: Van Nostrand, 1980. Compares the opinions of nine authorities regarding words, phrases, and usage.

Follett, Wilson. *Modern American Usage: A Guide*. Ed. and comp. by Jacques Barzun in collaboration with Carlos Baker and others. New York: Hill & Wang, 1966. Arranged in dictionary format; explains words and phrases, giving recommended forms of usage; articles vary in length; treats matters of style.

Fowler, H. W. *A Dictionary of Modern English Usage*. 2d ed. Rev. by Ernest Gowers. Oxford: Clarendon P, 1965. Gives definitions of terms, sometimes with disputed spellings and plurals; brief essays on use and misuse of words and expressions; reflects the author's personal opinions; many new articles; modernized and brought up to date in light of current usage; some terms dropped; new ones added. Emphasis is on British usage.

Morris, William, and Mary Morris. *Harper Dictionary of Contemporary Usage*. 2d ed. New York: Harper, 1985. Treats idioms, slang words, regionalisms, spelling and pronunciation; articles range in length from a few sentences to several pages; opinions of a panel of expert writers and speakers are cited on certain points; aims to direct attention to incorrect or awkward oral or written language, but does not prescribe usage.

Webster's Dictionary of English Usage. Springfield: Merriam, 1989. Examines and evaluates disputed English usage of words and terms from both popular and classic sources; treats historical and contemporary aspects; gives an essay on the history of English usage; is descriptive, not prescriptive; has illustrative quotations.

Wiener, E. S. C. *The Oxford Guide to English Usage.* Oxford: Clarendon P, 1983. Provides simple and direct guidance regarding the formation and use of English words—pronouns, spelling, grammar, meaning, etc.; highlights "correct and acceptable standard British English" (Preface).

HANDBOOKS

McArthur, Thomas. *The Oxford Companion to the English Language.* New York: Oxford UP, 1992. Provides broad coverage of the language: history, grammar, style, dialects, current expressions, influence of other languages; gives many illustrative examples.

BIOGRAPHICAL DICTIONARIES[6]

Directory of American Scholars. 8th ed. Vol. III: *Foreign Languages, Linguistics, and Philology.* Ed. Jaques Cattell Press. New York: Bowker, 1982. Includes living persons in the field of language.

EXAMPLES OF PROFESSIONAL JOURNALS[7]

American Speech, A Quarterly of Linguistic Usage. University: U of Alabama, 1925–. Quarterly. Provides general and scholarly studies of English language in North America; covers dialect, current usage, structural linguistics, phonetics, dialects, geography, semantics, names, and vocabulary.

Modern Language Journal. Madison: U of Wisconsin, 1916–. Quarterly, September–May. Published by the National Federation of Modern Language Teachers Associations; devoted to methods, pedagogical research, and topics of interest to all language teachers.

PMLA. New York: Modern Language Assoc. of America, 1884–. Six, Bimonthly. The journal of MLA; presents scholarly and critical articles, professional news and notes, and bibliography. The abbreviation PMLA stands for Publications of the Modern Language Association.

---

[6] See also Chapter 10, Biographical Dictionaries.

[7] See also *Ulrich's International Periodicals Directory,* 31st ed., and *Magazines for Libraries,* 6th ed., ed. Bill Katz and Linda S. Katz.

CHAPTER

❧ 21 ❧

Science and Technology

The word "science," deriving from a Latin word which means "to learn" or "to know," is in its broadest sense synonymous with learning and knowledge, and in general usage it means an organized body of knowledge. In a more restricted meaning, science is organized knowledge of natural phenomena and of the relations between them. Sciences are commonly classified as exact or descriptive. Exact sciences are those characterized by the possibility of exact measurement—for example, physics. Descriptive sciences are those which have developed a method of description or classification that permits precise reference to the subject matter—for example, zoology.

The 500 class of the Dewey Decimal Classification System and class Q in the Library of Congress Classification are assigned to pure sciences and include mathematics, astronomy and allied sciences, physics, chemistry and allied sciences, earth sciences, paleontology, anthropology and biological sciences, botanical sciences, and zoological sciences.

Technology, or applied science, is concerned with tools (machines, instruments) and the techniques (methods, ways) for carrying out the plans, designs, etc., created by science. It has been defined as "the totality of the means employed to provide objects necessary for human sustenance and comfort.[1]

Technology (applied science) is placed in the 600 class, which comprises the medical sciences, engineering and allied operations, agriculture and agricultural industries, domestic arts and sciences, business and related enterprises, chemical technology, manufactures, and buildings. The Library of Congress Classification devotes parts of classes R, S, and T to these areas.

[1] *Webster's Seventh New Collegiate Dictionary* (Springfield: Merriam, 1967) 905.

Books in science and technology become outdated more quickly than those in other subject fields, and the student who seeks material on a topic in any of these areas must consult periodicals, abstract journals[2], and original sources, such as papers read at scientific meetings, reports, and patent applications, for the latest information. In addition to these sources, there are reference sources designed to provide answers to the many questions which arise in this broad subject area. Among the most useful kinds of reference sources are bibliographies and guides, professional journals, abstract journals, indexes, handbooks, dictionaries and glossaries (both English and foreign language), encyclopedias, yearbooks, directories, biographical dictionaries, and general histories.[3]

The importance of frequently consulting the bibliographies in periodicals and abstract journals and the library catalogs in order to keep up with new materials in these rapidly changing fields cannot be overemphasized.

Useful Reference Sources in Science and Technology

BIBLIOGRAPHIES[4]

Antony, Arthur. *Guide to Basic Sources in Chemistry*. New York: Wiley, 1979. Arranges information sources by type with concise annotations; has a chapter on computer search strategy; includes nonprint, textbooks, and monographs; for students from freshman to graduate level.

Malinowsky, H. Robert, and Jeanne M. Richardson, *Science and Engineering Literature: A Guide to Reference Sources*. 3d ed. Littleton: Libraries Unlimited, 1980. Arranged by subject; describes the nature of the various fields of science and engineering; offers discussions of basic types of scientific literature; annotates a selective list of sources in these areas; gives attention to computer-searchable databases; energy, environment, and important current topics are covered.

Scientific and Technical Books and Serials in Print. New York: Bowker, 1978–1981. Annual. Lists by author, title, and subject, books and periodicals in print worldwide in all areas of the physical and biological sciences, engineering, and technology. Available online and on CD-ROM also.

---

[2] An abstract journal lists and provides digests or summaries of periodical articles and other literature. Abstracts may be in the original language in which the article appeared, or they may be translated into English or another language.

[3] See also Chapter 14, Nonbook Information Sources.

[4] See also Chapter 13, Bibliographies.

Ward, Dedrick C., et al., eds. *Geologic Reference Sources*. Metuchen: Scarecrow, 1981. Covers general information sources, bibliography, abstracting services, and current awareness services of interest to the geological sciences; gives some annotations; includes a regional section with maps.

GUIDES

Chen, Ching-Cheh. *Scientific and Technical Information Sources*. Cambridge: MIT P, 1987. Presents a classified list of print and nonprint sources—guides, dictionaries, treatises, etc.—some with brief annotations.

Smith, Roger, and others. *Guide to the Literature of the Life Sciences*. 9th ed. Minneapolis: Burgess, 1980. Offers material for research in the biological sciences and suggestions for finding and using it; gives an introductory discussion of the topics related to the life sciences; includes information on the use of the library.

INDEXES[5]

Applied Science and Technology Index. New York: Wilson, 1958–. Monthly except July. Indexes by subject more than 390 periodicals in aeronautics, automation, physics, chemistry, engineering, industrial and mechanical arts, computer technology, energy, electricity and electronics, and related fields; author listing of citations to book reviews follows main body of index; available in print, online, on tape, and on CD-ROM.

The Biological and Agricultural Index. New York: Wilson, 1964–. Monthly except August. Indexes by subject 225 periodicals in agriculture, biology, and related areas; includes book reviews in a separate section; available in print, online, on tape, and on CD-ROM.

Compendex Plus. Palo Alto: DIALOG, 1989–. Quarterly. On CD-ROM. Covers the world's important engineering and technological literature, providing citations to and abstracts of journal articles, books, and selected United States government reports; has controlled vocabulary: use *Engineering Index Thesaurus*; search by words, phrases, author, title.

Engineering Index, 1906–. New York: Engineering Information, 1982. Annual. International in scope, indexes literature in more than 2700 publications, including professional and trade journals, publications of engineering societies, technical and scientific associations, government agencies, conference proceedings, and selected books.

General Science Index. New York: Wilson, 1978–. Monthly, except June and December; annual cumulation. Indexes by subject more than 100 gen-

[5] See also Chapter 9, Indexes.

eral science periodicals published in the English language covering pure and applied science; each issue contains an index to book reviews. Available in print, online, on tape, and on CD-ROM.

Index Medicus. Washington: National Library of Medicine, 1960–. Monthly. Published in various forms and by various publishers since 1879. A comprehensive index to the world's medical literature; indexes completely or selectively 2300 biomedical journals by subject and name; cumulated annually into the *Cumulated Index Medicus*; journal articles are cited under the subject headings which represent the most important concepts discussed; all citations are stored in the computerized bibliographic database of the National Library of Medicine. Available online.

Science Citation Index. Compact Disk Edition. Philadelphia: Inst. for Scientific Information, 1988–. Quarterly. Indexes 3200 leading science and technology journals by cited author, work, patent, title, author, name; covers biology and life sciences, technology, and government information. Search by title, keyword, Boolean operators, author, citation, address, journal.

Technical Book Review Index. Comp. and ed. in the Technology Department, Carnegie Library of Pittsburgh. New York: SLA, 1933–. Monthly, except July and August.

DICTIONARIES

Science

Allaby, Ailsa, and Michael Allaby, eds. *The Concise Dictionary of Earth Sciences.* New York: Oxford UP, 1990. Covers astronomy, climatology, geology, geophysics, mineralogy, oceanography, etc.; includes biographical information about important figures.

Allaby, Michael. *Dictionary of the Environment.* 3d ed. New York: New York UP, 1989. Defines terms relating to the environment.

Barnhart, Robert. *Hammond Barnhart Dictionary of Science.* Maplewood: Hammond, 1986. An aid to students in their beginning study of the physical and biological sciences; defines terms in all areas of the sciences.

Bynum, William F., and others, eds. *Dictionary of the History of Science.* Princeton: Princeton UP, 1981. Explains the major ideas and concepts in western natural science developments over the last five centuries; also considers ideas important to natural science in antiquity, the Middle Ages, and nonwestern cultures; philosophical and metaphysical bases of science, historiography, and methods of scientific process are also treated.

Challinor, John. *A Dictionary of Geology.* 6th ed. Ed. Anthony Wyatt. New York: Oxford UP, 1986. Aims to give a critical and historical review of the subject; defines some 1500 terms, giving both meaning and usage; illustrative quotations showing usage are from geological literature.

Holmes, Sandra. *Henderson's Dictionary of Biological Terms*. 10th ed. New York: Van Nostrand, 1989. Defines about 22,500 terms, giving brief, concise definitions; includes the derivation of the term; explains acronyms.

Immelmann, Klaus, and Colin Beer. *A Dictionary of Ethology*. Cambridge: Harvard UP, 1989. Defines or explains more than 600 terms relating to the scientific study of animal behavior.

James, Glenn, and Robert C. James, eds. *James & James Mathematics Dictionary*. 4th ed. New York: Van Nostrand, 1976. Definitions range from terms in high school algebra and geometry to more advanced university topics in topology and analysis; designed for use by persons with some background in the field; includes brief biographical entries.

Leftwich, A. W. *A Dictionary of Zoology*. 3d ed. Princeton: Van Nostrand, 1973. For students as well as naturalists; includes brief, concise definitions of the principal phyla and classes of animals as well as a large number of orders, suborders, and families.

Little, R. John, and C. Eugene Jones. *A Dictionary of Botany*. New York: Van Nostrand, 1980. Defines some 5500 botanical terms.

Mitton, Jacqueline, ed. *A Concise Dictionary of Astronomy*. New York: Oxford UP, 1991. Covers all areas of astronomy; includes definitions of terms from physics and space science.

Parker, Sybil, ed. *McGraw-Hill Dictionary of Physics and Mathematics*. New York: McGraw, 1978. Defines some 20,000 terms in physics, mathematics, and related disciplines; uses basic vocabulary and current and specialized terminology; illustrated.

McGraw-Hill Dictionary of Scientific and Technical Terms. 4th ed. New York: McGraw, 1989. Provides more than 100,000 definitions, each definition identified with a field of science or technology; electronics, computer science, physics, and chemistry are emphasized; includes brief biographies of about 1000 Nobel Prize winners or persons associated with laws and phenomena defined in the dictionary; has many illustrations; shows mathematical signs and symbols and international graphic symbols.

Sax, N. Irving, and Richard J. Lewis. *Hawley's Condensed Chemical Dictionary*. 11th ed. New York: Van Nostrand, 1987. Defines and discusses many thousands of chemical entities, phenomena, and terms.

Thewlis, J. *The Encyclopaedic Dictionary of Physics*. 9 vols. New York: Pergamon, 1961–1963. An international work; presents the whole of physics and its related subjects; brief to lengthy articles, each complete in itself; provides bibliographies for further study; Vol. 9 is a multilingual glossary; annual supplements.

Thomson, Sir Arthur L., ed. *A New Dictionary of Birds*. New York: McGraw, 1964. Worldwide in scope; designed for both British and North American readers; provides long articles as well as short articles which define terms; includes bibliography; intended for both the general reader and the ornithologist; many illustrations in color and black and white.

Walker, Peter M. B., ed. *Chambers Biology Dictionary*. 4th ed. New York: Cambridge UP, 1989. Defines terms in zoology, botany biochemistry, etc.; covers 100 fields; treats new developments in all areas.

Technology

Black's Medical Dictionary. Ed. C. W. H. Harvard. 36th ed. New York: Barnes, 1990. The standard British dictionary of terminology; includes sections on drugs and new subjects in medicine.

Campbell, Robert J. *Psychiatric Dictionary*. 5th ed. New York: Oxford UP, 1981. Includes terminology from psychiatry and related sciences; gives pronunciation, illustrations, quotations, and some bibliography.

Clayman, Charles B., ed. *The American Medical Association Encyclopedia of Medicine*. New York: Random, 1989. Treats symptoms, diseases, medications, and procedures; discusses the current state of medical knowledge; defines terminology.

De Vries, Louis. *French-English Science and Technology Dictionary*. 4th ed. Revised and enlarged by Stanley Hochman. New York: McGraw, 1978. Includes 4500 terms; emphasizes new developments in electronics, automotive technology, astronautics.

De Vries, Louis, and Hermann De Vries, eds. *English-German Technical and Engineering Dictionary*. 2d ed., revised and enlarged. New York: McGraw, 1966. For the engineer, research worker, translator, and student; offers over 225,000 terms; includes new words in the fields of nuclear physics, space flight, and plastics.

Dorland's Illustrated Medical Dictionary. 26th ed. Philadelphia: Saunders, 1985. Frequently revised; provides broad coverage of the field; gives pronunciations; claims that it is not just a record of usage but maintains "certain standards of etymological propriety and selection."

Gibilsco, Stan, and Neil Schater, eds. *Encyclopedia of Electronics*. 2d ed. New York: TAB, 1990. Defines and explains terms used in electronics: illustrated.

Hunt, V. Daniel. *Energy Dictionary*. New York: Van Nostrand, 1979. Provides brief definitions of some 4000 terms in energy and in a variety of fields relating to energy production and use; has diagrams, charts, and other illustrations.

Liungman, Carl G. *Dictionary of Symbols*. Santa Barbara: ABC-Clio, 1991. Traces the historical development of symbols since their first appearance 20,000 years ago; covers all historical periods and geographical areas; gives meaning, origin, and use of symbols.

Melloni's Illustrated Medical Dictionary. 2d ed. Baltimore: Williams & Wilkins, 1985. Defines 25,000 health science terms; has more than 2000 drawings.

Rosenberg, Jerry M. *Dictionary of Computers, Data Processing and Telecommunications.* New York: Wiley, 1984. Defines terms; explains symbols, acronyms, and abbreviations, giving general and specialized meanings.

Spencer, Donald D. *Computer Dictionary for Everyone.* 3d ed. New York: Scribner's, 1985. Defines terms in language for the lay person; includes information about persons important in the development of computers; covers microcomputers.

Stedman's Medical Dictionary. 25th ed. Baltimore: Williams & Wilkins, 1990. Offers a vocabulary of medicine and allied sciences; gives pronunciation and derivation; includes biographical sketches of persons important in the history of medicine.

ENCYCLOPEDIAS

Ashworth, William. *The Encyclopedia of Environmental Studies.* New York: Facts on File, 1991. Treats environmental protection, environmental engineering, pollution, and other topics related to the environment.

Bitter, Gary, ed. *Macmillan Encyclopedia of Computers.* 2 vols. New York: Macmillan, 1992. Discusses the influence of computers on society; gives an overview of the field, treats major issues and the use of computers in various subject fields.

Brooks, Michael, and Tim Birkhead. *The Cambridge Encyclopedia of Ornithology.* New York: Cambridge UP, 1991. Covers all aspects of ornithology, including physiology, reproduction, evolution, behavior, migration, conservation, etc.; has maps, charts, and photographs.

Besançon, Robert M., ed. *The Encyclopedia of Physics.* 2d ed. New York: Van Nostrand, 1974. Provides short introductory articles on physics, the history of physics, measurements, symbols, and terminology; has general articles on the major areas of physics.

The Cambridge Encyclopedia of Life Sciences. Ed. Adrian Friday and David S. Ingram. Cambridge: Cambridge UP, 1985. Covers modern biology and related fields; has many photographs and drawings, many in color.

Considine, Douglas M., and Glenn D. Considine. *Van Nostrand's Scientific Encyclopedia.* 7th ed. New York: Van Nostrand, 1989. Covers all areas of science and technology; includes planetary astronomy, with information from Voyager; clear definitions; has many illustrations and diagrams.

Dulbecco, Renato, ed. *Encyclopedia of Human Biology.* 8 vols. San Diego: Harcourt, 1991. Aims to review the current state of contemporary biology, covering all fields; offers articles, illustrations, color plates, tables, and bibliographies.

Encyclopedia of Bioethics. 4 vols. New York: Free Press, 1978. A comprehensive source of information on ethical and social issues in the life sciences, medicine, health care, and the health professions; covers such ethical and legal problems as abortion, genetics, organ transplantation, sterilization, medical malpractice, and privacy; discusses basic concepts and principles, ethical theories, religious traditions, value questions, norms of right conduct, history of medical ethics, and subject fields related to bioethics; provides bibliographies and an index.

Groves Donald G., and Lee M. Hunt. *Ocean World Encyclopedia.* New York: McGraw, 1980. Presents oceanographic research relating to the physics, geophysics, chemistry, and biology of the world's oceans; covers the geography of the ocean, the ocean floor, plant and animal life, and waves and currents; includes information about important oceanographers and organizations.

Grzimek, Bernhard. *Grzimek's Encyclopedia of Mammals.* 2d ed. by Sybil Parker. 5 vols. New York: McGraw, 1990. A comprehensive basic zoological reference; provides text, charts, color photographs, drawings, and sketches of the anatomical features of the various classes of mammals.

Hora, Bayard. *The Oxford Encyclopedia of Trees of the World.* New York: Oxford UP, 1981. Covers a wide range of the most significant trees of the world; discusses the anatomy and morphology of trees and ecology of forest regions; explains the importance of certain trees in their geographical area; gives information on cultivation, history, and commercial use; has maps, photographs, and other illustrative materials, many in color.

Lapedes, Daniel, ed. *McGraw-Hill Encyclopedia of the Geological Sciences.* New York: McGraw, 1988. Covers geology, geochemistry, geophysics, and aspects of oceanography and meteorology which are essential to understanding the materials, processes, composition, and physical characteristics of the solid part of the earth; has photographs, maps, graphs, drawings, and diagrams.

Lerner, Rita, and George L. Trigg. *Encyclopedia of Physics.* 2d ed. VCH, 1990. Covers the major areas of physics and subdivisions and interfaces between physics and other sciences; illustrated; gives bibliographical references for each article.

McGraw-Hill Encyclopedia of Science and Technology. 7th ed. 20 vols. New York: McGraw, 1992. Presents factual, basic data in all the physical sciences, earth sciences, life sciences, and engineering; describes recent developments and advances in all fields of science including astronomy and space technology, computers and electronics, communications, aeronautical engineering, energy, genetics, medicine, psychology, printing, industrial engineering, and many others; for students and scholars. Available on CD-ROM. *McGraw-Hill Concise Encyclopedia of Science and Technology,* 2d ed., 1989.

Myers, Robert A., ed. *Encyclopedia of Astronomy and Astrophysics*. San Diego: Harcourt, 1989. Covers cosmic rays, the solar system, stars, stellar systems, observatories, techniques, etc.

Myers, Robert A. *Encyclopedia of Physical Science and Technology*. 2d ed. 18 vols. San Diego: Harcourt, 1992. Covers the physical sciences, mathematics, and engineering; provides illustrations, tables, a glossary and bibliography.

Nierenberg, William N., ed. *Encyclopedia of Earth System Science*. 4 vols. San Diego: Harcourt, 1992. Includes all the earth sciences: climatology, geology, geophysics, mineralogy, oceanography, etc.; provides definitions, illustrations, tables, color plates, and bibliographies.

Parker, Sybil P., ed. *McGraw-Hill Encyclopedia of Energy*. 2d ed. New York: McGraw, 1980. Covers energy consumption, energy reserves, world energy, energy choices, economic and social aspects of energy, and protecting the environment.

_____. *McGraw-Hill Encyclopedia of Environmental Science*. 2d ed. New York: McGraw, 1980. Offers articles on environmental protection, environmental analysis, precedents for weather extremes, urban planning, strip mining, noise pollution, water conversation, forests, and forestry.

_____. *McGraw-Hill Encyclopedia of Ocean and Atmospheric Sciences*. New York: McGraw, 1980. Covers marine resources, weather modification, atmospheric pollution, and satellites; arranged alphabetically; illustrated.

Rycroft, Michael, ed. *The Cambridge Encyclopedia of Space*. 3d ed. New York: Cambridge UP, 1992. Aims to cover every aspect of space flight: history, opening of the space age, early manned missions, launch centers, achievements, setbacks equipment, satellites, etc.; provides maps, illustrations, and tables.

HANDBOOKS

Burington, Richard Stevens. *Handbook of Mathematical Tables and Formulas*. 5th ed. New York: McGraw, 1973. A quick reference source of mathematical information, including a large collection of the most frequently needed tables.

Ganić, Ejup N., and Tyler Hickson. *The McGraw-Hill Handbook of Essential Engineering Information and Data*. New York: McGraw, 1991. Gives basic information with diagrams, charts, and tables.

Gray, Asa. *Gray's Manual of Botany*. 8th ed. New York: American Book Co., 1950. Identifies the flowering plants and ferns of the central and northeastern United States and nearby Canada. Centennial edition of a standard handbook.

Kreider, J. F., and F. Kreith, eds. *Solar Energy Handbook*. New York: McGraw, 1981. Covers the history of solar technology, law, design, wind power, and other aspects of solar energy; uses charts, conversion tables, bibliographies.

Lange's Handbook of Chemistry. Ed. John A. Dean. 13th ed. New York: McGraw, 1985. A compilation of facts, data, tabular material, and experimental findings; provides ready access to every aspect of chemistry; for students and professionals.

Loftness, Robert L. *The Energy Handbook*. New York: Van Nostrand, 1984. Covers energy resources, technology, and policies; has maps, tables, and charts.

The Peterson Field Guide Series. Boston: Houghton, 1934–. Under the editorship of Roger Tory Peterson; each title treats a specific subject, such as birds, shells, butterflies, mammals, rocks and minerals, animal tracks, ferns, trees, and shrubs, reptiles and amphibians, wildflowers, stars, and planets; usually regional in coverage; useful for identification purposes; illustrated. *A Field Guide to the Birds* (1980) is the latest work in the series.

Putnam's Nature Field Books. New York: Putnam, 1928–. This series includes separate volumes on specific scientific subjects. Titles include *Field Book of American Wild Flowers*, by F. S. Mathews; *Field Book of the Stars*, by W. T. Olcott; and *Field Book of Common Rocks and Minerals*, by F. B. Loomis.

Rickett, Harold William, ed. *Wildflowers of the United States*. 6 vols. in 14. New York: McGraw, 1966–1973. Prepared in cooperation with the New York Botanical Gardens; provides full-color photographs of thousands of wildflowers, most of them shown in their natural habitats; gives both Latin and common names. Vol. I: *The Northeastern States* (2 vols.). Vol. II: *The Southeastern States* (2 vols.). Vol. III: *Texas* (2 vols.). Vol. IV: *The Southwestern States* (3 vols.). Vol. V: *The Northwestern States* (2 vols.). Vol. VI: *The Central Mountains and Plains* (3 vols.). *Index*. 1975.

Walker, Ernest P. *Walker's Mammals of the World*. By Ronald M. Nowac. 5th ed. 2 vols. Baltimore: Johns Hopkins UP, 1991. Offers a world distribution chart showing geographical location of the various mammals; gives common names, numbers, characteristics, etc.

YEARBOOKS[6]

McGraw-Hill Year Book of Science and Technology. New York: McGraw, 1961–. Annual. Planned as an annual supplement to the *McGraw-Hill Encyclopedia of Science and Technology*; summarizes the significant events and advances of the previous year in every area of science and technology and serves to keep the *Encyclopedia* up to date.

---

[6] Most of the societies in the subject fields issue a yearbook, e.g., *The Yearbook of Mathematics*. Some encyclopedias issue a science supplement, e.g., *Science Year*, issued to supplement *World Book Encyclopedia* (1965–). Other yearbooks and annuals provide information on activities in the fields of science and technology during the preceding year.

BIOGRAPHICAL DICTIONARIES[7]

American Men and Women of Science: Physical and Biological Sciences. 18th ed. 8 vols. New York: Bowker, 1992. Gives biographical information on American and Canadian men and women now working and teaching in the physical, biological, and engineering sciences; online access to this database has been available since 1981. Vol. 9 is a geographic and descriptive index.

Dictionary of Scientific Biography. Published under the auspices of the Council of Learned Societies. 14 vols. New York: Scribner's, 1970–1990. Vol. XV, *Supplement*, 1977; Vol. XVI, *Index*, 1981; Vol. XVII and Vol. XVIII Suppl., 1990. Describes and evaluates the lives of more than 5000 scientists from all regions and periods; does not include living persons; gives biographical information and information on the contributions of each person in relation to other scientists; each biography has a bibliography of works by and about the biographee. *Concise Dictionary of Scientific Biography* (1981) is an abridgment of the basic work.

McGraw-Hill Modern Scientists and Engineers. 3 vols. New York: McGraw, 1980. Contains 1140 biographies of scientists and engineers from the 1920s to the present—living and not living.

Ogilvie, Marilyn. *Women in Science.* Cambridge, Mass.: MIT, 1986. Provides information about women who made a contribution to science from antiquity through the nineteenth century.

ATLASES

Andouze, Jean and Israel Guy, eds. *The Cambridge Atlas of Astronomy.* Cambridge: Cambridge UP, 1985. Presents what is currently known about the universe; in text and illustrations, color and black and white.

Cuff, David J., and William J. Young. *The United States Energy Atlas.* 2d ed. New York: Free Press, 1986. Uses maps, photographs, charts, diagrams, and tables to locate America's energy sources; gives comprehensive and comparative coverage to each energy source; has a glossary of energy terms, bibliographies, and an index.

Mason, Robert, and Mark T. Mattson, eds. *Atlas of United States Environmental Issues.* New York: Macmillan, 1991. Surveys in text and maps the condition of the environment throughout the United States, covering such problems as pollution, natural resources, and nature conservation.

The Rand McNally Atlas of the Oceans. Chicago: Rand, 1977. Gives a comprehensive survey of the ocean regions; the birth and evolution of oceans, marine life, and minerals.

---

[7] See also Chapter 10, Biographical Dictionaries.

EXAMPLES OF PROFESSIONAL JOURNALS
IN SCIENCE AND TECHNOLOGY[8]

American Chemical Society Journal. Washington: American Chemical Soc., 1879–. Fortnightly. Reports significant research in all branches of chemistry; has a section on short preliminary studies of importance; gives book reviews.

American Journal of Physics. Woodbury: 1933–. Monthly. Published by the American Inst. of Physics; represents the entire field; reports on new techniques and apparatus; includes some abstracts; gives book reviews.

American Journal of Public Health. Washington: APNA, 1911–. Monthly. Covers all aspects of public health; written for the expert but has information of interest to nonexperts; discusses current issues in health; gives book reviews.

American Mathematical Monthly. Washington: Mathematical Assoc. of America, 1894–. Ten times a year. The official journal of the association; aimed at the college-level mathematics student; presents papers and notes, including reports of research; includes book reviews.

Geological Society of America. *Bulletin.* Boulder: Geological Soc. of America, 1888–. Monthly. The official publication of the society; concerned with original research on any facet of geology, including geochemistry, geophysics, mineralogy, etc.; has long and short articles; illustrated.

JAMA: The Journal of the American Medical Association. Chicago: AMA, 1848–. Weekly. The official journal of the association; reviews current research; reports advances in the field of medical science; gives selected abstracts of world's medical literature; gives information on current topics of interest to the medical profession; includes news, views, and reviews of the profession.

Journal of Geology. Chicago: U of Chicago P, 1893–. Bimonthly. Concerned with original studies in all aspects of geology; some issues are devoted to a single subject; has book reviews; international in scope.

Natural History. New York: American Museum of Natural History, 1900–. Monthly. Provides a popular approach to many topics of interest to nature lovers, including conservation, anthropology, geography, astronomy, etc.; authoritative articles are written in semipopular style; has many photographs.

Nature. London: Macmillan, 1869–. Three weekly editions. A British publication; represents all branches of science; gives essay and review articles by leading scientists and some studies on original research; provides both general and specialized treatment; includes book reviews.

---

[8] See also *Ulrich's International Periodicals Directory.* 31st ed. *Magazines for Libraries.* 7th ed., ed. Bill Katz and Linda S. Katz.

Scientific American. New York: Scientific American, 1845–. Monthly. Reports scientific and technical advances and theories; for both general readers and specialists; has many illustrated articles; gives book reviews.

ABSTRACT JOURNALS[9]

Biological Abstracts. Philadelphia: Biological Abstracts, 1926–. Semimonthly. Covers the world's biological research literature in agronomy, genetics, behavioral sciences, and other related fields, including periodical publications, books, government reports, and reports of conferences; is the major abstracting source for the biological sciences; entries are arranged under broad subject headings with many subdivisions. Online: BIOSIS.

Chemical Abstracts. Washington: American Chemical Society, 1907–. Weekly. Provides abstracts from about 10,000 journals covering fifty languages, patents from twenty-five countries, and theses, books, conference proceedings, and government reports; makes available some 240,000 abstracts annually; not confined to chemistry but covers all scientific and technical literature; reports new chemical information from patent literature; covers all scientific and technical papers; now on machine-readable tape for computer searching. Online: BRS, DIALOG, ORBIT, STN.

Mathematical Reviews. Providence: American Mathematical Society, 1940–. Monthly. Abstracts and reviews mathematical literature appearing in some 1200 journals and books, conference proceedings, and translations grouped under general subject headings; international in scope.

Pollution Abstracts. Bethesda: Cambridge Scientific Abstracts, 1970–. Bimonthly. Divided into chapters by subject (such as air, fresh water, land, noise pollution) or by type of document cited (such as government documents, patents); includes books, journals, papers, government reports. On CD-ROM.

Science Abstracts. Piscataway: Institution of Electrical Engineers, 1898–. Monthly. Includes physics abstracts, electrical and electronics abstracts, and computer and control abstracts; covers journals, papers, books, and conference proceedings; arranged by classified subject headings; available on magnetic tape for computer searches. Online: BRS, DIALOG, STN.

---

[9] This is just a sample; there are abstract journals in every major area of science and technology.

CHAPTER

❦ 22 ❦

The Fine Arts and Recreation

Art—the word is derived from the Latin *ars*—is any skill or aptitude which enables its possessor to perform in a superior manner. This meaning of the word covers (1) the fine arts, which express ideas, emotions, and experiences in beautiful or significant forms; (2) the useful arts, which are both utilitarian and artistic; (3) the decorative arts, which adorn rather than create; and (4) the recreational arts, which afford relaxation and amusement.

The fine arts, as a branch of knowledge, are those arts (skills or aptitudes) concerned with creating, producing, or expressing what is beautiful, imaginative, or appealing for its own sake, rather than for some utilitarian purpose. Traditionally, the fine arts include music, painting, sculpture, dance, drama, architecture, and poetry.

In the fine arts class of the Dewey Decimal Classification System (700), all the above-named fine arts are included except poetry. Landscape and civic arts, drawing and decorative parts, prints and printmaking, photography, and recreation are also placed in the 700 class. In the Library of Congress Classification, M is music and N is fine arts. Recreation is placed in the G class (GV).

Works or art—that is, paintings, sculpture, musical scores, dramatic productions, etc.—constitute the primary source materials in the fine arts subject field. There are, however, many reference sources designed to aid the student in understanding and appreciating the works of art themselves; the artists who produced them; the technical terminology of the several areas; the historical backgrounds of schools, movements, and trends; and the actual techniques employed. Those reference aids include bibliographies, guides and catalogs, indexes to periodical literature and to paintings and illustrations, dictionaries and encyclopedias, biographical dictionaries, handbooks, histories, and professional journals.[1]

Useful Reference Sources in Painting, Sculpture, Architecture, and Decorative Arts

BIBLIOGRAPHIES, GUIDES, AND INDEXES[2]

Appel, Marsha, ed. *Illustration Index*. 4th ed. Metuchen: Scarecrow, 1980. Indexes photographs, paintings, drawings, and diagrams in major periodicals, 1972–1976; arranged by subject; includes wildlife, furniture, art works, and pictures and individuals. *Illustration Index V*, 1984; *Illustration Index VI*, 1988.

Arntzen, Etta, and Robert Rainwater, comps. *Guide to the Literature of Art History*. Chicago: ALA, 1981. Organizes and evaluates the literature of art history—the basic reference works and sources for advanced research; annotates more than 4000 sources, including general reference sources, bibliographies, directories, encyclopedias, handbooks, primary sources, histories, periodicals, and serials; includes basic monographs on each of the arts arranged by period and region.

The Art Index. New York: Wilson, 1929–. Quarterly. Indexes more than 200 selected art journals, museum publications, domestic art publications, and foreign journals by author and subject; includes fine arts and applied arts; citations to book reviews are arranged alphabetically by author in a separate section of the index. Available in print, on tape, online via WilsonLine, on CD-ROM.

British Humanities Index. London: Library Associations, 1962–. Quarterly; annual cumulations. Index to 400 British journals covering architecture, art, cinema, sports and games, language, law, music, politics, television, and theater.

Clapp, Jane. *Sculpture Index*. 2 vols. Metuchen: Scarecrow, 1970–1971. Indexes pictures of sculpture in some 950 art publications; traces sculpture from prehistoric times to the present; for each work, gives the present location of the sculpture, dimensions, materials of construction, and

---

[1] See also Chapter 14, Nonbook Information Sources.
[2] See also Chapter 9, Indexes, and Chapter 13, Bibliographies.

picture sources; Vol. I covers Europe and the contemporary Middle East; Vol. II covers the Americas, the Orient, Africa, the Pacific, and the classical world.

Ehresmann, Donald L. *Fine Arts: A Bibliographic Guide to Basic Reference Works, Histories, and Handbooks*. 3d ed. Englewood: Libraries Unlimited, 1990. Provides an annotated list of titles in these areas.

DICTIONARIES AND ENCYCLOPEDIAS

Baigell, Matthew. *Dictionary of American Art*. New York: Harper, 1980. Provides information about American painters, sculptors, printmakers, and photographers, as well as about movements in American art from the sixteenth century to the present. Emphasis is on artistic achievement rather than biographical information.

Chilvers, Ian, and Harold Osborne, eds. *The Oxford Dictionary of Art*. New York: Oxford UP, 1988. Discusses paintings, graphics, sculpture, architecture, periods, schools, techniques, terms; covers western art and western-inspired art since antiquity.

Encyclopedia of American Art. New York: Dutton, 1981. Gives a summary of American art and artists from pre-Revolutionary times to the present— painting, sculpture, architecture, prints, photography, folk arts, decorative arts, and contemporary handicrafts; covers styles, materials, and techniques; arranged alphabetically; lists some museums.

Encyclopedia of World Art. 15 vols. New York: McGraw, 1959–1968. Includes biographies of artists; has monographic treatments of periods, movements, and areas of art; gives discussions of types, media, technology, concepts, and problems of art; provides bibliographies. Supplements V.16, 1983; V.19, 1989.

Fleming, John, and Hugh Honour. *The Penguin Dictionary of Decorative Arts*. New York: Viking, 1990. Aims to be a guide to the decorative arts of Western Europe and North America from the Middle Ages to the present; includes some nonwestern art; covers all forms of art; defines and explains terms; has many illustrations, including color plates.

Goulart, Ron, ed. *The Encyclopedia of American Comics*. New York: Facts on File, 1990. Gives history and development of American comic strips and comic books from the beginning of the twentieth century, including both major and minor artists.

Gouring, Lawrence, ed. *The Encyclopedia of Visual Art*. 2 vols. Englewood Cliffs: Prentice, 1983. Vol. I. *History of Art*; Vol. II: *Biographies*.

Harris, Cyril M., ed. *Dictionary of Architecture and Construction*, 2d ed. New York: McGraw, 1987. Provides clear definitions of basic terminology in architecture and construction; has many illustrations.

————. *Historic Architecture Sourcebook*. New York: McGraw, 1977. Defines more than 5000 terms in both eastern and western architecture covering some 5000 years; has many line drawings.

Norwich, John Julian, ed. *Oxford Illustrated Encyclopedia of Art*. New York: Oxford UP, 1991. Covers all areas; discusses styles and techniques. This is Vol. 5 in the *Oxford Illustrated Encyclopedia* series, 1985–.

Praeger Encyclopedia of Art. 5 vols. New York: Praeger, 1971. Aims to provide a comprehensive and authoritative reference guide for students and general readers to the history of world art; includes biographies, chronological surveys, and articles on periods, styles, and schools; gives articles on civilizations for which no artists' names are known.

Savage, George. *Dictionary of Antiques*. New York: Praeger, 1970. Emphasizes style and fashion in art; has articles on almost every aspect of American and European decorative art; gives definitions for terms and explains techniques; provides biographical information on individual artisans; designed to help readers recognize fakes in antiques; includes bibliographies.

Stevenson, George A. *Graphic Arts Encyclopedia*. 3d ed. New York: McGraw, 1992. Provides information on terms, techniques, processes, concepts, equipment, and methods in the graphic arts profession; covers electronic text processing, copying machines, and other recent developments; has illustrations, tables, and charts.

Torbet, Laura, ed. *The Encyclopedia of Crafts*. 4 vols. New York: Scribner's, 1980. Provides basic information on the terminology, history, tools and materials, techniques, and processes of fifty major crafts from all over the world; has many illustrations.

Wilkes, Joseph A., ed. *Encyclopedia of Architecture: Design, Engineering and Construction*. New York: Wiley, 1987–. (In progress.) Covers construction, materials, design, planning, and energy considerations; includes biography and history of architectural building types; has many illustrations and tables. Four vols. completed.

Yarwood, Doreen. *The Encyclopedia of World Costume*. New York: Scribner's, 1978. Portrays costume and costume-related topics from the ancient world to the present in text and illustrations; covers various historical periods and geographical areas; gives the history and development of each garment as well as the forms and designs of that garment.

HANDBOOKS

Mayer, Ralph. *The Artist's Handbook of Materials and Techniques*. 5th ed. Rev. and updated by Steven Sheehan. New York: Viking, 1991. Discusses the materials and methods of the artist's craft: what they are and how they are used.

Osborne, Harold, ed. *The Oxford Companion to Twentieth Century Art*. New York: Oxford UP, 1982. Covers the entire range of twentieth century art; includes architects and photographers if their work is related to other art forms.

BIOGRAPHICAL DICTIONARIES AND DIRECTORIES[3]

American Art Directory. 1993–94. New York: Bowker, 1992. Biennial. Includes art associations and museums, periodicals, scholarships, art schools, and people and places in United States and Canadian art.

Cederholm, Theresa A., comp. and ed. *Afro-American Artists: A Bio-bibliographical Directory*. Boston: BPL, 1973. Provides biographical information on some 2000 American artists, identifies media used, titles of works, and locations of permanent collections.

Cummings, Paul. *A Dictionary of Contemporary American Artists*. 5th ed. New York: St. Martin's, 1988. Gives personal data and bibliographical references for further study on 923 contemporary painters, sculptors, and printmakers; has black-and-white illustrations.

Emanuel, Muriel, ed. *Contemporary Architects*. New York: St. Martin's, 1980. Provides detailed information on about 600 contemporary architects of international reputation, including landscape architects and structural engineers: biographical information; a chronological sketch of constructed works or projects; illustration of a significant work; a bibliography of books and articles by and about the architect; an essay about each one's career; some photographs.

Larousse Dictionary of Painters. New York: Larousse, 1981. Gives biographical information about more than 500 important western painters from medieval times to the present; includes evaluations of their work, the museums which have their paintings, and examples of each artist's work, most of them in color.

Macmillan Encyclopedia of Architects. 4 vols. New York: Macmillan/Free Press, 1982. Biographies cover more than 2450 architects from ancient times to recent times, giving information about their training, careers, and influence; has a glossary of technical terms; black-and-white illustrations.

Marks, Claude. *World Artists 1950–1980*. New York: Wilson, 1984. Presents 312 artists who have been influential in the post-WWII period: life, work, and methods; includes painting, sculpture, and graphic media; lists collections of each artist's work. *World Artists 1980–1990*. New York: Wilson, 1991. Adds 120 artists; is a guide to the art of the decade.

---

[3] See also Chapter 10, Biographical Dictionaries.

Naylor, Colin. *Contemporary Designers*. New York: St. James, 1990. Offers international coverage of prominent designers in every field, with personal information and writings by and about them.

Rubinstein, Charlotte S. *American Women Artists: From Early Indian Times to the Present*. Boston: Hall, 1982. Gives biography and criticism of leading women painters and sculptors; black-and-white illustrations.

Watson-Jones, Virginia. *Contemporary American Women Sculptors*. Phoenix: Oryx, 1986. Treats some 328 living American women sculptors briefly; gives personal information, including education, collections, awards, exhibitions, and media.

Who's Who in American Art, 1992–1993. Ed. Jaques Cattell Press. New York: Bowker, 1992. Gives biographies of U.S. and Canadian artists including professional painters, sculptors, illustrators, graphic artists, executives, collectors patrons, scholars, and critics; online.

EXAMPLES OF PROFESSIONAL JOURNALS[4]

Art Bulletin. New York: College Art Assoc. of America, 1913–. Quarterly. Contains articles for students of art history written by faculty members of the association and covering all facets and periods of fine arts.

Art in America. New York: Brant, 1913–. Bimonthly. Emphasis is on contemporary art; includes some historical articles; covers painting, sculpture, architecture, design, and photography.

Useful Reference Sources in Music

Music, according to *The Oxford English Dictionary*, is "that one of the fine arts which is concerned with the combination of sounds with a view of beauty of form and the expression of emotion; . . . the science of the laws or principles (of melody, harmony, rhythm, etc.) by which the art is regulated."[5]

The literature of music covers works on music as a whole or a part; the music of various nations and peoples; the technical aspects of music (theory, notation, tone, and harmony); the history of music and musicians; musical form and the means of executing it (instrument or voice, group or individual); the types of music (for example, jazz, folk songs, and Greek music); critical

---

[4] See also *Ulrich's International Periodicals Directory*, 31st ed., and *Magazines for Libraries*, 7th ed., ed. Bill Katz and Linda S. Katz.

[5] *The Oxford English Dictionary*, VI, 1933, 782.

studies of music and musicians; musical scores; biographical information on performers, composers, and lyricists; and the teaching of music.

There are many reference sources designed to aid in the study, interpretation, understanding, and appreciation of music. Some of these are: bibliographies, guides, indexes, dictionaries, encyclopedias, handbooks, biographical dictionaries, professional journals, and many kinds of nonbook sources. (See Chapter 14 for a discussion of nonbook information sources.)

BIBLIOGRAPHIES, GUIDES, AND INDEXES[6]

Cohn, Arthur. *Recorded Classical Music: A Critical Guide to Compositions and Performances*. New York, Macmillan, 1981. Describes and evaluates the best recordings of classical music; arranged alphabetically by composer; gives one or more recommended recordings with commentary for each one.

Duckles, Vincent Harris, and Michael A. Keller, comps. *Music Reference and Research Materials: An Annotated Bibliography*, 4th ed. rev. New York: Schirmer, 1992. Points out and describes the resources of the field: dictionaries, encyclopedias, histories, chronologies, bibliographies of music and music literature, guides to research methods in musicology, and catalogs of major music libraries and collections throughout the world; does not include biographical material.

The Music Index. Warren: Harmonie Park P, 1949–. International in coverage, indexes by subject and author over 350 periodicals; includes a broad range of subjects; indexes book reviews and reviews of recordings, tapes, and performances. Since 1981–88, on CD-ROM. *The Music Index on CD-ROM* (computer file), produced by Opus Publications, Inc., is a subject-author guide to music periodical literature.

Shapiro, Nat, ed. *Popular Music, An Annotated Index of American Popular Songs*. 10 vols. New York: Adrian, 1964–1985. Aims to provide selective annotated lists by decades of significant American popular songs, giving discussions of the decades in question and, for each song, information about the composer, lyricist, current publisher, recordings, film or stage show in which it was introduced, and performers associated with it. Vols. 7–10 published by Gale Research Company, 1984–1985.

DICTIONARIES

Ammer, Christine. *Harper's Dictionary of Music*. 2d ed. New York: Harper, 1991. Defines the most commonly used musical terms; gives material on

---

[6] See also Chapter 9, Indexes, and Chapter 13, Bibliographies.

music history and biographical material about composers; emphasizes popular music; includes information about musical forms and musical instruments.

Anderson, James. *The Harper Dictionary of Opera and Operetta.* New York: HarperCollins, 1992. Covers composers, operas, operettas, singers, conductors; especially useful for operettas.

Arnold, Denis, ed. *The New Oxford Companion to Music.* 2 vols. Oxford: Oxford UP, 1983. International in coverage; treats musicians' careers and achievements; the history of music in various countries, individual works, instruments, forms of music, music theory, etc.; emphasis is on classical music. Reprint with corrections, 1988.

Griffiths, Paul. *The Thames and Hudson Encyclopedia of 20th Century Music.* London: Thames & Hudson, 1986. International in scope; presents contemporary musical subjects, such as ensembles, instruments, techniques, biography; arranged chronologically 1901–1985.

Hitchcock, Wiley, and Stanley Sadie, eds. *The New Grove Dictionary of American Music.* New York: Grove, 1986. All aspects of specifically American music are included: jazz, popular, folk, serious, regional, ethnic, American composers and performers, music periodicals, etc.; has illustrations and musical notations.

Kennedy, Michael. *The Oxford Dictionary of Music.* New York: Oxford UP, 1985. Provides articles on composers, performers, and other persons in music; gives brief definition or identification of terms, titles of works, types of music and instruments; covers new developments in music.

Kernfeld, Barry, ed. *New Grove Dictionary of Jazz.* 2 vols. New York: Grove, 1988. Identifies about 3000 jazz performers, composers, and arrangers; covers styles, terms, theory, instruments, films, jazz clubs, groups, labels.

Morehead, Philip D., and Annie MacNeil. *The New American Dictionary of Music.* New York: Dutton, 1991. Emphasizes American music and current performers; covers all facets of music from early times to the present; gives musical illustrations and a glossary of musical terms.

Randel, Don Michael, ed. *The New Harvard Dictionary of Music.* Cambridge: Harvard UP, 1986. Brings the previous editions by Apel up to date and expands coverage of recent music, including jazz and rock; covers music of some ninety countries and regions, instruments from earliest times to the present, and history and theory of music.

Sadie, Stanley, ed. *The New Grove Dictionary of Musical Instruments.* 3 vols. New York: Grove, 1984. Based on *The New Grove Dictionary of Music,* (see below), covers instruments of classical and modern western music and their makers, nonwestern music, and folk instruments.

————. *The New Grove Dictionary of Music and Musicians.* 20 vols. New York:

Macmillan, 1980. Distributed by Grove's Dictionaries of Music. Both a dictionary and an encyclopedia; includes all types of music and performers up to the present; explains terms, concepts, forms, and genres; gives brief and lengthy critical biographies; covers nonwestern music; offers many illustrations (musical notations, facsimiles of manuscripts, and pictures of composers); has extensive bibliographies.

———. *The New Grove Dictionary of Opera*. New York: Grove's, 1992. Treats history, individual operas, artists, composers, librettists, etc.

ENCYCLOPEDIAS

Clarke, Donald, ed. *The Penguin Encyclopedia of Popular Music*. New York: Viking, 1989. Treats all forms of popular music: rock, country, jazz, gospel, heavy metal, ragtime, and more; identifies artists, composers, and labels.

Nite, Norm N. *Rock On: The Illustrated Encyclopedia of Rock 'n' Roll*. Updated ed. New York: Harper, 1982. Vol. I: *The Solid Gold Years*. Provides brief biographical and career information on the popular recording artists of the 1950s, 1960s, and 1970s. Vol. II: *The Modern Years, 1964–Present* (1978). Offers the same coverage for the period 1964–1978.

Orrey, Leslie, ed. *The Encyclopedia of Opera*. New York: Scribner's, 1976. Contains information on a limited number of operas and persons concerned with their production: composers, librettists, singers, conductors, and designers; includes operatic characters and opera companies; includes terminology; has some entries for musical comedies and their composers; illustrated.

Stambler, Irwin. *Encyclopedia of Pop, Rock and Soul*. Rev. ed. New York: St. Martin's, 1989. Gives major attention to pop and rock musicians; some attention given to soul, new world, and punk.

———. *Encyclopedia of Popular Music and Rock*. Rev. ed. New York: St. Martin's, 1973. Presents popular music from 1925, the people responsible for it, and its effects on modern life; gives definitions, biographical information, and synopses of musicals; lists award winners.

Stambler, Irwin, and Grelun Landon. *Encyclopedia of Folk, Country and Western Music*. 2d ed. New York: St. Martin's, 1983. Emphasizes biographical information on current and past performers; defines terms; describes instruments; gives some historical background; includes items of general interest in this field.

Thompson, Oscar, ed. *The International Cyclopedia of Music and Musicians*. 11th ed. Ed. Bruce Bohle. New York: Dodd, 1985. Provides definitions, bibliography, biography, synopses of opera plots, and pronunciation of names; has short articles and lengthy discussions; international in scope, but has strong emphasis on American music and the American scene.

HANDBOOKS

Barnes, Anthony. *The Oxford Companion to Musical Instruments*. New York: Oxford UP, 1992. Covers instruments ancient and modern; treats instruments of non-Western cultures and other regions of the world; includes ensembles of musical instruments; is illustrated.

Cross, Milton, and Karl Kohrs. *The New Milton Cross: More Stories of the Great Operas*. New York: Doubleday, 1980. Reviews seventy widely performed operas act by act, aria by aria.

Fuld, James J. *The Book of World-famous Music—Classical, Popular and Folk*. 3d ed., rev. and enl. New York: Crown, 1986. Gives information about many hundreds of the best-known musical compositions from twenty-five countries; includes music and words of songs, date of first appearance, and brief biographical information for composer, librettist, and lyricist; traces each melody to its original printed source; gives words of each work and first line of music in original key.

Gammond, Peter. *The Oxford Companion to Popular Music*. New York: Oxford UP, 1991. Covers a wide range of information about music of all kinds from about 1850: ballads, blues, calypso, music hall, light opera, gypsy, drawing-room, jazz, etc.; theaters, schools of music, and individuals and their careers are included.

Geiringer, Karl. *Instruments in the History of Western Music*. 3d ed. New York: Oxford UP, 1978. Explains the development of instruments and the relationship of instruments to artistic trends; discusses the musical trends of a period and the instruments in use (construction, manufacturers, and composers who used them); has drawings and photographs.

Kobbé, Gustav. *The New Kobbé's Complete Opera Book*. Ed. and rev. by the Earl of Harewood. New York: Bodley Head, 1987. Traces the development of opera; gives stories of more than 300 operas; gives brief notes on composers; includes old and modern works; arranged chronologically, subdivided by country and within each country arranged by dates of the composers; includes musical examples.

Lax, Roger, and Frederick Smith. *The Great Song Thesaurus*. 2d ed. New York: Oxford UP, 1989. Lists popular songs from 1558–1986: notable songs, top hits, revivals, musical shows, political songs, school songs, and many more; gives performance medium; provides a thesaurus of songs by subject, key word, and category; lists composer, lyricist, year of popularity, and recording artists.

Lazarus, John. *The Opera Handbook*. Boston: Hall, 1990. Gives information about 200 operas, a glossary of operatic terms, historical background, biographical sketches of contemporary artists, and black-and-white photos.

McRae, Barry. *The Jazz Handbook*. Boston: Hall, 1990. Covers jazz from pre-twenties to the present; gives brief biographies of jazz musicians and photos.

Marcuse, Sibyl. *A Survey of Musical Instruments*. New York: Harper, 1975. Offers historical and technical information on the musical instruments of the world, tracing the development of individual instruments from their origin to the present; quotations from scholarly works and bibliographical references are given.

Martin, George. *The Opera Companion to Twentieth-Century Opera*. New York: Dodd, 1979. Gives a synopsis of seventy-eight twentieth-century operas; translates key words in foreign-language operas; discusses personalities and aspects of twentieth-century opera.

The Simon and Schuster Book of the Opera: A Complete Reference Guide, 1597 to the Present. New York: Simon, 1977. Arranges 777 operas chronologically by premiere date; gives composer, librettist, original plot source, and synopsis of each opera; provides illustrations, some in color.

Slonimsky, Nicolas. *Music Since 1900*. 4th ed. New York: Scribner's, 1971. Presents chronologically events of musical importance in Europe and North America from January 1, 1900, through July 20, 1969; includes information on composers and their works and other items of musical interest; covers electronic music and instruments; includes a glossary. *Supplement to Music Since 1900*. By Nicolas Slonimsky. 1986. Brings coverage to 1985.

BIOGRAPHICAL DICTIONARIES[7]

Anderson, E. Ruth, comp. *Contemporary American Composers: A Biographical Dictionary*. 2d ed. New York: Hall, 1982. Gives brief biographical information for some 4000 composers born in 1870 or later who did the major part of their work in the United States; includes information about career, compositions, professional positions, awards, etc.

Baker's Biographical Dictionary of Musicians. 8th ed. Rev. by Nicholas Slonimsky. New York: Schirmer, 1992. Gives biographical information on many pop stars as well as the most recently notable classical performers, composers, librettists, musicologists, publishers, instrument makers, etc.; includes some bibliographies.

---

[7] See also Chapter 10, Biographical Dictionaries.

Cummings, David M., and Dennis K. McIntire, eds. *International Who's Who in Music and Musicians' Directory*. Cambridge: International Who's Who In Music, 1990. Focuses on individuals in classical and light classical music.

Ewen, David, comp. and ed. *Great Composers, A Biographical and Critical Guide: 1300–1900*. New York: Wilson, 1966. Supplies detailed biographical, historical, and analytical information on 198 composers of the past whose works are significant in the development of music; includes lesser masters and composers. *Composers Since 1900 (1969)* and *Composers Since 1900: First Supplement (1981)*, companion volumes, bring the coverage of composers up to date.

———. *Musicians Since 1900*. New York: Wilson, 1978. Gives detailed biographical information about 432 performing artists; includes photographs and bibliographical references; has a classified list of performers by instrument or voice.

EXAMPLES OF PROFESSIONAL JOURNALS[8]

The Musical Quarterly. New York: Oxford UP, 1915–. Quarterly. Aims to present the best musical thought throughout the world; publishes research in the field of serious music; gives reviews of recordings and musical examples. Available on CD-ROM.

Opera News. New York: Metropolitan Opera Guild, 1936–. Monthly May –Nov., biweekly Dec.–Apr. Emphasizes performers and performances; has book reviews.

Billboard: The International Newsweekly of Music and Entertainment. New York: BPI Communications, 1894–. Weekly, except the last week in Dec. Gives information about artists, news, new techniques, etc. Online from DIALOG.

Rolling Stone. New York: Straight Arrow, 1967–. Biweekly. Covers current events, popular music, video, radio, etc.

Useful Reference Sources in the Performing Arts

The performing arts include dance in its various forms; dramatic and musical theatre; motion picture films; television productions; writers, directors, composers, producers, performers, and choreographers; drama; and the history of each medium. The original performances are primary sources in the performing arts.

---

[8] See also *Ulrich's International Periodicals Directory*, 31st ed., and *Magazines for Libraries*, 7th ed., ed. Bill Katz and Linda S. Katz.

Reference materials (secondary sources) which are designed to aid in studying, understanding, and appreciating the performing arts include dictionaries, encyclopedias, handbooks, biographical dictionaries, and professional journals.

BIBLIOGRAPHIES, GUIDES, AND INDEXES[9]

The Art Index. (See p. 219.)

Banham, Martin, ed. *The Cambridge Guide to World Theatre.* New York: New York UP, 1988. Emphasizes performance, but also the theatrical history and traditions of most of the countries of the world; traces the development of various types of theatrical performance, e.g., the Broadway musical, provides information on actors, designers, etc.

Humanities Index. New York: Wilson, 1974–. Includes opera, ballet, drama, television, and film reviews; lists important persons in various fields under appropriate subject headings. Available in print, online via Wilson-Line, on tape, on CD-ROM via WilsonDisc.

Epstein, Lawrence S., ed. *A Guide to Theatre in America.* New York: Macmillan, 1985. Gives addresses of people, companies, and organizations associated with the theater, such as awards, agents, foundations, schools, colleges, and theater groups; arranged by state and city.

DICTIONARIES AND ENCYCLOPEDIAS

Bordman, Gerald. *American Musical Theatre: A Chronicle.* 2d ed. New York: Oxford UP, 1991. Covers the period 1866–1978; gives a season-by-season account of the Broadway stage; includes a brief summary of the plot of each musical covered, together with its major credits and comments on its place in the history of the musical; the appendix covers major figures in the theatre.

Bronner, Edwin. *The Encyclopedia of the American Theatre, 1900–1975.* Rev. ed. Cranbury: Barnes, 1980. Gives brief information about every major theatrical presentation on and off-Broadway in this century: author, director, New York opening date, theater, number of performances, cast, and excerpt from a review; does not include musicals.

Clarke, Mary, and David Vaughan, eds. *The Encyclopedia of Dance and Ballet.* New York: Putnam, 1977. Discusses ballet and contemporary dance, especially of the twentieth century; traces the development of the major ballet companies; describes more than 300 ballets and modern dance

[9] See also Chapter 9, Indexes, and Chapter 13, Bibliographies.

works; gives biographical information on the choreographers, composers, designers, and dancers who created them; has numerous photographs and a glossary of terms.

Green, Stanley. *Encyclopedia of the Musical Film*. New York: Oxford UP, 1981. Gives brief plot outlines and credits; provides factual information about singers, actors, actresses, songs, and awards.

Hodgson, Terry. *The Drama Dictionary*. New York: Amsterdam, 1988. Defines practical and critical terms used in the theater by theater critics, including terms from several languages.

Koegler, Horst. *The Concise Oxford Dictionary of Ballet*. 2d ed. New York: Oxford UP, 1982. Covers all aspects of ballet for the past four centuries (ballets and their sources, dancers, choreographers, schools, theaters, companies, cities important to ballet); defines terms; includes information on ethnic, ballroom, and modern dancing.

McGraw-Hill Encyclopedia of World Drama. 2d ed. 5 vols. New York: McGraw, 1984. International in scope; gives articles on 910 dramatists and important movements and schools in world drama; has biographical articles; includes critiques of the work of all dramatists listed and synopses of their most important plays.

Wilson, G. B. L. *A Dictionary of Ballet*. 3d ed. New York: Theatre Arts, 1974. Emphasizes dance in English-speaking countries, with special emphasis on classical ballet; covers individual ballets, dancers, steps, technical terms.

HANDBOOKS

Bawden, Liz Anne. *The Oxford Companion to Film*. New York: Oxford UP, 1977. A guide to feature films; gives information about the art of films; has biographies of actors, actresses, directors, and producers; provides histories of major film companies and discussions of movements and genres; includes some critics; gives history of films in each country.

Bordman, Gerald. *The Oxford Companion to American Theatre*. 2d ed. New York: Oxford UP, 1992. Arranged in dictionary style, with brief articles; covers social history of the theater, personalities, schools of acting, companies, plays, musical and nonmusical films, foreign plays, and theater-related subjects, both well known and obscure.

Halliwell, Leslie. *Halliwell's Film Guide*. 9th ed. New York: Scribner's, 1988. Provides information about some 12,000 sound and silent feature films from the United States and the United Kingdom and some from other countries released up to 1980; arranged alphabetically; for each film, gives a quality rating, country of origin, release date, running time, cast credits, author, producer, music credits, and a brief annotation.

Hardy, Phil. *The Film Encyclopedia.* 2 vols. New York: Morrow, 1983–1984. Vol. I: *The Western*; Vol. II: *Science Fiction.* Both volumes give synopses, credits, review of each film; arranged alphabetically by decade. Additional volumes will cover comedy, romance, horror, musicals, and war epics.

Hartnoll, Phyllis, ed. *The Oxford Companion to the Theatre.* 4th ed. New York: Oxford UP, 1983. Provides information on every aspect of the theater; deals with the theater in all ages and in all countries; includes new playwrights and players. *The Concise Oxford Companion to the Theatre,* 1992.

Robertson, Allen, and David Hutera. *The Dance Handbook.* Boston: Hall, 1990. Treats Western ballet and modern dance; does not include ethnic or social dancing; gives factual data and critical evaluations; discusses specific types of ballet, such as classical, romantic; gives the stories of selected ballets.

The Simon and Schuster Book of the Ballet. New York: Simon, 1979. A complete guide from 1581 to 1979.

BIOGRAPHICAL DICTIONARIES[10]

Directory of American Scholars. 8th ed., Vol. II. *English, Speech, and Drama.* Ed. Jaques Cattell Press. New York: Bowker, 1982. Provides information about the education, positions, research, publications, etc., of persons in these fields.

Mapp, Edward. *Directory of Blacks in the Performing Arts.* 2d ed. Metuchen: Scarecrow, 1990. Identifies performers, composers, directors, playwrights, and others, living and not living; emphasizes contemporary American artists.

Robinson, Alice M., Vera Mowry Roberts, and Milly S. Barranger, eds. *Notable Women in the American Theatre: A Biographical Dictionary.* Westport: Greenwood, 1989. Identifies 300 women: actresses, dancers, choreographers, playwrights, designers, critics, agents, and managers who were born in or had their major career in the United States; gives significant achievement, influence, and contribution of each one.

Who's Who in the Theatre. 17th ed. 2 vols. Ed. Ian Herbert. Detroit: Gale, 1981. Vol. 1, *Biographies*, gives biographical information for actors, actresses, directors, playwrights, and other persons associated with the English-speaking stage. Vol. 2, *Playbills*, covers the period 1976–1979 for Broadway, off-Broadway, London, Stratford-on-Avon, and Stratford, Ontario.

---

[10] See also Chapter 10, Biographical Dictionaries.

EXAMPLES OF PROFESSIONAL JOURNALS[11]

Broadcasting: The Fifth Estate. Washington: Broadcasting Magazine, 1931–.
Weekly. Covers tv, radio, cable, etc.; new technology; FCC regulations;
news; and marketing.

Dance Magazine. New York: Dance Magazine, 1926–. Monthly. A general-
coverage dance magazine; includes all aspects of the dance, national and
international (costumes, schools, dance companies, and tours); gives
information about choreographers, dancers, and various kinds of dance
(ballet and modern, ethnic and variety dancing).

Useful Reference Sources in Sports and Recreation

Art, meaning "any skill or aptitude which enables the possessor to perform in
a superior manner," includes sports and other forms of recreation.

There are reference sources which are useful for both the participant and
the spectator in studying and understanding the numerous sports and games.
They include encyclopedias, dictionaries, handbooks, and periodical publications.

ENCYCLOPEDIAS, DICTIONARIES, AND HANDBOOKS

Arlott, John, ed. *The Oxford Companion to World Sports and Games.* New York:
Oxford UP, 1975. Traces the development of specific sports; introduces
the sports that are played in national or international competition; explains the way a sport is played; gives a digest of the rules of each game,
line drawings and diagrams, action photographs; provides information
on prominent players, teams, and stadiums; traces the historical development of each sport; intended to help the reader understand a sport when
watching it for the first time.

*The Baseball Encyclopedia: The Complete and Official Record of Major League
Baseball.* 8th rev. ed. New York: Macmillan, 1990. Gives history, team
and player records, rules, special achievements, statistical tables, and all-
time leaders.

Dickson, Paul. *The Dickson Baseball Dictionary.* New York: Facts on File,
1989. Gives the etymology, meaning, form, and first use of over 5000
baseball terms.

---

[11] See also *Ulrich's International Periodicals Directory*, 31st ed., and *Magazines for Libraries*, 7th ed.,
ed. Bill Katz and Linda S. Katz.

Hollander, Zander, and Alex Sachare. *The Official NBA Basketball Encyclopedia*. New York: Villard, 1989. Traces the game from the first pro game in 1896 to the present; provides statistics for games and players.

Neft, David, and Richard M. Cohen. *The Sports Encyclopedia: Pro Football*. 9th ed., rev. and updated. New York: St. Martin's, 1991. Covers the era 1960–1990; arranged chronologically by season, then every team and its score, player and team statistics; includes playoffs and superbowl games.

Wallechinsky, David. *The Complete Book of the Olympics*. 1992 ed. New York: Little, Brown, 1991. Traces the history of the Olympics; gives statistics for every event since 1896, summer and winter games.

Webster's Sports Dictionary. Springfield: Merriam, 1976. Defines briefly and concisely terms used in the principal sports of the English-speaking countries; gives common sports abbreviations, specifications for playing fields, and discussions of sports equipment, officials' signals, and scoring; has many drawings.

EXAMPLES OF PROFESSIONAL JOURNALS[12]

Journal of Physical Education, Recreation, and Dance. Reston: AHPER, 1896–. Monthly, Sept.–June. Covers physical education and related areas, such as dance, intramural sports, athletics; gives some history; gives news, notes and workshops.

Sports Illustrated. Chicago: Time, 1954–. Weekly. Covers all the usual spectator sports; includes information about sports personalities, sports records, news of interest; has many illustrations. Online from DIALOG.

---

[12] See also *Ulrich's International Periodicals Directory*, 31st ed., and *Magazines for Libraries*, 7th ed., ed. Bill Katz and Linda S. Katz.

Literature

Any discussion of reference and information sources in the field of literature must be prefaced by a definition and a delimiting of the term "literature."

In its broadest sense, "literature" includes all preserved writings. In a more limited but still general denotation, it is the total written works of a people, such as the literature of America or the literature of England. It is also the name given to all writings upon a particular subject, such as the literature of geography, the literature of education, or the literature of history.

Specifically and as a subject area, literature is that class of writing which is notable for imaginative and artistic qualities, form, or expression. The forms of literature are poetry, drama, prose, fiction, and essay. The Dewey Decimal class assigned to literature is 800. In the Library of Congress Classification, literature and language share class P.

Reference sources in the field of literature are more numerous than in any other subject field. There are both print and nonprint materials which cover all forms of literature, and there are both print and nonprint materials in each of the literary genres, such as poetry, drama, and fiction.

Since each print and nonprint source is designed to serve a particular purpose, the representative titles listed below are grouped according to the purposes they serve and the kinds of questions they answer. Distinguishing features are noted with the bibliographical entry.

Useful Reference Sources in Literature

BIBLIOGRAPHIES AND GUIDES[1]

Bibliographies and guides in literature, as in other areas of knowledge, are designed to locate and evaluate the literature of a field. They may group

[1] See also Chapter 13, Bibliographies.

works according to form, such as poetry, drama, fiction, or essay; they may be complete and include all works; or they may be selective, listing only a part of the literature. Not all bibliographies and guides do all these things. These materials are accessible in print forms or online from a database or a CD-ROM.

Atlick, Richard Daniel, and Andrew Wright. *Selective Bibliography for the Study of English and American Literature*. 6th ed. New York: Macmillan, 1979. Provides a guide to a highly selective group of materials for research; includes more than 600 items; lists, does not annotate.

Bateson, Frederick Wilse, et al., eds. *A Guide to English and American Literature*. 3d ed. New York: Gordian, 1976. Formerly *A Guide to English Literature*; now includes American literature and American authors; arranged chronologically according to periods; intended for the serious student of English literature.

Blanck, Jacob, comp. *Bibliography of American Literature*. Vols. 1–9. New Haven: Yale UP, 1955–1990. (In progress.) A selective bibliography limited to the past 150 years of American literature; describes but does not evaluate; arranged chronologically.

Fiction Catalog. 12th ed. New York: Wilson, 1991. An annotated list of more than 500 of the best new and established English-speaking fiction titles, including literary classics and recent popular works; has author, title, and subject index.

Gohdes, Clarence Louis Frank, and Sanford E. Marovitz. *Bibliographical Guide to the Study of the Literature of the U.S.A.* 5th ed. Completely rev. and enl. Durham: Duke UP, 1984. Lists types and sources of bibliography, biography, and other materials on forms and periods of the literature of the United States; includes allied fields such as folklore, theater, history, and literature on or by racial and other minority groups, and materials on methods of research; gives sources on the book trade, publishing, and areas of literary study, e.g., women's studies.

Leary, Lewis Gaston. *Articles on American Literature 1950–1967*. Compiled with the assistance of Carolyn Bartholet and Catharine Roth. Durham: Duke UP, 1970. Based on the quarterly checklists of articles appearing in *American Literature*; supplements author's volume which covered articles from the first half of the century (1900–1950), published in 1954. Continued by *Articles on American Literature: 1968–1975*. Comp. Lewis Leary with John Auchard. Durham: Duke UP, 1979.

The Literary History of the United States: Vol. II, Bibliography. Ed. Robert E. Spiller, et al. New York: Macmillan, 1974. Classifies literature by author, period, and literary type; describes and evaluates.

Ludwig, Richard M. and Clifford A. J. Nault, eds. *Annals of American Literature*. New York: Oxford UP, 1986. Arranges American literature chronologically, with social history, journals, and foreign literature in parallel columns; year by year and alphabetically by author, gives the most influential works of fiction, poetry, drama, and nonfiction published; examines related contributing facts, such as current events, prominent works published abroad as well as in America.

Mainiero, Lina, ed. *American Women Writers: A Critical Reference Guide from Colonial Times to the Present.* 4 vols. New York: Ungar, 1979–1982. Provides bio-bibliographical and critical information about American women writers from colonial times to 1981; includes writers in many subject areas.

Modern Humanities Research Association. *Annual Bibliography of English Language and Literature.* Cambridge: Cambridge UP, 1920–. Annual. Lists books, pamphlets, and periodical articles in English and American literature with references to reviews of works; arranged chronologically.

Modern Language Association of America. *MLA International Bibliography of Books and Articles on the Modern Languages and Literatures.* 1921–. Annual. A classified list of books, articles, and monographs covering general literatures, criticism, linguistics, folklore, and other related topics; lists materials in English and in foreign languages. Available on CD-ROM via WilsonDisc; online via Dialog and WilsonLine.

Reardon, Joan, and Kristine A. Thorsen. *Poetry by American Women, 1900–1975: A Bibliography.* Hamden: Scarecrow, 1979. Lists some 9500 separately published volumes of poetry by more than 5500 American women between 1900 and 1975. *Poetry by American Women, 1975–1989,* 1990.

Rubin, Louis D., Jr., ed. *A Bibliographical Guide to the Study of Southern Literature.* Southern Literary Studies. Baton Rouge: Louisiana State UP, 1969. Aims to be "a compilation of some of the most useful materials available for the student who would begin work in the field of Southern literary study" (Preface); gives discussions of general topics and historical periods and 100 selected writers; covers folklore, drama, popular literature, and local color; gives a checklist of aids to the study of each area. *Southern Literature, 1968–1975,* compiled by the Committee on Bibliography of the Society for the Study of Southern Literature (Boston: Hall, 1978), contains the annotated entries from the annual checklists published in the spring issue of the *Mississippi Quarterly.*

Stapleton, Michael. *The Cambridge Guide to English Literature.* Cambridge: Cambridge UP, 1984. Gives factual information about authors, major works, literary terms, subjects and periods; articles are brief; arranged alphabetically. Includes writings in English of all English-speaking countries.

Watson, George, ed. *The Concise Cambridge Bibliography of English Literature, 600—1950.* 2d ed. Cambridge: Cambridge UP, 1965. Lists books (and a few articles) about some 400 English writers; includes significant works by and about each writer; provides a concise statement of the bibliography of all periods of English literature through the early twentieth century; includes only writers native to or mainly resident in the British Isles.

————, ed. *The New Cambridge Bibliography of English Literature.* 5 vols. Cambridge: Cambridge UP, 1969–1977. Covers works by and about authors in both primary and secondary sources; covers belles lettres, philosophy, book publication, religion, history, travel, education, sports, newspapers, and magazines; the location of manuscripts and papers of some authors is given; Vol. V, *Index*, comp. J. D. Pickles, 1977.

INDEXES[2]

An index in the field of literature locates an article in a periodical or locates a poem, quotation, fairy story, play, essay, or other work in an anthology. Since the person seeking information does not always know the title and the author of a poem, play, or essay, a means of locating these items by subject is also necessary. It may be necessary to locate quotations by means of key words. The following indexes provide some or all of these kinds of listings; they are representative of the indexes available.

Chapman, Dorothy. *Index to Poetry by Black American Women.* Westport: Greenwood, 1986. First of a two-volume work, provides information about black women poets from 1746 to the present; covers more than 80 authors and over 4000 poems from 400 publishers.

Essay and General Literature Index. New York: Wilson, 1934–. Semiannual. Indexes, by author and subject, collections of essays and other collected works in many areas, particularly in the humanities and the social sciences; emphasizes literary criticism, indexes only twentieth-century publications, but includes authors of all ages and nationalities. Print; CD-ROM on WilsonDisc; online on WilsonLine.

The Columbia Granger's Index to Poetry. 9th ed. New York: Columbia UP, 1990. Indexes, by title, first line, and subject, poems appearing in anthologies published through June 1989.

Columbia Granger's World of Poetry. New York: Columbia UP, 1990. This CD-ROM provides access to more than 90,000 poems in anthologies plus the full text of 8000 classic poems and quotations. Includes *Granger's Index to Poetry*, 8th ed., the *Columbia Granger's Index to Poetry*, 9th ed., and *Dictionary of Poetry Quotations.*

Humanities Index. New York: Wilson, 1974–. Quarterly. Indexes by author and subject 295 English language periodicals in the humanities; includes

[2] See also Chapter 9, Indexes.

poems, short stories, and other fiction in the periodicals as well as essays. In print; online on WilsonLine; CD-ROM on WilsonDisc.

Ottemiller's Index to Plays in Collections. 7th ed., rev. and enl. Ed. John M. Connor and Billie M. Connor. Metuchen: Scarecrow, 1988. Indexes, by author and title, plays which appear in collections published from 1900 through early 1985.

Play Index. 7 vols. New York: Wilson, 1953–1987. Covers plays published from 1949 to 1986, including plays in collections; single plays; radio, television, and Broadway plays; and plays for children and young adults. Gives plot, cast, set, and other information; lists plays under author, title, and subject.

Short Story Index. New York: Wilson, 1953–. Annual. Indexes by author, title, and subject short stories in more than 8000 collections published 1900–1988 and 300 stories in periodicals published 1974–1988. 9 vols. to date.

Sutton, Roberta B. *Speech Index*, 4th ed., rev. and enl. New York: Scarecrow, 1966. Indexes world-famous orations and speeches for various occasions found in more than 250 collected works; covers works published through 1965; four *Supplements* cover the period 1966–1988.

BOOK REVIEWS[3]

A book review is a notice, usually in a periodical publication, of a current book or play. Its purpose is to tell enough about the work under consideration to enable the reader to decide whether or not to read it. Therefore, it describes the subject matter, discusses the method and technical qualities, and may examine the work's value or usefulness when it is compared with similar works. A book review may be only descriptive; it may also be critical and evaluative. Among the sources of book reviews are the book review sections of newspapers, notably *The New York Times Book Review*; professional and scholarly journals which review materials in specific subject fields, for example, *The American Historical Review*; trade publications, which announce and sometimes promote newly published books (see Chapter 13, Bibliographies); and bibliographies in the subject fields. The sources below cover book reviews in several fields and in several kinds of publications.

Book Review Digest. New York: Wilson, 1905–. Monthly except February and July. Indexes reviews of books published or distributed in the United States, Britain, and Canada which appear in more than ninety-five periodicals and journals; each book reviewed is entered by author, with a descriptive note; gives citations to all reviews (which appear in the periodicals indexed) and excerpts from selected reviews; indicates the

---

[3] See also Chapter 9, Indexes.

number of words in the review; has a title and subject index in each issue
and a cumulated subject and title index every five years, covering the
preceding five-year period. (See Figure 9.1, page 100.) Online on
WilsonLine; CD-ROM on WilsonDisc; also available in print.

Book Review Index. Detroit: Gale, 1965–. Bimonthly; annual cumulations. An
index to reviews appearing in more than 300 periodicals (both magazines
and newspapers) including the major adult and children's book review-
ing media and many special-interest magazines; gives book title, name,
date, and pages of the publication in which the review is located; does
not give excerpts from the reviews. Since 1976, has a title index.

An Index to Book Reviews in the Humanities. Vol. 1, No. 1, March 1960–.
Williamston: Philip Thomson, 1960–. Annual. Indexes reviews appearing in English in some 700 periodicals, American and foreign; does not
include theology and archaeology; does not give excerpts from reviews.

DICTIONARIES AND ENCYCLOPEDIAS

Dictionaries and encyclopedias of literature define words and phrases; identify references to fictional, mythical, and legendary places, characters, and
events; explain the historical, geographical, social, economic, and cultural
backgrounds of literature; provide biographical and critical information
about authors and their works; and in some cases give pronunciation, summaries of plots, and bibliographical references. Some useful dictionaries and
encyclopedias of literature follow.

Dictionaries

Baldick, Chris. *The Concise Dictionary of Literary Terms.* New York: Oxford
UP, 1990. Aims to clarify words and terms most often confusing to
students and general readers; terms are from literature, history, criticism, and drama; gives pronunciation, illustrative examples, and use.

Bédé, Jean-Albert, and William B. Edgerton. *Columbia Dictionary of Modern
European Literature.* 2d ed., rev. and enl. New York: Columbia UP,
1980. Covers the period from the end of the nineteenth century to the
present; gives biographical and critical discussions of authors and over-
views of the various national literatures, arranged alphabetically; provides brief biographies.

Cuddon, J. A. *A Dictionary of Literary Terms and Literary Theory.* Cambridge:
Cambridge UP, 1991. Defines terminology used in literary criticism.

Hammond, N. G. L., and H. H. Scullard, comps. *The Oxford Classical
Dictionary.* 2d ed. Oxford: Oxford UP, 1970. Revised in light of new
discoveries and recent scholarship; covers ancient Greek and Roman
periods; includes archaeology, geography, history, literature, mythol-

ogy, philosophy, religion, and science; arranged alphabetically by topic; includes bibliographies.

Pickering, David, Alan Isaacs, and Elizabeth Martin, eds. *Brewer's Dictionary of Twentieth Century Phrase and Fable*. Boston: Houghton, 1992. Emphasizes literary characters, political events, popular culture, popular movements, and slang expressions of the twentieth century.

Reed, Joyce, M. H., ed. *The Concise Dictionary of French Literature*. New York: Oxford UP, 1976. An abridgment and updated version of the *Oxford Companion to French Literature* (1959); reflects developments since 1959; gives essential facts on writers, works, forms, genres, and trends that have influenced French literature.

Encyclopedias

Cassell's Encyclopedia of World Literature. Rev. and enl. Ed. J. Buchanan-Brown. 3 vols. New York: Morrow, 1973. Provides general articles on literary genres, movements, and terms; brief histories of national literature and biographical articles; aims to cover all periods and peoples.

Klein, Leonard S., ed. *Encyclopedia of World Literature in the 20th Century*. New ed. 4 vols. New York: Ungar, 1981–1984. Contains essays on national literature; critical articles on individual writers; covers more than eighty-five Asian and African literatures; has pictures, bibliographies, and index.

Preminger, Alex, et al., eds. *Princeton Encyclopedia of Poetry and Poetics*. Enlarged ed. Princeton: Princeton UP, 1974. Covers the full range of poetry from oral tradition to recent trends (history, theory, technique, and criticism); international in scope; provides entries on the history of each major body of world poetry.

Tierney, Helen, ed. *Women's Studies Encyclopedia*. Westport: Greenwood, 1989–. A projected three-volume work, it will cover women's contribution to the sciences, literature, arts and language, history, philosophy, and religion.

HANDBOOKS

Handbooks provide short, concise answers to questions about literary authors, terminology, works, and trends; movements affecting literature; and events, places, and characters referred to in literature. The Oxford Companions, which are listed below, provide this kind of information, although each volume may vary in points of emphasis. The other handbooks listed provide some or all of the types of information mentioned above.

Renét's Reader's Encyclopedia. 3d ed. New York: Harper, 1987. Covers all nations and all peoples; explains literary expressions and terms; identifies literary schools and movements; describes plots and characters; gives information on musical compositions, works of art, writers, philosophers, scientists and musicians; treats myths, legends, and folklore; lists recipients of major literary awards; covers both classic and contemporary literature.

Blain, Vivian, et al., eds. *The Feminist Companion to Literature in English: Women Writers from the Middle Ages to the Present.* New Haven, Yale UP, 1990. Discusses the writings of some 2700 women writing in English in various English-speaking cultures; includes popular forms such as memoirs, diaries, and travel.

Brewer's Dictionary of Phrase and Fable. 14th ed. Ed. Ivor H. Evans. New York: Haper, 1989. Emphasizes the unusual; includes words which are not in the traditional dictionary; defines, identifies, and explains words, phrases, and allusions in nonfiction, folklore, and legend; gives pronunciation for some words; universal in scope.

Burke, W. J., and Will D. Howe, eds. *American Authors and Books.* 3d rev. ed. Rev. Irving Weiss and Anne Weiss. New York: Crown, 1972. Has articles on authors, books, periodicals, newspapers, publishing firms, literary societies, regions, and locations in the United States; primarily about authors and their works; secondarily about aspects of American literature; covers all types of writing, including western and detective stories; limited to the United States; covers the period 1940–1970.

Deutsch, Babette. *Poetry Handbook: A Dictionary of Terms.* 4th ed. New York: Funk & Wagnalls, 1974. Defines and explains literary terms; arranged alphabetically.

Drabble, Margaret. *The Oxford Companion to English Literature.* 5th ed. New York: Oxford UP, 1985. Broad in scope, provides information about classical allusions in literature; gives biographical and background material; identifies characters; offers brief synopses of literary topics, institutions, and movements. Appendixes include treatment of censorship, English copyright law, and the calendar.

Frye, Northrop, et al., eds. *The Harper Handbook to Literature.* New York: Harper, 1984. Defines literary terms and phrases; covers forms, styles, movements and periods.

Hart, James David. *The Oxford Companion to American Literature.* 5th ed. New York: Oxford UP, 1983. Provides biographical information on American authors; gives summaries of American literary works: novels, poems, essays, short stories, and plays; discusses movements and events that influenced American literature; presents literary and social history of America from 1578 to 1982 in chronological listing in parallel columns.

Harvey, Paul, and Janet E. Heseltine, eds. *The Oxford Companion to French Literature.* New York: Oxford UP, 1961. Surveys French literary life from the emergence of the vernacular.

Holman, Hugh, and William Harmon. *A Handbook to Literature*. 5th ed. New York: Macmillan, 1986. A comprehensive dictionary of terminology and literary history and criticism; defines and explains terms, words, phrases, and movements peculiar' to English and American literature; emphasizes terminology related to literary study.

Howatson, M. C., ed. *The Oxford Companion to Classical Literature*. New York: Oxford UP, 1989. Covering the period from 2200 B. C. through the Renaissance, provides information on the backgrounds of classical literature: the theater, authors, religion, philosophy, politics, places, literary works, historical figures, myths, etc.; gives chronological tables and maps.

The Penguin Companion to World Literature. 4 vols. New York: McGraw, 1971. The four volumes cover English literature; European literature; American literature; and classical, oriental, and African literature. Includes biography, critical evaluation of work, plot, and bibliography for each entry.

Perkins, George, Barbara Perkins, and Phillip Leininger, eds. *Benét's Reader's Encyclopedia of American Literature*. New York: HarperCollins, 1991. Covers American literature from the period of European exploration to the early 1900s; includes literature of the United States, Canada, and Latin America; gives factual information about thousands of authors, significant texts, movements, and ideas in literature and the related arts; points out religious, social, political influences on literature; includes biographical information.

Salzman, Jack. *The Cambridge Handbook of American Literature*. Cambridge: Cambridge UP, 1986. Treats the major landmarks in American literature; covers 500 authors from Henry Adams to the present; includes novels, plays, poetry, and historical narratives; emphasis is on authors; includes literary movements, literary magazines; gives chronological tables of American history and literature.

Toye, William, ed. *The Oxford Companion to Canadian Literature*. New York: Oxford UP, 1983. Surveys periods of literature; ethnic literature, e.g., Indian, Yiddish; literary genres, e.g., fiction, drama, poetry, folklore, science fiction; covers writers of French and French Canadian literature; provides literary and historical background; gives attention to the period since WWII.

BOOK DIGESTS

Magill, Frank N., ed. *Masterpieces of World Literature in Digest Form*. Series 1–4. New York: Harper, 1952–1969. Emphasizes poetry and philosophical works; has some essay-type reviews; is universal in scope.

———. *Masterplots*. Rev. ed. Story ed., Dayton Koehler. 12 vols. Englewood

Cliffs: Salem, 1976. "2,010 plot stories and essay reviews from the world's fine literature" (subtitle); begun in 1949, now covers more than 1000 authors; arranged alphabetically by title, gives plot summaries and essay-reviews of each; identifies form, author, period, type of plot, locale, date of first publication, principal characters, and themes; gives an evaluation of the work; poems, philosophy, and speeches have essay-reviews only.

————. *Masterplots II: Drama Series*. 4 vols. Pasadena: Salem, 1990. Summarizes the plots of 327 plays, popular and serious, by 148 twentieth-century authors, British or American. For each drama, gives the author, type of plot, locale, date first produced and published, and the number of characters.

BOOKS OF QUOTATIONS

Books of quotations provide (1) quotations on a subject for speeches or papers and (2) the correct wording and source of a given quotation. There are many collections of quotations; each one includes some quotations omitted in others, and thus they supplement each other. The usefulness of a book of quotations depends on (1) the kind of quotations included, (2) the kind of reference provided (name of author, work from which the quotation is taken, collection in which it can be located, with page, stanza, or line), and (3) the ways each quotation is indexed (author, title, subject, first line, key word). Some useful collections of quotations follow.

Augarde, Tony. *The Oxford Dictionary of Modern Quotations*. New York: Oxford UP, 1991. Offers about 5000 of the most widely known and used popular quotations from books, magazines, newspapers, novels, plays, speeches, films, radio, television, advertising, etc.; quotations are from persons living after 1900; gives a printed source for all quotations.

Bartlett, John. *Familiar Quotations*. 15th ed., rev. and enl.; 125th anniversary ed. Ed. Emily Morison Beck and the staff of Little, Brown and Company. Boston: Little, Brown, 1980. "A collection of passages, phrases and proverbs traced to their sources in ancient and modern literature" (subtitle). Arranged by author chronologically by birth dates; quotations arranged under author chronologically; keyword index; includes quotations from many contemporary authors.

Bartlett, John. *Familiar Quotations*. 16th ed. Ed. Justin Kaplan. Boston: Little, 1992. Follows the format of previous editions; quotations date from ancient to modern times and include many from contemporary sources; women, minorities, and popular personalities are represented.

Bohle, Bruce. *The Home Book of American Quotations*. New York: Dodd, 1967. Companion volume to Stevenson's *Home Book of Quotations*; emphasizes distinctly American subjects and American writers and speakers who have commented on them; quotations are exclusively American and chiefly contemporary; sources are American or deal specifically with America.

Magill, Frank Northen. *Magill's Quotations in Context*. 2 vols. New York: Harper, 1966. Offers quotations of prose, poetry, and proverbs from all periods of western literature in context, with emphasis on English and American writers; arranged alphabetically with historical background information. *Second Series*, 1969.

Mieder, Wolfgang, Stewart Kingsbury, and Kelsie Harder, eds. *A Dictionary of American Proverbs*. New York: Oxford UP, 1991. A collection of more than 15,000 proverbs, adages, and maxims in common use in the United States and Canada; based on oral, not written sources; includes traditional proverbs from Biblical, classical, and European literature which are in common use.

The Oxford Dictionary of English Proverbs. 3d ed. Rev. by F. P. Wilson. Oxford: Clarendon, 1970. Arranged alphabetically; gives dated uses in chronological order. *Concise Oxford Dictionary of English Proverbs*. Ed. by J. A. Simpson. 1983.

The Oxford Dictionary of Quotations. 3d ed. New York: Oxford UP, 1989. A comprehensive collection of quotations from English and foreign authors; thousands of new quotations reflecting recent events and writers have been added, including quotations from politicians and public figures; arranged alphabetically by author with an extensive keyword index.

Partnow, Elaine. *The New Quotable Woman from Eve to the Present*. Rev. and updated. New York: Facts on File, 1992. Gives noteworthy quotations from women from the beginning to the present; arranged chronologically; gives brief biographical information about the more than 800 women quoted.

Quotation Database, the online version of *The Oxford Dictionary of Quotations*, 3d ed., 1980.

Stevenson, Burton Egbert, ed. *The Home Book of Quotations, Classical and Modern*. 10th ed. New York: Dodd, 1967. Provides quotations from important contemporary figures; arranged alphabetically by subject.

BIOGRAPHICAL DICTIONARIES[4]

General encyclopedias, biographical dictionaries, handbooks, and histories of literature provide much information on the lives and works of authors. In

---

[4] See also Chapter 10, Biographical Dictionaries.

addition to these sources, there are biographical dictionaries devoted exclusively to authors.

Contemporary Authors. 4-vol. cumulations. Detroit: Gale, 1962–. Vols. 1 to 134 in print, 1992. Aims to be an up-to-date source of bio-bibliographical information on authors in many fields and of many nationalities; includes little-known authors. On CD-ROM with *Dictionary of Literary Biography* and volumes from *Literary Criticism—Authors*. Title of the disk: *Discovering Authors*.

Dictionary of Literary Biography. Detroit: Gale, 1978–. A multi-volume series, each volume treats a specific literary movement or period in bio-critical essays; gives personal and career information and discussion of all major works; arranged alphabetically; 108 volumes had been published by 1991. On CD-ROM.

Evory, Ann, ed. *Contemporary Authors*. Rev. Series. Detroit: Gale, 1981–. Gives biographical and bibliographical information about current writers in fiction, nonfiction, drama, motion pictures, television, and other fields. Vols. 1–36 in 1992.

Kunitz, Stanley J. and Howard Haycraft, eds. *The Junior Book of Authors*. 2d ed., rev. New York: Wilson, 1951. Covers the lives of writers and illustrators of books for young readers from Lewis Carroll and Louisa M. Alcott to the present time. Companion volumes are *More Junior Authors* (1963), *Third Book of Junior Authors* (1972), *Fourth Book of Junior Authors & Illustrators* (1978), *Fifth Book of Junior Authors and Illustrators* (1983), and *Sixth Book of Junior Authors and Illustrators* (1989).

Newby, James Edward. *Black Authors: A Selected Annotated Bibliography*. New York: Garland, 1990. Lists black American and selected African and Caribbean writers in the social sciences and humanities from 1845 to 1990; has some annotations.

Rush, Theressa Gunnels, et al., eds. *Black American Writers Past and Present: A Biographical and Bibliographical Dictionary*. 2 vols. Metuchen: Scarecrow, 1975. Covers the period from the early eighteenth century to the present; gives brief biographical information, list of works, some quotations from the author, and references to critical materials on the author; includes more than 2000 authors; writers from Africa and the West Indies who live in or publish in the United States are included.

Showalter, Elaine, ed. *Modern American Women Writers*. New York: Scribner's 1991. Offers critical and evaluative biographical essays for more than forty women writers who have published in the United States since the 1870s, representing a wide range of social/ethnic groups.

Smith, Valerie, et al., eds. *African-American Writers*. New York: Scribner's 1991. Introduces works of African-American writers who have made a significant contribution to American literature, society, and history; for each one, gives a brief biography, principal writings, an appraisal of work, and references for further study.

The Wilson Authors Series. New York: Wilson, 1936–1985. This series provides biographical information about some 9000 authors living from about 800 B.C. to 1985. The eleven-volume series includes:

Grant, Michael. *Greek and Latin Authors: 800 B.C.–A.D. 1000.* 1980.

Kunitz, Stanley J., and Vineta Colby, eds. *European Authors 1000–1900: A Biographical Dictionary of European Literature.* 1967.

Kunitz, Stanley J., and Howard Haycraft, eds. *American Authors: 1600–1900.* 1938.

————, eds. *British Authors before 1800.* 1952.

————, eds. *British Authors of the Nineteenth Century.* 1936.

————, eds. *Twentieth Century Authors.* 1942.

————, eds. *Twentieth Century Authors, First Supplement.* 1955.

Wakeman, John, ed. *World Authors, 1950–1970.* 1975.

————, ed. *World Authors, 1970–1975.* 1979.

Colby, Vineta, ed. *World Authors, 1975–1980.* 1985.

Index to the Wilson Authors Series. Rev., 1991.

CRITICISM

American Writers. 6 vols. New York: Scribner's, 1974. *Supplement*, 1979. 2 vols. A collection of 155 articles of literary criticism covering authors from the seventeenth century to the present; gives information about the author's life, style, and genre, and an analysis and evaluation of his or her works; includes poets, novelists, essayists, playwrights, short story writers, and philosophers. *Supplement I*, 1974; *Supplement II*, 1981; *Supplement III*, 1991. 2 vols.

Contemporary Literary Criticism. Ed. Sharon R. Gunton. Detroit: Gale, 1972–. A continuing series, provides lengthy excerpts from current criticism of major authors and playwrights now living (or deceased since 1960); 68 vols. in print in 1991.

Curley, Dorothy Nyren, et al. *Modern American Literature.* A Library of Literary Criticism. 4th enl. ed. 3 vols. New York: Ungar, 1969. An index to hundreds of critical books, essays, articles, and reviews dealing with works of some 300 important twentieth-century American poets, novelists, dramatists, essayists; includes excerpts from the criticism. Vol. IV: *Supplement* to the 4th ed., 1976. *Second Supplement*, comp. Paul Schlueter, et al., 1985. *Third Supplement*, comp. Paul Schlueter, et al., 1992.

Davis, Lloyd. *Contemporary American Poetry: A Checklist.* Metuchen: Scarecrow, 1980. Lists interpretations of poetry of British and American writers published in America. *Second Series*, 1973–1982.

Eddlemen, Floyd Eugene, comp. *American Drama Criticism: Interpretations 1890–1977*. 2d ed. Hamden: Shoe String, 1979. "Lists interpretations of American plays published 1890–1977 in books, periodicals, and monographs" (Preface). *Supplement One*, 1984.

Eichelberger, Clayton L., comp. *A Guide to Critical Reviews of United States Fiction 1870–1910*. Metuchen: Scarecrow, 1971. Lists reviews from thirty American and English periodicals, including some regional sources, of the period covered. Vol. II, 1974; covers ten additional periodicals.

Gerstenberger, Donna, comp. *The American Novel: A Checklist of Twentieth Century Criticism on Novels Written since 1789*. 2 vols. Chicago: Swallow, 1970. Vol. I: *The American Novel 1789–1959*; Vol. II: *Criticism Written 1960–1968*. Does not include reviews; is a listing by novelist of critical writings on particular works.

Guide to American Poetry Explication. Boston: Hall, 1989. Vol. I: *Colonial and Nineteenth Century*, ed. James Ruppert; and Vol. II: *Modern and Contemporary*, ed. John R. Leo. Indexes explications published through 1987.

Inge, Thomas, et al., eds. *Black American Writers: Bibliographical Essays*. 2 vols. New York: St. Martin's 1978. Identifies and evaluates bibliographies, editions, manuscript material, biographies, and criticism for major black American writers.

Kearney, Elizabeth, and Louise S. Fitzgerald, comps. *The Continental Novel: A Checklist of Criticism in English, 1900–1966*. Metuchen: Scarecrow, 1968. Lists criticism from books and periodicals of the period covered. *1967–1980*, ed. Louise Fitzgerald, 1983.

Kuntz, Joseph M., and Nancy E. Martinez. *Poetry Explication: A Checklist of Interpretation Since 1925 of British and American Poems, Past and Present*. 3d ed. Boston: Hall, 1980. Indexes poetry explications in collected works and literary periodicals.

Luce, T. James, ed. *Ancient Writers: Greece and Rome*. 2 vols. New York: Scribner's, 1982. Introduces the classical writers in clear nontechnical style; covers the entire Classical Age.

Magill, Frank Northen, ed. *Magill's Bibliography of Literary Criticism*. 4 vols. Englewood Cliffs: Salem, 1979. "Selected sources for the study of more than 2,500 outstanding works of Western literature" (subtitle). Emphasizes criticism published in the 1960s and 1970s.

Palmer, Helen H. *European Drama Criticism 1900–1975*. Hamden: Shoe String, 1977. A checklist of criticism in books and periodicals in English and foreign languages; extends coverage through 1975.

Palmer, Helen H., and Anne Jane Dyson, comps. *English Novel Explication: Criticisms to 1972*. Hamden: Shoe String, 1972. A checklist of critical articles arranged alphabetically by author and then by novel; lists criticism from 1957 to 1972 which is found in books and journals. Four *Supplements* cover the period 1975–1990.

Scott-Kilvert, Ian, ed. *British Writers*. 8 vols. New York: Scribner's, 1979–1984. A survey of major British writers from Langland and Chaucer to the present; gives for each author a biographical sketch, survey and evaluation of the author's principal works, and a bibliography of works by and about the author. *Supplement I*, 1987, adds writers who have become prominent during the period 1950–1980. *Supplement II*, ed. George Stade, 1991.

Stade, George, et al., eds. *European Writers*. 14 vols. New York: Scribner's, 1983–1991. Gives biographical sketches, and plot summaries; emphasis is on criticism; examines events which influenced an author; covers Middle Ages to the twentieth century. *European Writers: The Twentieth Century*, 1991.

Temple, Ruth Z., and Martin Tucker, eds. *Modern British Literature. A Library of Literary Criticism*. 3 vols. New York: Ungar, 1966. Presents over 400 twentieth-century British and Commonwealth authors, giving excerpts from criticism of their works found in British and American sources; includes bibliography of author's works. Vol. IV, 1975.

Todd, Janet. *A Dictionary of British and American Women Writers 1660–1800*. Totowa, N. J.: Rowman and Allanheld, 1985. In bio-critical essays, provides information on 500 women writers, their achievement and place in literary history.

Tucker, Martin, ed. *The Critical Temper: A Survey of Modern Criticism on English and American Literature from the Beginnings to the Twentieth Century*. 3 vols. New York: Ungar, 1969. Gives a view of the best twentieth-century criticism; shows wide range of thought within the criticism; gives excerpts from criticism and bibliographical references. Vol. IV (1979) adds criticism published during the past ten years.

Walker, Warren S. *Twentieth Century Short Story Explication*. 3d ed. Hamden: Shoe String, 1977. A bibliography of explications published in books, monographs, and periodicals; explications are listed alphabetically by critic's name; coverage is through 1975. Four supplements cover 1980–1989.

YEARBOOKS

American Literary Scholarship. 1963–. Durham: Duke UP, 1963–. Annual. Reviews the year's work in American literature.

Year's Work in English Studies. London: English Assoc., 1921–. Annual. Surveys studies of English literature appearing in books and periodicals published in Britain, Europe, and America; includes material on the English language and on American literature.

EXAMPLES OF PROFESSIONAL AND LITERARY JOURNALS[5]

American Literature: A Journal of Literary History, Criticism and Bibliography. Durham: Duke, 1929–. Quarterly. Published with the cooperation of the American Literature Section of the Modern Language Association; gives research articles on history, criticism, and bibliography of American literature; includes critical book reviews; reports dissertations completed or under way and research in progress.

Poetry. Chicago: Poetry, 1912–. Monthly. Publishes work of poets from the least known to the best established; offers essays on poetry and critical reviews of books about poetry.

Sewanee Review: A Library Quarterly Devoted to Criticism, Fiction, and Poetry. Sewanee: Univ. of the South, 1892–. Quarterly. The oldest literary magazine in the United States; contains original fiction, poetry, book reviews, essays, and recent criticism on literary figures.

ABSTRACT JOURNAL

Abstracts of English Studies. Calgary: U of Calgary P, 1958–. Four times a year, Sept.–June. Contains abstracts of articles on English and American literature from both American and foreign journals; each issue has a subject index.

---

[5] See also *Ulrich's International Periodicals Directory*, 31st ed., and *Magazines for Libraries*, 7th ed., ed. by Bill Katz and Linda S. Katz.

CHAPTER

🌿 24 🌿

History and Geography

History

History is the area of study which is concerned with the recording of past events and with the interpretations of the relationships and significance of these events. It is divided into ancient, medieval, and modern, and each of these divisions may be subdivided geographically, as the history of medieval Europe or the history of modern England. History can be subdivided further into its economic, cultural, social, political, military, and literary aspects. The history class of the Dewey Decimal Classification System, 900, includes geography. G is assigned to geography in the Library of Congress Classification; C, D, E, and F are the classes assigned to history and its subdivisions.

Many of the general reference sources—encyclopedias, dictionaries, handbooks, atlases, gazetteers, indexes, and bibliographies—provide material in the field of history. There are, however, specialized reference materials that have been prepared for the primary purpose of aiding students of history. They include bibliographies, guides, indexes, encyclopedias, chronologies, handbooks, dictionaries, historical atlases, general histories, and professional journals.[1]

Representative Reference Sources in History

BIBLIOGRAPHIES, GUIDES AND INDEXES[2]

America: History and Life. Santa Barbara: ABC-Clio, 1964–. Five issues per
    year. *Part A: Article Abstracts and Citations* offers abstracts and citations

---

[1] See also Chapter 14, Nonbook Information Sources, and Chapter 10, Government Publications.

[2] See also Chapter 9, Indexes, and Chapter 13, Bibliographies.

of articles on the history and culture of the United States and Canada from prehistoric times to the present from more than 2000 serial publications in 30 languages. *Part B: Index to Book Reviews* is an index to book reviews in more than 100 journals published in the United States and Canada. *Part C: American History Bibliography* lists books, articles, and dissertations. *Part D: Annual Index*. In print, online, and on CD-ROM. Since Vol. 26, abstracts, reviews, and citations are published together in the first four issues; the fifth issue is the Annual Index.

Freidel, Frank, ed. *Harvard Guide to American History*. Rev. ed. 2 vols. Cambridge: Harvard UP, 1974. A selection of the more important works; covers research methods and materials, biographies, general histories, and histories of special subjects; includes political science, constitutional and economic history; intended for the intelligent general reader, student, and scholar.

Frey, Linda, and others. *Women in Western European History*. 2 vols. Westport: Greenwood, 1982–1984. V. I: *Antiquity to the French Revolution*. V. II: *19th and 20th Centuries*. "A select chronological, geographical, and topical bibliography" (subtitle). Lists more than 17,000 citations from books and articles covering major topics relating to women, such as marriage, politics, education, and religion; *First Supplement*, 1986, adds more than 6500 citations from books and articles, United States and foreign.

Fritze, Ronald H., Brian E. Coutts, and Louis A. Vyhnanek. *Reference Sources in History: An Introductory Guide*. Santa Barbara: ABC-CLIO, 1990. Aims to provide an introduction to the major reference works for all periods of history and all geographical areas.

Harrison, Cynthia E. *Women in American History: A Bibliography*. Vol. II. Santa Barbara: ABC-Clio, 1985. Abstracts cover American history and life from periodical literature in history and related sources from 1976 to 1984; lists articles relating to women in such areas as women and religion, women and politics, women and education. Vol. I, 1979.

Humanities Index (See pp. 238–239)

Paetow, Louis John. *A Guide to the Study of Medieval History*. Rev. ed. Prepared under the auspices of the Medieval Academy of America. New York: Kraus Reprint Corporation, 1959. Lists general books useful in the study of medieval history; provides readings to accompany the study of major areas of medieval history; gives some critical notes. *Literature of Medieval History 1930–1975: A Supplement to Louis John Paetow's A Guide to the Study of Medieval History*. Compiled and edited by Gray Cowan Boyce. Millwood, N.Y.: Kraus International Publications, 1981, 5 vols.

DICTIONARIES AND ENCYCLOPEDIAS

Bedini, Silvio, ed. *The Christopher Columbus Encyclopedia*. 2 vols. New York: Simon, 1991. Views the age of exploration from the late fifteenth century to the middle of the seventeenth century; treats the life of Columbus, his writings, and the controversies surrounding him; discusses the Columbian legacy in literature, the arts, popular culture; gives information about other men and women of the period; provides numerous maps, documents; and facsimiles.

Brownstone, David, M. and Irene M. Franck. *Dictionary of 20th Century History*. New York: Prentice, 1990. Identifies the significant people, movements, ideas and discoveries of the twentieth century; treats politics, economics, religion, science, medicine, the military, and cultural influences.

Carruth, Gorton. *The Encyclopedia of American Facts and Dates*. 8th ed. rev. New York: Harper, 1987. Presents some 15,000 facts and dates arranged by subject in chronological order from A.D. 986 through July 4, 1986; includes events in four fields of interest: politics and government, literature and the arts, sciences, and sports.

Champion, Sara. *A Dictionary of Terms and Techniques in Archaeology*. New York: Facts on File, 1980. Explains terms dealing with artifact analysis and classification, soil analysis, ceramics, excavation, stone tools, dating methods, and other techniques; has many illustrations.

Dictionary of American History. Rev. ed. 8 vols. New York: Scribner's 1976. Provides coverage of almost all aspects of American history; does not include biographical entries. Vol. 8 is the index. *Concise Dictionary of American History*, 1982.

Drexel, John, ed. *The Facts on File Encyclopedia of the 20th Century*. New York: Facts on File, 1991. Offers articles on the most significant places, events, and scientific and artistic developments of this century; includes prominent figures from politics, literature, medicine, and sports; all countries of the world are included; has black-and-white illustrations and 250 maps.

Dupuy, R. Ernest, and Trevor N. Dupuy. *The Encyclopedia of Military History from 3500 B.C. to the Present*. 2d rev. ed. New York: Harper, 1987. A survey of the history of wars and military affairs; offers a series of narratives on these topics; organized chronologically by period; each period is prefaced by an essay on military trends and followed by a chronological arrangement of events and battles; gives a list of nations that have achieved independence since World War II.

Grant, Michael. *A Guide to the Ancient World*. New York: Wilson, 1986. "A dictionary of classical places and names." Includes maps.

Kohn, George C. *Dictionary of Wars*. New York: Facts on File, 1986. Concisely describes major human conflicts from 2000 B.C. to the present; gives the name of the war, dates, how it began, outcome or significance; alphabetically arranged by key word.

Morris, Richard B., ed. *Encyclopedia of American History*. 6th ed. New York: Harper, 1982. Cites essential historical facts about American life and institutions in both chronological and topical arrangements from the period of discovery; gives attention to recent developments in science and technology, to minorities and ethnic groups, and to film, dance, and popular music; includes biographical information for 500 notable Americans.

Olson, James S., ed. *Dictionary of the Vietnam War*. Westport: Greenwood, 1988. Covers locations of the Vietnam War, concepts, key people; gives biographical information and bibliographies.

Parrish, Thomas, ed. *The Simon and Schuster Encyclopedia of World War II*. New York: Simon, 1978. Aims to cover every aspect of the war: issues, strategy, campaigns, battles, intelligence sources, conferences, treaties, ships, airplanes, guns, and persons connected with the war. Has maps and photographs; arranged alphabetically.

Roller, David D., and Robert W. Twyman. *The Encyclopedia of Southern History*. Baton Rouge: Louisiana State UP, 1979. Arranged alphabetically; treats all aspects of southern history from the first discoveries of the Spanish in the fifteenth century to 1978: historical events, biographical information, history of each southern state—its art, literature, agriculture, economics, industry, music, folklore, and humor; defines and discusses usage of regional expressions; has maps and tables.

Sherratt, Andres, ed. *The Cambridge Encyclopedia of Archaeology*. New York: Crown, 1980. Concentrates on the contributions of archaeology to our knowledge of human culture; covers history and techniques; gives chronologies, has maps and charts.

Stillwell, Richard, ed. *The Princeton Encyclopedia of Classical Sites*. Princeton: Princeton UP, 1976. Presents more than 2200 articles on the archaeology of Greek and Roman civilization covering the period 750 B.C. to A.D. 565; gives sources for further reading.

Strayer, Joseph R., ed. *Dictionary of the Middle Ages*. 13 vols. New York: Scribner's, 1982–1989. Published under the auspices of the American Council of Learned Societies; covers the intellectual, cultural, philosophical, and socioeconomic accomplishments of western Europe, Byzantium, Islam, and the Slavic world from about 500 to 1500; articles range in length from brief descriptions and definitions to monographic treatment of major medieval subjects; includes biographies; each article has a bibliography. Vol. 13, Index, 1989.

Teed, Peter. *A Dictionary of Twentieth Century History 1914–1990*. New York: Oxford, 1992. Treats military, political, economic, technological, and social events.

HANDBOOKS

Dupuy, Trevor Nevitt, et al., eds. *The Almanac of World Military Power*. 4th ed. San Rafael: Presidio, 1980. Arranged by geographical area; gives information about the military and defense structure of every nation and summaries of factors that affect its military potential; includes maps and a glossary of military terms.

Foner, Eric, and John A. Garraty. *The Reader's Companion to American History*. Boston: Houghton, 1991. Gives an overview of social issues, popular culture, movements, and personalities.

Grun, Bernard. *The Timetables of History: A Horizontal Linkage of People and Events*. 3d ed. New York: Simon, 1991. Presents a columnar listing of major events in seven areas for each year from about 5000 B.C. to A.D. 1990; history, literature, theater, religion, philosophy, science and technology, music, and visual arts are represented; emphasis is on the western world.

Handbook of American Women's History. New York: Garland, 1990. Covers social movements, popular culture, laws, court cases, people, and associations.

Johnson, Thomas H., in consultation with Harvey Wish. *The Oxford Companion to American History*. New York: Oxford UP, 1966. Summarizes lives, events, and places of significance in the founding of the nation; gives attention to social, political, and labor movements; includes the fields of art, science, commerce, education, law, sports, and entertainment; provides some bibliographies.

Trager, James. *The Peoples Chronology*. New York: Holt, 1992. Covers all major areas of human endeavor from 3 million B.C. through 1991 in more than 30,000 entries.

Wetterau, Bruce. *The New York Public Library Book of Chronologies*. New York: Prentice, 1990. Chronicles happenings in specific subject areas, e.g., technology, accidents and disasters, war and military operations, sports, education, etc.

HISTORICAL ATLASES

Atlas of American History. 2d rev. ed. Kenneth T. Jackson, Editor in Chief. New York: Scribner's 1984. Portrays in maps all facets of American history from the earliest settlement to 1982, including all twentieth-century wars, shifts in population, and recent changes in the political, social, and economic characteristics of the country.

Barraclough, Geoffrey, ed. *The Times Atlas of World History*. 3d ed. Maplewood: Hammond and The London Times, 1989. For the general reader and the student; covers world history from the earliest times to the late 1980s; symbols, color, and other devices are used on maps to show political, social, cultural, and economic development important to each period; each map is accompanied by commentary; has a world chronology and a glossary of names; has new maps and photographs.

Cappon, Lester J., and others, eds. *Atlas of Early American History: The Revolutionary Era, 1760–1790*. Published for the Newberry Library and Institute of Early American History and Culture. Princeton: Princeton UP, 1976. Covers in maps aspects of life in the period of the Revolution: political, economic, religious, cultural, demographic, and military.

Coe, Michael, et al., eds. *Atlas of Ancient America*. New York: Facts on File, 1986. Treats prehistoric people, their behavior, and their culture; provides an introduction to the art and archaeology of North, Central, and South America; relief maps show site locations, political boundaries, cultural boundaries, etc.; provides text, illustrations.

Ferrell, Robert H., and Richard Natkiel. *Atlas of American History*. New York: Macmillan, 1987. Covers American history from 1492 to the 1980s in maps and charts, treating events, people, movements, population, international involvements, etc.

Finely, M. I., ed. *Atlas of Classical Archaeology*. New York: McGraw, 1977. An introduction to classical sites, covers the Greco-Roman world of 1000 B.C. through A.D. 500; describes archaeological sites; has diagrams, maps, and photographs.

Heyden, A. A. M. Van Der, and H. H. Scullard, eds. *Atlas of the Classical World*. New York: Nelson, 1959. Includes maps, illustrations, and text relating to the religious, economic, military, literary, artistic, and political history of Greece and Rome.

Keegan, John, ed. *The Times Atlas of the Second World War*. New York: Harper, 1989. Depicts military formations; gives chronology; has maps and text.

Moore, R. I., ed. *Rand McNally Historical Atlas of the World*. Chicago: Rand, 1981. Traces the history of mankind in maps and text; includes middle eastern and oriental cultures as well as western; devotes a special section to the United States; gives an overview of the events shown in maps.

Schwartzberg, Joseph E., ed. *A Historical Atlas of South Asia*. Chicago: The U of Chicago P, 1978. Seeks to provide a comprehensive record in maps of the history of South Asia from the Old Stone Age to 1975; includes text, maps, bibliography, and charts; text is keyed to maps. 2d impression with additional material. New York: Oxford UP, 1992.

Shepherd, William R., ed. *Historical Atlas*. 9th rev. and updated ed. New York: Barnes, 1976. Provides maps of world history from 1450 B.C. to the 1960s; new maps since 1929.

Talbert, Richard J. A. *Atlas of Classical History*. New York: Macmillan, 1985. Gives information about cities, battles, trade, countries, and other areas of ancient history; has maps and illustrations.

DOCUMENTS

Brownlie, Ian, ed. *Basic Documents on Human Rights*. 3d ed. Oxford: Clarendon P, 1991. Includes documents from 1688 to the late 1980s.

Documents of American History. Ed. Henry Steele Commager and Milton Cantor. 10th ed. 2 Vols. Englewood Cliffs: Prentice, 1988. Contains reprints of selected original documents designed to illustrate the course of American history starting with the age of discovery; arranged chronologically. Vol. 1: to 1988; Vol. 2: since 1988.

BIOGRAPHICAL DICTIONARIES[3]

Directory of American Scholars. 8th ed. Vol. I, *History*. Ed. by the Jaques Cattell Press. New York: Bowker, 1982.

Who Was Who in America, Historical Volume, 1607–1896. Chicago: Marquis, 1963. Provides biographical material on more than 13,000 persons from 1607 to 1896; historical and statistical data on federal government, states, major cities; major American events. Rev. ed., 1967, adds about 200 biographies.

EXAMPLES OF PROFESSIONAL JOURNALS[4]

American Heritage: The Magazine of History. New York: American Heritage, 1949–. Bimonthly. Covers all aspects of American history, major and minor; social, educational, and cultural trends; many illustrations in color. Online via DIALOG.

American Historical Review. Washington: AHA, 1895–. Five issues per year. The official journal of the American Historical Association; has scholarly articles based on original research; gives book reviews.

---

[3] See also Chapter 10, Biographical Dictionaries.

[4] See also *Ulrich's International Periodicals Directory*, 31st ed., and *Magazines for Libraries*, 7th ed., ed. Bill Katz and Linda S. Katz.

English Historical Review. London: Longman, 1886–. Quarterly. Covers history of all periods with some emphasis on Great Britain and the British Empire; offers scholarly articles; includes lengthy and critical book reviews.

Journal of American History. Bloomington: Organization of American Historians, 1914–. Quarterly. Formerly *Mississippi Valley Historical Review*; the scope is almost entirely American; articles include biographical sketches as well as historical theory.

Journal of Modern History. Chicago: U of Chicago P, 1929–. Quarterly. Published in cooperation with the Modern European History Section of the American Historical Association; articles cover European history from the Renaissance to the present; important documents are often published; has book reviews.

The Journal of Negro History. Washington: The Association for the Study of Negro Life and History, Inc., 1916–. Quarterly. Aims to promote historical research and writing; articles are concerned with black life and history; has book reviews.

Geography

Geography—the term is derived from *geo*, the Greek combining form for "earth," plus *graphia*, "writing"—is the science concerned with the description of the earth's surface; its form and physical features; its natural and political subdivisions; and its climate, products, and population. Geography is frequently divided into mathematical, physical, and political geography.

In addition to atlases and gazetteers, which are recognized as being essential aids in the study of geography, there are bibliographies of, and indexes to, the literature of geography, dictionaries of place names and terminology, and guidebooks which provide descriptive material and maps not usually found in gazetteers and atlases.

Representative Reference Sources in Geography[5]

BIBLIOGRAPHIES, GUIDES, AND INDEXES[6]

Lock, Clara B. M. *Geography and Cartography: A Reference Handbook.* Hamden: Shoe String, 1976. A revision of two earlier works; gives short articles on geographers (not living), societies, organizations, schools of geography, and journals, atlases, and other geographical sources.

Social Sciences Index. (See p. 211.)

---

[5] See also Chapter 11, Atlases and Gazetteers.
[6] See also Chapter 9, Indexes, and Chapter 13, Bibliographies.

ATLASES[7]

The Bartholomew/Scribner Atlas of Europe: A Profile of Western Europe. New York: Scribner's 1974. Uses text, diagrams, maps, and graphs to present a comprehensive picture of the eighteen countries of western Europe; gives statistical information on business and industry, economic conditions, transportation, trade, and other topics in addition to the physical-political maps.

Glassborow, Jilly, and Gillian Freemen. *Atlas of the United States.* New York: Macmillan, 1986. Using maps, compares the states with one another; other thematic maps show population, climate, personal wealth, land use, etc.; maps are accompanied by text; twenty five maps are devoted to the nation as a whole, comparing it with the rest of the world in such areas as health care, military expenditures, food production, and consumption.

The New York Times Atlas of the World. 3d rev. ed. New York: Times Books, 1992. Gives information about the physical earth, the stars, the solar system, the universe, space flight, Earth's moon, climate, vegetation, food, population, and patterns of human selection; provides both text and maps.

Rand McNally Commercial Atlas and Marketing Guide. Chicago: Rand, 1876–. Annual. Gives general information about each state in the United States and the territories and possessions regarding agriculture, communications, manufacturing, population, business centers, transportation, distance; covers the United States, Canada, and the world; has maps, tables, etc.

The Times Atlas of the World. Comprehensive 9th ed. New York: Times Books, 1992. Provides information on physiography, oceanography, climatology, the universe, stars, population, vegetation, Earth's moon, food; includes information on each country; maps by John Bartholomew & Son, Ltd., Edinburgh.

GAZETTEERS

For a discussion of gazetteers and examples, see pp. 118, 120–123.

DICTIONARIES, ENCYCLOPEDIAS, AND HANDBOOKS

British Association for the Advancement of Science. Research Committee. *A Glossary of Geographical Terms.* 3d ed. Ed. by L. Dudley Stamp and Audrey N. Clark. London: Longman, 1979. Gives agreed-upon definitions and sources of definitions; includes references to origin and to

---

[7] See also pp. 120–122.

current use and misuse; uses quotations from original and standard sources to clarify several meanings of a term; includes foreign terms and new terms in geography.

Harder, Kelsie B., ed. *Illustrated Dictionary of Place Names, United States and Canada*. Hudson Group Book. New York: Van Nostrand, 1976. Has more than 15,000 place names, including towns, villages, cities, counties, states, provinces, parks, and historic sites.

Monkhouse, F. J., ed. *A Dictionary of Geography*. 2d ed. London: Edward Arnold, 1970. Covers terms relating to landforms, oceanography, climate, soil, vegetation, archaeology, and cartography.

Rand McNally and Company. *The Earth and Man*. Chicago: Rand, 1976. Describes the planet Earth; discusses the preservation of the environment; uses colored illustrations to show the history of the earth and its present condition; includes diagrams, text, and maps.

Rand McNally's Encyclopedia of World Rivers. Chicago: Rand, 1980. Locates and describes 1750 rivers which have made a contribution to man's progress and development (selection based on length of the river, natural beauty, and importance); for each river, includes the source, length, tributaries, dams, and history; combines maps and text; arranged by country.

Schmieder, Allen A., and others. *A Dictionary of Basic Geography*. Boston: Allyn, 1970. Covers basic geographic terminology needed for an understanding of general geography; includes a brief, basic annotated bibliography.

Stewart, George R. *American Place Names: A Concise and Selective Dictionary for the Continental United States of America*. London: Oxford UP, 1970. Has 12,000 American place names; gives derivation, state, historical, geographical, or other interpretation of the name; includes unusual names.

GUIDEBOOKS

Other sources of geographical information are guidebooks. Produced by local or state chambers of commerce, state development commissions, local historical societies, travel bureaus, airlines, railroads, hotels, commercial publishers, and other sources, they are designed for the tourist and traveler, to attract trade and industry, or for purposes of historical record or local interest. They include certain types of information not found in gazetteers or atlases, such as maps of small towns and areas; places of strictly local or historical interest; and information about schools, churches, hotel accommodations, communications, transportation, and natural resources. If guidebooks are produced locally, they reflect the local interpretation of the social, economic, cultural, industrial, and other advantages of a given area.

Guidebooks are available from the local, state, or national agencies responsible for industrial development and tourism; from historical societies, tourist bureaus, and book stores; and from commercial publishers.

The American Guide Series. Prepared by the Federal Writers' Project of the Works Progress Administration, 1937–1949. Reprinted and distributed by various publishers. Includes guides to each state and to many cities and regions, giving basic economic, historical, and sociological information about each one.

Baedeker Handbook for Travellers. Various publishers, 1828–. Published in English, French, and German editions, these handbooks cover Europe, North and South America, Egypt, and the Near East, giving information useful to the sightseeing traveler.

Fodor's Modern Guides. Ed. Eugene Fodor. New York: David McKay, 1953–. Cover Europe, Asia, South America, Japan, and other areas.

EXAMPLES OF PROFESSIONAL JOURNALS[8]

Association of American Geographers. *Annals.* Washington: Association of American Geographers, 1911–. Quarterly. Provides a scholarly approach to any geographical subject—human, historical, economic, or cultural—in articles by professional geographers; illustrated with maps, photographs, tables, and charts; includes abstracts of papers given at professional meetings.

Economic Geography. Worcester: Clark University, 1925–. Quarterly. For geographers, economists, generalists in education and the professions; covers economic and urban geography; gives maps, tables, black-and-white illustrations, and book reviews.

Geographical Review. New York: American Geographical Society, 1913–. Quarterly. Offers scholarly articles on all aspects of geography, historical and current; includes illustrations, maps, and charts; gives book reviews.

Historical Abstracts. Santa Barbara: ABC-Clio, 1955–. Quarterly. Publisher varies. Abstracts more than 20,000 articles appearing in some 2000 journals published worldwide in history, the social sciences, and related humanities. *Beginning with Vol. 3 (1910),* added listing of new books. *Part A: Modern History Abstracts; Part B: Twentieth Century Abstracts,* 1914–present. Indexed by subject.

---

[8] See also *Ulrich's International Periodicals Directory,* 31st ed., and *Magazines for Libraries,* 7th ed., ed. Bill Katz and Linda S. Katz.

PART

5

*Using Library Resources
for a Research Paper*

The Research Paper

The word "research" means "search, inquiry, pursuit" and comes from the French *rechercher*, "to seek again."

The true research paper involves not only studious inquiry into a subject but also critical and exhaustive investigation of that subject for the purpose of revising accepted conclusions concerning it in the light of facts uncovered by the investigation.

It may be said that elementary research begins when the first encyclopedia the student consults fails to provide the information needed to answer a question or to carry out an assignment, and it becomes necessary to consult several sources.

In general, the college research paper on the undergraduate level is an exposition, designed to present the results of the student's inquiry into, or investigation of, a chosen subject.

The undergraduate-level research paper—sometimes called a "term paper"—may be one of several kinds.

1. It may be a report which relates facts for the purpose of informing the reader or of showing progress over a period of time.
2. It may be a report, based on the student's investigations, which analyzes an event, a situation, or a period.
3. It may be a thesis,[1] that is, a paper which states and maintains by argument a position or a proposition.
4. It may be a thesis taking the form of a presentation and evaluation of facts for the purpose of persuading or recommending.

---

[1] "Thesis" is also the name given to a dissertation presented by a candidate for an academic degree, usually the M.A. or M.S. degree.

The successful completion of any research paper depends upon:

1. Careful investigation of a subject
2. Ability to choose and evaluate materials
3. Ability to take clear, well-documented notes
4. Understanding of the purpose and forms of footnotes and bibliography
5. Clear, logical, and orderly development and presentation of facts in keeping with the purpose of the paper

Procedure

Some of the basic steps in writing a research paper are listed below.

1. Select a subject. In making the choice of a topic, consider the following factors:
    a Is this a subject of sufficient interest to you that you can make it interesting to your readers?
    b Can you study it seriously in the length of time allotted for writing the paper?
    c Can you cover it adequately in the number of words prescribed by your instructor?
    d Is it likely that you will find sufficient material on it to write a paper, or is it too new, too highly specialized, or too limited in appeal to have received coverage in books, newspapers, magazines, or other sources?
2. Restrict your subject if the topic you have chosen is too broad or too general for the assigned paper.
    a Look in the library catalog under your subject and read the subject headings immediately following to see how that subject is subdivided. Notice the subject headings listed at the bottom of each catalog record to find further subdivisions and related headings. For example, if you are looking for material on the general topic "music," you may find in the catalog:

Music	Music, Gipsy
Music, American	*See* Folk music—Gipsy
Music, American—	Music, National
Discography	Music, Popular (songs, etc.)
Music as a profession	Musical fiction
(*See* Music—Vocational	Musical instruments, Electronic
guidance	
Music festivals	

b Find the subject in a periodical index; notice the subdivisions; e.g.:[2]

Music	Musical instruments,
Music, Black	Electronic
See Black music	Musical performance
Music festivals	*See* Music—Performance
Music in advertising	Musicians
Musical instruments	*See also*
	Orchestras
	Rock Musicians

c See how a general encyclopedia index subdivides your subject.[3]

Music	Music box
Acoustics	Music festivals
Band	Music history
Computers	Musical comedy
Dance	Musical instruments: types
Folk	Musical theater
Jazz	
Rhythm	

d Consult the *Library of Congress Subject Headings* for subjects and subdivisions of subjects.
e You may restrict your topic according to period of time or geographical location or according to historical, social, cultural, or political significance. For example:

Music in Colonial America
The Contribution of Music to Media Production
Military Marches
Music in Television Commercials
The Influence of the Computer on Music

[2] Entries from *Readers' Guide to Periodical Literature*, May 10, 1981, issue. *Readers' Guide to Periodical Literature* Copyright © 1981 by the H. W. Wilson Company. Material reproduced by permission of the publisher.
[3] *Encyclopedia Americana*. 30: *Index* (1981), 550–551. Reprinted with the permission of the *Encyclopedia Americana* Copyright © 1981, Grolier, Inc.

f In the following list of subjects, notice the progression from general to specific:

Music
National music
National music—United States
Music for national holidays
Music for the Fourth of July
Yankee Doodle Dandy

3. Choose the aspect of your subject that you wish to investigate:
   a Social, economic, or other conditions that influenced it
   b Historical background
   c Important persons associated with it
   d Current status
   e Other
4. Determine the chronological period in which your subject falls.
   a Is the time period ancient, medieval, modern, recent, current, on-going?
   b Does the subject cover several periods?
   c If the subject is current, is it influenced by past events? To what extent?
5. Decide upon the purpose of your paper.
   a Is it to inform?
   b Is it to show progress?
   c Is it to analyze an event, a situation, or a period?
   d Is it to persuade and recommend?
6. Make a tentative statement of your thesis or purpose—that is, the proposition you will attempt to defend, clarify, or develop. For example, "Monasticism was of major importance in the preservation and development of literature during the Middle Ages," or "The printing press hastened the era of discovery and exploration."
   a Analyze your thesis as to the subject areas it includes or touches: geography, sociology, economics, history, literature, politics.
   b Decide what kinds of sources will provide the information you will need to write your paper.
      (i) Primary sources[4]—interviews, questionnaires, letters, diaries, manuscripts, memoirs

---

[4] Primary sources are those materials which have not been interpreted by another person. Secondary sources are materials which have been reported, analyzed, or interpreted by other persons.

(ii) Secondary sources—books, journals, encyclopedias, other reference books, nonbook materials.

7. Begin your preliminary search for material. In the preceding chapters, reference sources have been discussed, with emphasis upon their usefulness in providing material on a subject. Since subject headings are the key to the library catalog, the indexes, and most reference books, it is necessary, before using any of these sources, to determine the headings under which your subject may be listed.[5]

   a Consult the library catalogs and appropriate indexes and bibliographies—science, social science, humanities, etc.—to find books and other materials in your library in which your subject or any aspect of it is discussed. Read the complete catalog record, bibliographic entry, or index citation to see what the source covers:

   (i) The number of topics treated and the topic which is given the greatest emphasis
   (ii) The amount and kinds of illustrative material included
   (iii) The bibliographical references provided
   (iv) The subject headings and *see* references as indications of other topics which will lead to more material. For example, if your subject is "folk music," some of the headings under which you will find material are:

Folk Music	Country music
See also	*See also*
Folk dance music	Bluegrass music
Folksongs	Fiddle tunes
Folk dancing	Gospel music
Folk lore	Guitar—Methods (country)
Folk music, American	Country and Western music
See also Country music	Country musicians
Folk music, French	
Folk music, Gipsy	

   (v) Utilize various search options: subject, browsing, word, Boolean operators, etc.
   (vi) Consult several types of sources: printed reference sources; CD-ROM versions of indexes, abstracts, etc.; union catalogs via the OPAC. If your library does not have a source you need, it may be available through interlibrary loan (ILL).

---

[5] See pp. 62–64.

b Take the class number or numbers and browse in those sections of the stacks, looking at the tables of contents and the indexes of books which may be helpful.

c Consult a printed bibliography or guide to find material on your subject which may not be listed in the library catalog, such as parts of books, pamphlets, and reports.

d Use a general dictionary for general definitions; use a subject dictionary for specialized definitions and terminology.

e Find an overview of your topic in a general encyclopedia, and then consult a subject encyclopedia for technical and specialized information. Consult the bibliography at the end of the article for additional readings and the index volume for other headings under which to look; remember that an encyclopedia is *only* the starting point.

f Use general and subject indexes to find recent material in periodicals and to find selections in collected works.

g Consult a handbook for statistical information or for identification of allusions to persons, events, dates, and legendary or mythological figures.

h Look up important persons connected with your subject in a biographical dictionary.

i Establish geographical locations and facts with the aid of an atlas or a gazetteer.

j Consult nonbook sources—microforms and visual and audiovisual materials—for information on your subject; you may want to use pictures, slides, a film, a video, a sound track, or other forms to illustrate, clarify, or support points you wish to make in your paper.

k Look for current information and statistics in government publications, especially on topics in the social sciences, history, education, and the sciences.

l Use primary sources whenever possible.

It is essential that you use a variety of sources in order to obtain a broad view of your subject; to see its various aspects; to discover the factors which influenced or contributed to it; to know the individuals, groups, or organizations associated with it; to become acquainted with current thinking as well as with past opinion regarding it; and to have some understanding of the terminology of the field in question.

8. Begin preliminary reading.
   a Read a background or overview article in a textbook or in a history of the subject.

b Examine a general article in an encyclopedia and a specialized article in a subject encyclopedia.

c Read a popular article in a periodical.

d Skim through the material at first.

e Make brief notes of references for later serious reading, giving adequate information for finding these references easily.

9. As you examine material, make a tentative bibliography of the materials which you think you will use. (See Figure 25.1.)

a You may make the bibliography on cards, paper slips, or computer print-outs, if you are using a computer to take notes.

(i) Choose a format of uniform size that will be easy to alphabetize, file, and consult.

(ii) Use a separate card or page for each bibliographical reference.

(iii) Label each card or page with a subject heading, which will be a subdivision of your outline.

b Give basic information for each reference.

(i) Author

(ii) Title

(iii) Facts of publication; volume, date, and pages, if it is a periodical

(iv) Page or pages on which the information you are using can be found

c Include a brief descriptive statement of each work, indicating the content and its usefulness for your subject.

10. Make a tentative outline of the major divisions of your paper. A possible outline of the major topics in a paper on "The Music Festival in the United States" is as follows:

I Definition and origin of the music festival

II Beginnings in the United States

A Nineteenth century

B Early twentieth century

III Development in the United States since the 1960s

A Sponsors

B Themes

C Artists, performers

D Seasons

IV Popularity

A Number

B Locations

C Attendance

V Contribution to the cultural life in the United States

Ref
ML   Fuld, James J. The Book of World-Famous
113   Music --Classical, Popular and Folk.
F8   Rev. and enl. ed. New York: Crown, 1971.

            Gives information about hundreds of the
        best known musical compositions.

        Vinton, John. "Change of Mind."
            Music Review 35 (Nov. 1974) 301-318.

        Discusses changes in music in the
        19th and 20th centuries

    Ref
    ML   New Oxford History of Music. 10 vols.
    160   London: Oxford UP, 1974.
    N4

        The background of music in the United
        States during the period 1918-1960 is
        discussed in Vol. X, 569-594.

FIGURE 25.1
Sample bibliography cards.

11. Begin serious reading. As you read, you may discover that even the limited aspect of your topic is still too broad. Preliminary reading and exploration of the topic will aid in restricting it.

12. Take notes. (See Figure 25.2.)

   a The kinds of notes you may take include:

     (i) A restatement, in your own words, of the thought or thoughts of an author. It is important that in your paraphrase you do not lose the meaning of the original statement when you take it out of context.

     (ii) A direct quotation, copied exactly, including punctuation. Any omission must be indicated by an ellipsis (...); any interpolation must be indicated by brackets ([ ]). Credit for a quotation must be given in a footnote.[6] Failure to give the source for a quotation or a paraphrase in which the language, thoughts, or ideas of another person are used as one's own is plagiarism.

     (iii) A critical or evaluative comment about a book or a person.

   b You may use cards, paper slips, or print-outs—if you are taking notes on a computer.

     (i) Use cards or paper of uniform size throughout; if more than one card or page is needed for a reference, number each one and put the author's last name on all cards or pages after the first.

     (ii) Give complete bibliographical information on the first card or page for each reference:[7]

       (a) Author's full name

       (b) Complete title

       (c) Imprint: place of publication, publisher, date

       (d) Pages and volume

       (e) Month, day, year, volume, and pages of periodical articles

       (f) Month, day, year, and pages of newspaper articles.

   c Leave space at the top of the card for the subject headings, which will be the subdivisions of your outline.

13. Formulate your thesis.

   a State it simply, expressing the basic idea which you will develop.

   b Restrict it to one approach to the subject.

   c Avoid using ambiguous words or phrases.

14. Study your notes in order to restrict your subject further.

15. Make a preliminary detailed outline, in either topical or sentence form. Whatever form you choose, use it throughout your outline.

   a Make sure that your outline is organized in a logical manner, that each

---

[6] A footnote gives credit for—or explains—a specific part of the text. See also pp. 275–277, 278–282.

[7] For additional information on nonbook sources, see pp. 135, 137–138.

Ref
ML   Thompson, Oscar, ed. The International
100   Cyclopaedia of Music and Musicians.
T47   10th ed. Ed. Bruce Bohle. New
            York: Dodd, 1975.

            Before primitive man could speak
            intelligibly, he expressed feelings of
            joy, grief, and fear in bodily movements
            accompanied by rhythmic noises.

Ref
N   Encyclopedia of World Art. 15 vols.
31   New York: McGraw, 1959-1968.
E533

            "Among the most important factors
            that influence the evolution of musical
            instruments are . . . the prevailing style
            of a period and . . . the status of
            technology." Vol. X, 431.

Ref
ML   Fink, Robert, and Robert Ricci. The
100   Language of Twentieth Century Music:
F55   A Dictionary of Terms. New York:
            Schirmer, 1975.

            Useful for brief definitions of terms
            used in contemporary music.

FIGURE 25.2
Sample note cards: (top) restatement or paraphrase; (center) quotation; (bottom) evaluative comment.

division and subdivision receives proper emphasis, and that each part
of the outline is in the appropriate relationship to other parts of the
outline.[8]

b Fill in the gaps in your outline by additional reading and note taking.

c Discard irrelevant material.

16. Remake your outline.
17. Write the first draft of your paper.
18. Use footnotes or endnotes when necessary.
    a Give the source of a direct quotation.
    b Acknowledge the source of an opinion or a discussion which you have
       paraphrased or of any specific material which cannot be considered
       common knowledge.
    c Give credit for statistical information, graphs, and charts you have
       used.
    d Suggest additional reading on a particular point.
    e Add an explanation to clarify or expand a statement in the text of your
       paper.
    f Make cross references to other parts of your paper.
19. Make a bibliography.
    a Give sources of materials you have used in writing the paper.
    b Suggest additional reading materials.
    c Include an entry for each work mentioned in a footnote.
20. Revise your paper.
21. Evaluate the entire paper as to:
    a Clarity of purpose
    b Proper emphasis of important ideas and divisions
    c Elimination of gaps and irrelevant material
    d Accuracy in presenting or intepreting facts
    e Appropriateness of the choice of words
    f Correctness of grammatical structure and form
    g Unity and coherence in writing
    h Adequacy of documentation
    i Consistency of bibliographical and footnote form
22. Write the final draft of your paper.

Footnotes and Bibliography

Footnotes explain or give credit for specific items of information used in the
text of the research paper and the exact location of any quotation used.

---

[8] Show the relationship of subdivisions in an outline (or of items in an enumeration) by
indentation and the use of letters and numerals in the following order: I, A, B, 1, a, b, (1), (a),
(b), (i).

Bibliography describes, as a whole, the work or works from which the citations are taken. The forms for footnotes and bibliography—that is, the order of listing the items and the punctuation, capitalization, and underlining of words in the title—vary according to the manual of style[9] which is followed by a college or by a department within a college. Each department may adopt a different form. In general, the variations are not in the items included but in the style in which they are presented. Footnote and bibliographical forms are not the same, and entries for books, periodical and newspaper articles, encyclopedia articles, and special materials differ from each other.

Before writing a research paper, students must understand the forms which they are required to use in making footnotes and bibliography, and they must follow those prescribed forms consistently.

GENERAL RULES FOR FOOTNOTES

In general, footnotes are numbered consecutively; they may be placed at the bottom of the page in numerical order; they may be separated from the text by a solid line across the page; they may be placed at the end of the paper in a section labeled "Notes."

Arabic numerals are generally used as footnote reference indexes, but asterisks and other symbols may be used also. Whatever reference symbol is employed, it must follow the passage to which it refers and must be placed after it (following the punctuation mark if there is one), just above the line.

The first citation of a footnote reference must give complete information in logical order.

1. Author's name (usually not inverted)
2. Title of publication
3. Facts of publication: place, publisher, and date
4. Volume and page numbers
5. Date of periodicals

The order in which these items are given depends upon the style manual followed.[10]

---

[9] Footnote and bibliographic form in this text follow *MLA Handbook for Writers of Research Papers*, ed. Joseph Gibaldi and Walter S. Achtert, 3d ed. (New York: MLA, 1988). Among other style manuals available are: Kate L. Turabian, *A Manual for Writers of Term Papers, Theses, and Dissertations*, 5th ed. (Chicago: U of Chicago, 1987); *Webster's Standard American Style Manual* (Springfield: Merriam-Webster, 1985); William Giles Campbell, et al., *Form and Style: Theses Reports, Term Papers*, 6th ed. (Boston: Houghton, 1982). Other style manuals can be found in the library catalog under the subject "report writing."

[10] See footnote above.

Listed below are examples of one form which may be used in making footnotes:[11]

[1] Ludwig Bieler, *Ireland, Harbinger of the Middle Ages* (New York: Oxford UP, 1963) 24.
[2] Mabel M. Smythe, ed., *Black American Reference Book* (Englewood Cliffs: Prentice, 1976) 40.
[3] "Phoenicia," *Encyclopedia Americana*, 1958 ed.

Usually the complete form of a reference is not repeated after it is first given; a shortened form is used as follows:[12]

[1] Louis B. Wright, *The Cultural Life of the American Colonies, 1607–1763* (New York: Harper, 1957) 70.
[2] Wright 80–85.

GENERAL RULES FOR BIBLIOGRAPHY

There are numerous forms for making a bibliography; there are different forms for government documents and for science, medicine, and other disciplines. (See footnote p. 276, for titles of some style manuals.) It is necessary to know which form you are required to follow, and it is essential that you follow it consistently throughout your paper. Several principles must be adhered to in any form:

1. All bibliographical entries must be in accord with the purpose of the research paper.
2. All items must be presented accurately, clearly, and logically.
3. The bibliographical form which is prescribed for a given paper must be followed consistently in every entry.

The following items are included in a bibliographical entry:

1. Name of the author
2. Title of the work as it appears on the title page
3. Edition, if it is other than the first
4. Number of volumes in the set, if the entire set is used
5. Place of publication, name of publisher, and date of publication

[11] See *MLA Handbook for Writers of Research Papers* for additional forms.
[12] The abbreviations *ibid.* and *op. cit.* are not recommended in the *MLA Handbook for Writers of Research Papers.* See Kate L. Turabian, *A Manual for Writers of Term Papers, Theses, and Dissertations*, 5th ed. (Chicago: U of Chicago P, 1987). See also footnote p. 276.

6. Number of pages in the book and price, if these items are required by the instructor

Bibliographical entries may be grouped according to kind—books, newspapers, periodicals, nonbook sources—or according to the main divisions in the research paper. They are arranged alphabetically within the groups.

Examples of Bibliography and Footnotes

Some examples of one form for making bibliography and footnotes are give below:[13]

BOOKS

One author

Bieler, Ludwig. *Ireland, Harbinger of the Middle Ages*. New York: Oxford UP, 1963.

[1] Ludwig Bieler, *Ireland, Harbinger of the Middle Ages* (New York: Oxford UP, 1963) 24.

Two authors

Brown, James W., and Kenneth D. Norberg. *Administering Educational Media*. New York: McGraw, 1965.

[2] James W. Brown, and Kenneth D. Norberg, *Administering Educational Media* (New York: McGraw: 1965) 100–102.

Several authors

Pickering, David, Alan Isaacs, and Elizabeth Martin, eds. *Brewer's Dictionary of Twentieth Century Phrase and Fable*. Boston: Houghton, 1992.

[3] David Pickering, Alan Isaacs, and Elizabeth Martin, eds., *Brewer's Dictionary of Phrase and Fable* (Boston: Houghton, 1992) 25.

More than three authors

King, Gilbert, W., et al. *Automation and the Library of Congress*. Washington: Library of Congress, 1963.

[6] Gilbert W. King, et al., *Automation and the Library of Congress* (Washington: Library of Congress, 1963) 4.

[13] See *MLA Handbook for Writers of Research Papers* for additional examples.

Organization or institution as author

American Institute of History and Art. *Hudson Valley Painting, 1700–1750*.
    Albany: Inst. of Hist. and Art, 1959.

[4] American Institute of History and Art, *Hudson Valley Painting, 1700–1750* (Albany: Albany
Inst. of Hist. and Art, 1959) 3.

Edition of an author's work

Deutsch, Babette. *Poetry Handbook: A Dictionary of Terms*. 4th ed. New York:
    Funk, 1974.

[5] Babette Deutsch, *Poetry Handbook: A Dictionary of Terms*, 4th ed. (New York: Funk, 1974) 73.

Author's work edited by another person

Cary, Joyce. *Selected Essays*. Ed. A. G. Bishop. New York: St. Martin's,
    1976.

[7] Joyce Cary, *Selected Essays*, ed. A. G. Bishop (New York: St. Martin's, 1976) 60.

Translation

Chastel, André. *The Age of Humanism: Europe, 1480–1530*. Trans. Katherine
    M. Delavenay and E. M. Gwyer. New York: McGraw, 1963.

[8] André Chastel, *The Age of Humanism: Europe, 1480–1530*, trans. Katherine M. Delavenay (New
York: McGraw, 1963) 40.

Edited work

Smythe, Mabel M., ed. *The Black American Reference Book*. Englewood Cliffs:
    Prentice, 1976.

[9] Mabel M. Smythe, ed., *The Black American Reference Book* (Englewood Cliffs: Prentice, 1976)
25–30.

Volume in a series

Lunt, William Edward. *History of England*. 4th ed. Harper's Historical Se-
    ries. New York: Harper, 1957.

[10] William Edward Lunt, *History of England*, Harper's Historical Series, 4th ed. (New York:
Harper, 1957) 1.

Multivolume work

McGraw-Hill Dictionary of World Art. 5 vols. New York: McGraw, 1969.

[11] *McGraw-Hill Dictionary of World Art*, vol. 1 (New York: McGraw, 1969) 80–85.

Reprint edition

Hansen, Waldemar. *The Peacock Throne: The Drama of Mogul India*. New York: Holt, 1972. Delhi, India: Banarsidass, 1981.

[12] Waldemar Hansen, *The Peacock Throne: The Drama of Mogul India* (New York: Holt, 1972; Delhi, India: Banarsidass, 1981) 2.

No author given

Webster's Standard American Style Manual. Springfield: Merriam, 1985.

[13] *Webster's Standard American Style Manual* (Springfield: Merriam, 1985) 8.

ARTICLES

Encyclopedia

"Phoenicia." *Encyclopedia Americana*. 1958 ed.

[14] "Phoenicia," *The Encyclopedia Americana*, 1958 ed.

Periodical article—magazine

Trippett, Frank. "The Weather: Everyone's Favorite Topic," *Time*, 6 Feb. 1978: 76–77.

[15] Frank Trippett, "The Weather: Everyone's Favorite Topic," *Time*, 6 Feb. 1978: 76.

Essay, article, or chapter in a collected work

Morgan, E. "Women and the Future." *Images of the Future: The Twenty-First Century and Beyond*. Ed. R. F. Bundy. Buffalo: Prometheus, 1976.

[16] E. Morgan, "Women and the Future," *Images of the Future: The Twenty-First Century and Beyond*, ed. R. F. Bundy (Buffalo: Prometheus, 1976) 143–151.

Newspaper—signed

Jonas, Jack. "A Visit to a Land of Many Facets." *The Sunday Star*, 5 Mar. 1961: F1.

[17] Jack Jonas, "A Visit to a Land of Many Facets," *The Sunday Star*, 5 Mar. 1961: F1.

Periodical article—journal

Dodson, Carolyn. "CD-ROMs for the Library." *Special Libraries* 78 (Summer 1987): 191–194.

[18] Carolyn Dodson, "CD-ROMs for the Library," *Special Libraries* 78 (Summer 1987): 191–194.

Book review in a magazine

Morrison, Philip. Rev. of *The Cosmic Inquirers: Modern Telescopes and Their Makers*, by Wallace Tucker and Karen Tucker. *Scientific American* 255 (October 1986): 38.

[19] Philip Morrison, rev. of *The Cosmic Inquirers: Modern Telescopes and Their Makers*, by Wallace Tucker and Karen Tucker, *Scientific American* 255 (October 1986): 38.

NONBOOK MATERIALS

American Men in Space, The Story of Project Mercury. Phonodisc. Nar. John H. Powers and Fred Hanney. N.p.: CMS Records, CMS 71000, 1964. 2 s, 12 in, 33⅓ rpm, microgroove, stereophonic.

[20] *American Men in Space, The Story of Project Mercury*, Phonodisc, nar. John H. Powers and Fred Hanney (N.p.: CMS Records, CMS 71000, 1964).

The Book Takes Form. Motion Picture. Los Angeles: Department of Cinema, USC. Released by NET Film Service, 1956. 29 min, sd., b&w, 16 mm.

[21] *The Book Takes Form*, Motion Picture (Los Angeles: Department of Cinema, USC, released by NET Film Service, 1956).

Duché, Jacob. *Observations on a Variety of Subjects, Literary, Moral and Religious* . . . Microfilm. Philadelphia: Printed by John Dunlap, 1974.

[22] Jacob Duché, *Observations on a Variety of Subjects, Literary, Moral and Religious*, Microfilm (Philadelphia: Printed by John Dunlap, 1974.)

Video

Whales Weep Not. Videocassette. Dir. Lana Jokel and James R. Donaldson. 26 min. Coronet/MTI Film & Video, 1986.

[23] *Whales Weep Not*, videocassette, dir. Lana Jokel and James R. Donaldson, 26 min., Coronet/MTI Film & Video, 1986.

Interview

Moore, Fred. Personal interview. 12 April 1988.

[24] Fred Moore, personal interview, 12 April 1988.

GOVERNMENT PUBLICATIONS

United States, Bureau of Labor Statistics. *Jobs for Which a College Education is Usually Required*. Washington: U.S. Dept. of Labor, 1976.

[25] United States, Bureau of Labor Statistics, *Jobs for Which a College Education Is Usually Required* (Washington: U.S. Dept. of Labor, 1976) 16.

ERIC PUBLICATION[14]

Parker, Judy. *Accessing the Media*. Kent: Kent Public Schools, 1991. ERIC ED 339337.

[26] Judy Parker, *Accessing the Media* (Kent: Kent Public Schools, 1991) 7 ERIC ED 339337.

[14] From Turabian, p. 218.

Subject Index

Abstract journals, 78, 206N
  on CD-ROM, 17?
Alcuin, 11
Alexandrian libraries, 8–9
Almanac, 77, 124, 127
  definition of, 77, 124
  examples of, 127
Alphabet, 7–8
American Library Association, 17
American Memory, 20
Appendix as part of a book, 28
Architecture, reference sources (*see* Fine
    arts, painting, sculpture, architec-
    ture, decorative arts)
Aristotle, 7–8
Arrangement of entries in the library
    catalog, 64–66
Assurbanipal, 4–5
Assyria, books and libraries in, 4–5
Atlases, 118–122, 162, 259, 270
  definition of, 77, 119
  electronic format, 121
  examples of, 120–122
  selection and use of, 119–120
  (*See also specific subjects*)
Audiovisual materials, 136–137, 270
  bibliographical form for, 281

Audiovisual materials (*Cont.*):
  kinds of, 136
  organization and arrangement
    of, 137
  sample catalog cards, 135
Author entry, 60
Automated information sources,
    139–145
  kinds, 144
  reference sources on, 145–147
  search strategy for, 144
  selection and use of, 147
  standardization of, 143
Babylonia, books and libraries in, 4–5
Bay Psalm Book, The, 16
Behistun Inscription, 5
Bibliography(ies), 129–133, 270,
    271–273, 275–278
  definition, 26N, 28, 77, 160
  general rules for, 277–278
  printed, 129–133
    examples of, 131–133
    kinds of, 129–130
    of periodical publications, 131–132
    on CD-ROM, 131–132
    online, 131–133
    selective and evaluative, 132–133

Bibliography(ies) (*Cont.*):
    trade, 133
    union catalogs, 131
    usefulness of, 130
    (*See also specific subjects*)
  sample cards, 272
  sample forms, 278–282
Binding as part of the book, 25
Biographical dictionaries, 77, 108–112,
    162, 270
  definition of, 108
  examples of, 113–117
  kinds of, 110
  on CD-ROM, 103, 117
  online, 102, 117
  selection and use of, 110–112
  (*See also specific subjects*)
Biography:
  definition of, 108–109
  indexes to, 116–117
Block books, 14N
Book, parts of a, 25–28
Book catalogs, 57–58
Book forms, 4, 14, 15, 20
Booklist, xii
Boolean operators, 69–70
Borsippa, 4
Byzantine Empire, 11

Caesar, Julius, 10
Call number, 43–45, 49–50
Card catalog, 57, 59–66
Carnegie, Andrew, 18
Carolingian Renaissance, 11
Cassiodorus, 11–12
Catalog cards (*see* Catalog entries)
Catalog entries, 59–64
  arrangement in catalog, 64–66
  definition of, 59
  examples of, 60–62, 67–69
  kinds of, 60–64
Caxton, William, 14
CD-ROM, 20, 70–71, 142–145, 209
  advantages and disadvantages of,
    141–142
  data bases, 142
  definition of, 142

CD-ROM (*Cont.*):
  instructions for use, 143
  kinds, 142
  reference sources on, 145–146
  search options for, 71
  search strategy for, 71, 143, 144
  selection and use, 145
  standardization of, 143
  trends, 144–145
  workstation, 142
  (*See also subject fields*)
CD-ROM catalogs, 70–71
  definition of, 70–71
  entries in, 71
  instructions for use, 71
  search options for, 71
Champollion, Jean Franqis, 6
Charlemagne, 11
China:
  books and libraries in, 7, 13–14
  movable types in, 13–14
Choice, xii
Classification in libraries, 37–53
  classification systems, purposes and
    characteristics of, 38–39
  definition of, 37
  Dewey Decimal Classification Sys-
    tem, 17, 38–45
  Library of Congress Classification
    System, 45–53
  Superintendent of Documents Classi-
    fication System, 53–54, 151
Clippings, 134, 136
Codex, 9
Collation, definition of, 56N
COMcats (*see* Computer output micro-
    form catalogs),
Companion, definition of, 125
Computer output microform catalogs,
    58–59
  microfiche catalog, 58
  microfilm catalog, 58
Computer searches, 31, 139–140
Computers, 19–20, 24, 70, 139–142
  data bases, 140–141
  instructions for use, 140
  reference sources for, 146

Computers (*Cont.*):
  search options for, 140
  search strategy for, 144
  selection and use, 145
  standardization of, 143
  use in libraries, 140
  use in online catalogs, 140
Copyright, 15
Copyright legislation, 31
Crete, development of alphabetic characters in, 7
Cutter, C. A., 44

Data bases, 140–141, 146
Decorative arts, reference sources (*see* Fine arts, painting, sculpture, architecture and decorative arts)
Dedication page as part of the book, 27
Depository libraries, 149
Dewey, Melvil, 17, 38
Dewey Decimal Classification System, 17, 38–45
DIALOG, 140, 142
Diamond Sutra, 14N
Dictionaries, 81–87, 160, 270
  biographical (*see* Biographical dictionaries)
  characteristics of, 82
  definition of, 82
  determining usefulness of, 82–83
  examples of, 84–87
  kinds of, 84
  on CD-ROM, 84
  online, 85
  (*See also specific subjects*)
Directories:
  definition of, 77, 124
  examples, 127

Edition, definition of, 26
Education, 192–196
  definition of, 192
  reference sources, 193–196
    abstract journals, 195–196
    bibliographies, 193
    biographical dictionaries, 195

Education (*Cont.*):
    dictionaries, 193–194
    directories, 194
    encyclopedias, 193–194
    guides, 193
    handbooks, 195
    indexes, 193
    on CD-ROM, 193
    online, 193
    professional journals, 195
    yearbooks, 196
Educational Resources Information Center (ERIC), 54, 124, 126, 196
Egypt, books and libraries in, 5–6
Electronic Numerator, Integrator, and Computer (ENIAC), 19
Encyclopedias, 89–95, 161, 267, 270
  definition of, 76, 90
  examples of, 92–95
  on CD-ROM, 92–93, 94
  online, 92–93, 94
  selection and use of, 90–92
  (*See also specific subjects*)
Encyclopedia annuals, 124, 126
Endnotes (*see* Footnotes)
Endpapers as part of a book, 25
ERIC (*see* Educational Resources Information Center)

Fertile Crescent, 6
Fine arts and recreation, 218–234
  definition of, 218
  music, 223–229
    reference sources, 224–229
      bibliographies, 224
      biographical dictionaries, 228–229
      dictionaries, 224–226
      encyclopedias, 226–227
      guides, 224
      handbooks, 224
      indexes, 224
      on CD-ROM, 224, 229
      online, 219, 229, 230
      professional journals, 229
  painting, sculpture, architecture and decorative arts, 218–223

Fine arts and recreation (*Cont.*):
  reference sources, 219–223
    bibliographies, 219
    biographical dictionaries,
      222–223
    dictionaries, 220–221
    directories, 222–223
    encyclopedias, 220–221
    guides, 219
    handbooks, 221–222
    indexes, 219
    on CD-ROM, 219
    online, 219
    professional journals, 223
  performing arts, 229–233
    reference sources, 229–233
      bibliographies, 230
      biographical dictionaries,
        232–233
      dictionaries, 230–231
      encyclopedias, 230–231
      guides, 230
      handbooks, 231–232
      indexes, 230
      on CD-ROM, 230
      online, 230
      professional journals, 233
    primary source materials, 218
    reference sources, examples, 219–234
Fly-leaves as part of the book, 26
Footnotes, 28, 273, 275, 277–282
  definition of, 273, 275
  examples of, 275–282
  general rules for, 273, 275–277
Franklin, Benjamin, 16
Frontispiece as part of the book, 26

Geographia, 118
Geography, 258–261
  definition of, 258
  reference sources, 258–261
    atlases, 259
    bibliographies, 258
    dictionaries, 259–260
    encyclopedias, 259–260
    gazetteers, 259
    guidebooks, 260–261

Geography (*Cont.*):
    guides, 258
    handbooks, 259–260
    indexes, 258
    professional journals, 261
Glossary, definition of, 28
Government publications, 148–155,
  161, 163, 270
  definition of, 148
  kinds of, 149–150
  on CD-ROM, 153–155
  online, 153–155
  organization and arrangement in li-
    braries, 150–151
  purpose of, 149
  reference sources, 153–155
    bibliographies and guides, 153
    Congressional information sources,
      153–154
    handbooks and yearbooks, 154–155
    statistical information sources,
      155
  usefulness of, 150
Greeks, books and libraries of, 7–9
Guidebooks, 260–261
Guides, definition of, 160
Gutenberg, Johann, 14
Gutenberg Bible, 14

Half-title page as part of the book, 26
Hammurabi, Code of, 5
Handbooks, 124–128, 161, 270
  definition of, 77, 124
  examples of, 127–128
  selection and use of, 125–126
  types of, 125
  (*See also specific subjects*)
Harvard, John, 16
History, 251–258
  definition of, 251
    reference sources, 251–258
    atlases, 255–256
    bibliographies, 251–252
    biographical dictionaries, 257
    dictionaries, 253–255
    documents, 257
    encyclopedias, 253–255

History (*Cont.*):
    guides, 251–252
    handbooks, 255
    indexes, 251–252
    on CD-ROM, 252
    online, 252
    professional journals, 252–258

Illumination, definition of, 11, 14
Imprint, definition of, 26
Incunabula, definition of, 14
Index as part of the book, 28
Indexes, 28, 96–107, 160, 270
    definition of, 76–77, 96
    examples of, 101–107
    excerpts from, 99, 100, 103
    formats, 98
    kinds of, 96
    on CD-ROM, 101, 103, 105
    online, 102, 103, 105
    to literature in collections, 106–107
    to newspapers, 104–105
    to periodicals, 98–104
    selecting and using, 99–101
    (*See also specific subjects*)
INFOTRAC data base, 102N
Instruction in the use of the library, 30
Interlibrary loan, 30–31, 140, 269
INTERNET, 141
Introduction as part of the book, 27
Ireland, books and libraries in, 11

Jefferson, Thomas, 38

Language, 197–204
    definition of, 197
    reference sources, 198–204
        bibliographies, 198–199
        biographical dictionaries, 204
        dictionaries, 199
            kinds of, 198
            of specific aspects of, 199–204
            on CD-ROM, 198
            online, 198
        encyclopedias, 199
        guides, 198–199
        professional journals, 204
Legislation, federal, 18

Libraries,
    academic, 12–13, 16–17, 18, 20, 29–33
    classification in (*see* Classification in libraries)
    depository, 149
    electronic technologies in, 20, 66–71, 139–144
    orientation visit to, 33
    private, 16
    public, 17, 20
    research, 18
    school, 18
    special, 20
    state, 17
    subscription (social), 16
Library catalog, 39, 55–71, 266–269
    common characteristics of, 56–57
    definition of, 55
    entries in, 59–64
        arrangement of, 64–66
    forms of, 57
        book, 57–58
        COMcat, 58–59
        card, 59–66
        CD-ROM, 70–71
        online, 66–70, 140, 269
    kinds of, 59
Library classification systems, purposes and characteristics of, 38–39
Library Journal, xii
Library materials, kinds of, 32–33
Library of Congress, 17, 19–20, 45–46
Library of Congress Classification System, 45–53
Library of Congress Subject Headings, 63, 67–68, 267
Library staff, 33
Linguistics, definition of, 197
Literature, 235–250
    definition of, 235
    in collections, 106
        indexes to, 107
    reference sources, 235–250
        abstract journals, 250
        bibliographies, 235–238
        biographical dictionaries, 245–247

Literature
  reference sources (*Cont.*):
    book digests, 243–244
    book reviews, 239–240
    books of quotations, 244–245
    criticism, 247–249
    dictionaries, 240–241
    encyclopedias, 241
    guides, 235–238
    handbooks, 241–243
    indexes, 238–239
    on CD-ROM, 238, 239, 240, 246
    online, 238, 239, 240, 245
    professional journals, 250
  yearbooks, 249–250

Machine-Readable Cataloging (MARC),
    19–20, 139
Main entry, 60–61
Manual, definition of, 125, 161
Manuals of style, 276–277
Manutius, Aldus, 15
MARC (*see* Machine-Readable Cata-
    loging)
Microcard, 138
Microfiche, 137–138
Microfilm, 137
Microforms, 137–139, 270
  kinds of, 138
  organization and arrangement of,
    138–139
  uses of, 138
Microprint, 138
Miscellany, definition of, 125
Monasteries, 10–12
Morphology, definition of, 197
Music, 223–229
  definition of, 223
  references sources, 224–229
  (*See also* Fine Arts, music and recre-
    ation)
Mythology, 180–181
  definition of, 180
  reference sources, 180–181

Networks, 141
Newspapers,
  indexes to, 104–105
  on CD-ROM, 105

Nineveh Library, 4–5
Nonbook information sources, 18, 78,
    134–147, 163, 270
  bibliographical form for, 281–282
  determining usefulness of, 139
  examples of reference materials on,
    145–147
  footnote form for, 281–282
  kinds of, 134
  sample catalog cards, 135
NOTIS Systems, Inc., 69
Note-taking, 273
  examples of note cards, 274

Online catalog, 20, 66–70, 140, 269
  instruction for use of, 68–70, 140
  search options, 68–70, 140
Online Public Access Catalog (OPAC)
    (*See* Online catalogs)
ORBIT Search Service, 141
Orientation visit to library, 33
Outlining, 271, 273

Painting, reference sources (*see* Fine
    arts: painting, sculpture, architec-
    ture and decorative arts)
Pamphlets, 134, 136
Paper, 13
Papyrus, 5, 8
Parchment, 8–9
Performing arts, reference sources,
    229–233
Pergamum Library, 9
Periodicals, 77, 96–97
  indexes to, 98–104
  usefulness of, 97–98
Philology (*see* Language)
Philosophy, 165–169
  definition of, 165–166
  reference sources, 166–169
    bibliographies, 166–167
    biographical dictionaries, 168
    dictionaries, 167
    digests, 168
    encyclopedias, 167
    handbooks, 168
    indexes, 167–168
    professional journals, 169

Phoenicians, books and libraries of, 6–7
Photocopying in libraries, 31
Plagiarism, definition of, 273
Preface as part of the book, 27
Primary sources, 229, 268
Printing with movable types, 13–15
Professional journals, 97, 162–163
  (*See also specific subjects*)
Psychology, 169–172
  abstract journals, 171–172
  definition of, 169–170
  reference sources, 170–172
    bibliographies, 170
    biographical dictionaries, 171
    dictionaries, 170–171
    directories, 171
    encyclopedias, 170–171
    indexes, 172
    on CD-ROM, 172
    online, 172
    professional journals, 171–172
    yearbooks, 171
Ptolemy, Claudius, 118
Public Printer, The, 149

Rameses II, 6
Rawlinson, Sir Henry, 5
Recuyell of the Histories of Troy, 14
Reference sources, 32, 75–76
  characteristics of, 75–76
  general, 76–78
    definition of, 76
  kinds of, 76–78
  nonbook forms, 78
  subject, 159–164
    (*See also* Subject information
      sources)
  selection and use of, 78–80
Reference service, 30
Religion, 173–180
  definition of, 173–174
  reference sources, 174–180
    atlases, 178
    bibliographies, 174
    biographical dictionaries, 179
    books of quotations, 177
    concordances, 175
    dictionaries, 175–176

Religion
  reference sources (*Cont.*):
    digests, 177–178
    encyclopedias, 176–177
    guides, 174
    handbooks, 178–179
    hymns, 178
    indexes, 174
    professional journals, 179
    yearbooks, 178–179
Renaissance, the, 13
Research paper, 265–282
  basic steps in writing, 266–275
  bibliography for, 271, 277–278
    examples of bibliographical form,
      278–282
    sample cards, 272
  footnotes, 273, 275–277
    examples of, 278–282
  kinds of, 268
  note-taking, 273
    sample cards, 272
  outlining, 273–274
  search strategy, 266–275
  using library resources for, 266–271
Reserve materials, 30
Romans, books and libraries of the,
  9–10
Rosetta Stone, 6

Science, 205–217
  definition of, 205
  reference sources, 206–217
    abstract journals, 217
    atlases, 215
    bibliographies, 206–207
    biographical dictionaries, 215
    dictionaries, 208–209
    encyclopedias, 211–213
    guides, 207
    handbooks, 213–214
    indexes, 207–208
    on CD-ROM, 206–208, 217
    online, 206–208, 212, 217
    professional journals, 216
    yearbooks, 214
Scribes, 4, 6, 11
Scriptorium, 11–12

Sculpture, reference sources (*see* Fine arts, painting, sculpture, architecture, and decorative arts)
Search options, 68, 101–102, 140, 142, 269
Search strategy, 71, 143, 144, 266–275
Search instructions, 68, 71, 140
Secondary sources, 268–269
Semantics, definition of, 197
Serial, definition of, 55N
Series, definition of, 26
Social sciences, 182–192
  definition of, 182
  reference sources, 182–192
    atlases, 190–191
    bibliographies, 182–183
    biographical dictionaries, 191
    dictionaries, 184–185
    encyclopedias, 185–188
    guides, 182–183
    handbooks, 188–189
    indexes, 183–184
    on CD-ROM, 183–184, 196
    online, 183–184, 195
    professional journals, 191–192
    yearbooks, 190
Social studies, 182
Spine as part of the book, 25
Sports and recreation, reference sources, 233–234
Subject entry, 62–64
Subject headings, 62–64, 144, 269
Subject information sources, 159–164
  definition of, 159
  kinds and purposes of, 160–163
  selection and use of, 163–164
  usefulness of, 159–160
Sumerians, books, and libraries of, 4
Superintendent of Documents, the, 149, 151
Superintendent of Documents Classification System, 151
Syntax, definition of, 197

Table of contents as part of the book, 27

Technology, 205–217
  definition of, 205
  reference sources, 206–217
    abstract journals, 215
    atlases, 215
    bibliographies, 206–207
    biographical dictionaries, 215
    dictionaries, 210–211
    encyclopedias, 211–213
    guides, 207
    handbooks, 213–214
    indexes, 207–208
    on CD-ROM, 206–208, 212, 217
    online, 206–208, 212, 217
    professional journals, 216–217
    yearbooks, 214
Text, as part of the book, 28
Thesaurus, definition of, 30, 64
Thesis, definition of, 265
Title entry, 61
Title page:
  as part of the book, 26
  as part of the nonbook, 27

Ulpian Library, 10
Union catalogs, 67, 140
United States Government, Printing Office, 149

Vellum, 8–9
Vertical file, 136

Watermark, definition of, 27
Wilson Library Bulletin, xii
WilsonDisc, 103
WilsonLine, 103
Writing materials, 3–13
Writing styles, 3–11

Yearbooks, 124–127
  definition of, 77, 124, 161
  examples of, 126–127
  selection and use of, 125–126
  types of, 124
  (*See also specific subjects*)

Title Index

Abbreviations Dictionary, 199
Abingdon Dictionary of Living Religions, 175
Abi/Inform, 183
ABS Guide to Recent Publications in the Social and Behavioral Sciences, The, 182
Abstracts of English Studies, 250
Academic American Encyclopedia, 92
Acronyms, Initialisms, and Abbreviations Dictionary, 199
Africa Contemporary Record, 188
African-American Writers, 246–247
Afro-American Artists: A Biobibliographical Directory, 222
Almanac of American Politics, The, 188
Almanac of American Women in the 20th Century, 115
Almanac of World Military Power, The, 255
Almanack, 127
America: History and Life, 251–252
American Academy of Political and Social Science, *Annals*, 191
American Art Directory, 222
American Authors and Books, 242
American Authors: 1600–1900, 247

American Chemical Society Journal, 216
American Drama Criticism: Interpretations 1890–1977, 248
American Economic Review, 191
American Educators' Encyclopedia, 193
American Guide Series, The, 261
American Heritage Dictionary of the English Language, 85
American Heritage: The Magazine of History, 257
American Historical Review, 257
American Hymns Old and New, 178
American Journal of Economics and Sociology, 191–192
American Journal of Physics, 216
American Journal of Psychology, 171
American Journal of Public Health, 216
American Library Directory, 77
American Medical Association Encyclopedia of Medicine, The, 210
American Literary Scholarship, 249
American Literature: A Journal of Literary History, Criticism and Bibliography, 250
American Mathematical Monthly, 216
American Men and Women of Science, 171, 191, 215

American Musical Theatre: A Chronicle, 230

American Novel: A Checklist of Twentieth Century Criticism on Novels Written since 1789, The, 248

American Place Names: A Concise and Selective Dictionary for the Continental United States of America, 260

American Political Dictionary, The, 185

American Political Science Review, 192

American Reference Books Annual, 133

American Sign Language: A Comprehensive Dictionary, 202

American Speech, A Quarterly of Linguistic Usage, 204

American Statistics Index, 155

American Thesaurus of Slang, 202

American Universities and Colleges, 194

American Usage and Style: The Consensus, 203

American Women Artists: From Early Indian Times to the Present, 223

American Women Writers: A Critical Reference Guide from Colonial Times to the Present, 237

American Writers, 247

Americana Annual, 126

Analytical Concordance to the Revised Standard Version of the New Testament, An, 175

Anchor Bible, The, 175

Ancient Writers: Greece and Rome, 248

Annals of American Literature, 236–237

Annual Bibliography of English Language and Literature, 198, 237

Annual Register: A Record of World Events, The, 77, 190

Annual Review of Psychology, 171

Appleton's Cyclopaedia of American Biography, 112, 114

Appleton's New Cuyás English-Spanish and Spanish-English Dictionary, 87–88

Applied Science and Technology Index, 207

Art Bulletin, 223

Art in America, 223

Art Index, 219, 230

Articles on American Literature 1950–1967, 236

Artist's Handbook of Materials and Techniques, The, 221

Association of American Geographers, *Annals*, 261

Atlas of American History, 162, 255–256

Atlas of American Women, 191

Atlas of Classical Archaeology, 256

Atlas of Classical History, 257

Atlas of Early American History The Revolutionary Era, 1760–1790, 256

Atlas of Southeast Asia, 191

Atlas of the Classical World, 256

Atlas of the Environment, 121, 215

Atlas of the United States, 259

Atlas of United States Environmental Issues, 121, 215

Audiocassette, Finder, 147

AV Market Place, 145

Baedeker Handbook for Travellers, 261

Baker's Biographical Dictionary of Musicians, 228

Barnhart Dictionary of Etymology, The, 200

Bartholomew/Scribner Atlas of Europe: A Profile of Western Europe, The, 259

Baseball Encyclopedia, The Complete and Official Record of Major League Baseball, 233

Basic Documents on Human Rights, 257

Benet's Readers Encyclopedia, 241–242

Benet's Reader's Encyclopedia of American Literature, 243

Bibliographic Index, The, 131

Bibliographical Guide to the Study of Southern Literature, A, 237

Bibliographical Guide to the Study of the Literature of the U.S.A., 236

Bibliography of American Literature, 236

Billboard: The International Weekly of Music and Entertainment, 229

Biographical Directory, 171

Biography and Genealogy Master Index, 116

Biography Index, 102, 116, 117

Biological Abstracts, 216

Biological and Agricultural Index, The, 207

Black American Writers: Bibliographical
Essays, 248
Black American Writers Past and Present:
A Biographical and Bibliographical
Dictionary, 241
Black Authors: A Selected Annotated Bibliography, 246
Black's Law Dictionary, 185
Black's Medical Dictionary, 210
Book of the States, The, 154
Book of World-Famous Music—Classical,
Popular and Folk, The, 227
Book Review Digest, 100, 102, 239–240
Book Review Index, 102
Books in Print, 77, 133
Books in Print with Book Reviews
Plus, 133
Bowker's Complete Video Directory, 147
Brewer's Dictionary of Phrase and
Fable, 242
Brewer's Dictionary of Twentieth Century
Phrase and Fable, 241
Britain: An Official Handbook, 190
Britannica Book of the Year, 126
British Authors before 1800, 247
British Authors of the Nineteenth
Century, 247
British Humanities Index, 219
British Writers, 249
Broadcasting: The Fifth Estate, 233
Brockhaus Encyklopädic in zwanzig
Banden, 94
Business Information Sources, 183
Business Periodicals Index, 184
Business Periodicals on Disc, 184

Cambridge Atlas of Astronomy, The, 215
Cambridge Biographical Dictionary, 113
Cambridge Encyclopedia, The, 93
Cambridge Encyclopedia of Archaeology,
The, 254
Cambridge Encyclopedia of Language,
The, 199
Cambridge Encyclopedia of Latin America
and the Caribbean, The, 186
Cambridge Encyclopedia of Life Sciences,
The, 211

Cambridge Encyclopedia of Ornithology,
The, 211
Cambridge Encyclopedia of Space, The, 213
Cambridge Guide to English Literature,
The, 237
Cambridge Guide to World Theatre,
The, 230
Cambridge Handbook of American Literature, The, 243
Cambridge Italian Dictionary, The, 87
Cambridge World Gazetteer, 122–123
Canada Yearbook, 196
Canadian Almanac and Directory, 127
Canadian Encyclopedia, The, 92–93
Canadian Periodical Index, 102
Cassell's Encyclopedia of World
Literature, 241
Cassell's German Dictionary: German-English, English-German, 86
Cassell's Italian Dictionary: Italian-English,
English-Italian, 87
Cassell's New Latin Dictionary: Latin-English, English-Latin, 87
Catholic Periodical and Literature
Index, 102
CD-ROM Information Products: An Educational Guide and Directory, 145
CD-ROMS in Print 1992: An International Guide to CD-ROMS, CDI, CDTV
and Electronic Book Products, 146
Chambers Biology Dictionary, 210
Chambers English Dictionary, 85
Chambers World Gazetteer, 77
Chemical Abstracts, 216
Children's Catalog, 132
Christopher Columbus Encyclopedia,
The, 253
Church History, 179
CIS/Annual, 154
College Blue Book, The, 194
Collier's Encyclopedia, 93
Collier's Year Book, 126
Columbia Dictionary of Modern European
Literature, 240
Columbia Granger's Index to Poetry, 238
Columbia Granger's World of Poetry, 238
Commonwealth Universities Yearbook,
195

Comparative Guide to American
Colleges, 194
Compendex Plus, 207
Complete Book of the Olympics, 234
Complete Concordance to the Bible (Douay
Version), 175
Complete Concordance to the Holy Scrip-
tures of the Old and New Testaments,
A, 175
Composers Since 1900: First Supplement
(1981), 229
Comprehensive Etymological Dictionary of
the English Language, A, 200
Computer Dictionary for Everyone, 211
Computer Readable Data Bases: A Directory
and Data Sourcebook, 146
Concise Cambridge Bibliography of English
Literature, 600–1950, The, 237–238
Concise Columbia Encyclopedia, 93
Concise Dictionary of American
History, 253
Concise Dictionary of Astronomy, A, 209
Concise Dictionary of Earth Science,
The, 208
Concise Dictionary of French Literature,
The, 241
Concise Dictionary of Literary Terms,
The, 240
Concise Dictionary of National Bio-
graphy, 114
Concise Dictionary of Scientific Bio-
graphy, 215
Concise Encyclopedia of Islam, The, 177
Concise Oxford Dictionary of Ballet,
The, 231
Concise Oxford Dictionary of Current En-
glish, The, 201
Concise Oxford Dictionary of English Ety-
mology, 200
Concise Oxford Dictionary of English
Proverbs, 245
Congress A to Z, 153
Congressional Quarterly Almanac, 154
Contemporary American Composers: A Bio-
graphical Dictionary, 228
Contemporary American Poetry: A Check-
list, 247

Contemporary American Women
Sculptors, 223
Contemporary Architects, 222
Contemporary Atlas of the United
States, 121
Contemporary Authors, 246
Contemporary Designers, 223
Contemporary Literary Criticism, 247
Continental Novel: A Checklist of Criticism
in English, 1900–1966, The, 248
Core List of Books and Journals in Educa-
tion, 193
County and City Data Book, 155
CQ Weekly Report, 154
Critical Temper: A Survey of Modern Crit-
icism on English and American
Literature from the Beginnings to the
Twentieth Century, The, 249
Crowell's Handbook of Classical
Mythology, 181
Cumulative Book Index, 133
Current Biography, 113
Current Index to Journals in
Education, 196

Dance Handbook, The, 232
Dance Magazine, 233
Data Base, 147
Dial-In 1992: An Annual Guide to Online
Public Catalogs, 146
DIALOG on Disc: Newspapers, 105
Dickson Baseball Encyclopedia, The, 233
Dictionary of American Art, 220
Dictionary of American Biography, 77,
109, 112, 114
Dictionary of American English on Histori-
cal Principles, A, 200
Dictionary of American History, 253
Dictionary of American Proverbs, A, 245
Dictionary of American Regional
English, 202
Dictionary of American Religious Biogra-
phy, 179
Dictionary of American Slang, 202
Dictionary of Americanisms on Historical
Principles, A, 201

Dictionary of Antiques, 221
Dictionary of Architecture and Construction, 220
Dictionary of Ballet, A, 231
Dictionary of Basic Geography, A, 260
Dictionary of Bible and Religion, The, 176
Dictionary of Botany, A, 209
Dictionary of British and American Women Writers, 1660–1800, A, 249
Dictionary of Business and Economics, 185
Dictionary of Canadian Biography/Dictionaire Biographique du Canada, 114
Dictionary of Canadianisms on Historical Principles, A, 200–201
Dictionary of Christianity in America, 176
Dictionary of Comparative Religion, A, 175–176
Dictionary of Computers, Data Processing and Telecommunication, 211
Dictionary of Contemporary American Artists, A, 222
Dictionary of Contemporary Slang, The, 200
Dictionary of Education, 197
Dictionary of Ethology, 209
Dictionary of Foreign Phrases and Abbreviations, 200
Dictionary of Foreign Terms, 200
Dictionary of Geography, A, 260
Dictionary of Geology, A, 208–209
Dictionary of Human Geography, 185
Dictionary of Literary Terms and Literary Theory, A, 240
Dictionary of Modern English Usage, A, 203
Dictionary of National Biography, 109, 112, 114
Dictionary of Non-Christian Religions, A, 176
Dictionary of Philosophy, A, 167
Dictionary of Philosophy and Psychology, 167
Dictionary of Philosophy and Religion: Eastern and Western Thought, 167
Dictionary of Poetry Quotations, 238–239
Dictionary of Scientific Biography, 112, 115

Dictionary of Slang and Unconventional English, A, 202
Dictionary of Symbols, 210
Dictionary of Terms and Techniques in Archaeology, A, 253
Dictionary of the Bible and Religion, The, 176
Dictionary of the Environment, 208
Dictionary of the History of Ideas: Studies of Selected Pivotal Ideas, 167
Dictionary of the History of Science, 208
Dictionary of the Middle Ages, 254
Dictionary of the Social Sciences, A, 185
Dictionary of the Vietnam War, 254
Dictionary of 20th Century History, 253
Dictionary of Twentieth Century History, 1914–1990, A, 255
Dictionary of Wars, 253–254
Dictionary of Word and Phrase Origins, 201
Dictionary of World Mythology, A, 180
Dictionary of Zoology, A, 209
Directory of American Philosophers, 168
Directory of American Scholars, 168
Directory of Blacks in the Performing Arts, 232
Directory of Portable Databases, 146
Discovering Authors CD-ROM, 246
Dissertation Abstracts International, 195
Documents of American History, 162, 257
Dorland's Illustrated Medical Dictionary, 210
Drama Dictionary, The, 231

Earth and Man, The, 260
Economic Geography, 261
Education Index, The, 193
Educational Leadership, 195
Eighth Mental Measurements Yearbook, 171
Electromap World Atlas, 121
Emily Post's Etiquette, 128
Enciclopedia Italiana di Scienze Lettere ed Arti, 94
Enciclopedia Universal Ilustrada Europeo-Americana, 95
Encyclopaedia Britannica, 90, 93
Encyclopaedia Judaica, 177

Encyclopaedia of Language, An, 199
Encyclopaedia Universalis, 95
Encyclopaedic Dictionary of Physics,
  The, 209
Encyclopedia of American Art, 220
Encyclopedia Americana, The, 76, 93
Encyclopedia of American Biography, 115
Encyclopedia of American Comics, 220
Encyclopedia of American Economic History:
  Studies of the Principal Movements and
  Ideas, 187
Encyclopedia of American Facts and Dates,
  The, 253
Encyclopedia of American History, 254
Encyclopedia of American Religions, 177
Encyclopedia of American Theatre,
  1900-1975, 230
Encyclopedia of Architecture: Design, Engi-
  neering and Construction, 221
Encyclopedia of Astronomy and Astrophysics,
  The, 213
Encyclopedia of Bioethics, 212
Encyclopedia of Black America, 187
Encyclopedia of Crafts, The, 221
Encyclopedia of Dance and Ballet, The, 230
Encyclopedia of Earth System Science, 213
Encyclopedia of Eastern Philosophy and Reli-
  gion: Buddhism, Hinduism, Taoism,
  Zen, The, 177
Encyclopedia of Economics, 186
Encyclopedia of Education, The, 193
Encyclopedia of Educational Research, 194
Encyclopedia of Electronics, 210
Encyclopedia of Environmental Studies,
  The, 211
Encyclopedia of Ethics, 167
Encyclopedia of Folk, Country and Western
  Music, 226
Encyclopedia of Higher Education, 193
Encyclopedia of Human Behavior: Psychol-
  ogy, Psychiatry, and Mental Health,
  The, 170
Encyclopedia of Human Biology, 211
Encyclopedia of Human Rights, 187
Encyclopedia of Military History from 3500
  B.C. to the Present, The, 253
Encyclopedia of Opera, The, 226
Encyclopedia of Philosophy, The, 167

Encyclopedia of Physical Science and Tech-
  nology, 213
Encyclopedia of Physics, The, 211, 212
Encyclopedia of Pop, Rock, and Soul, 226
Encyclopedia of Popular Music and
  Rock, 226
Encyclopedia of Psychology, 170
Encyclopedia of Religion, The, 176-177
Encyclopedia of Sociology, 185-186
Encyclopedia of Southern Culture, 187-188
Encyclopedia of Southern History, The, 254
Encyclopedia of the American Constitu-
  tion, 187
Encyclopedia of the Musical Film, 231
Encyclopedia of the Third World, 186
Encyclopedia of Visual Art, The, 220
Encyclopedia of World Art, 220
Encyclopedia of World Costume, The, 221
Encyclopedia of World Culture, 187
Encyclopedia of World Literature in the
  20th Century, 241
Encyclopedic Dictionary of Psychology,
  The, 171
Energy Dictionary, 210
Energy Handbook, The, 214
Engineering Index, 207
English-German Technical and Engineering
  Dictionary, 210
English Historical Review, 258
English Novel Explication: Criticisms to
  1972, 248-249
ERIC, 195
Essay and General Literature Index, 77,
  106-107, 238
Europa Yearbook, 126
European Authors 1000-1900: A Bio-
  graphical Dictionary of European
  Literature, 247
European Drama Criticism 1900-
  1975, 248
European Writers, 249
Expanded Academic Index, 102

Facsimile User's Directory, 147
Facts About the Cities, 188
Facts About the Presidents, 154
Facts About the States, 189
Facts on File Dictionary of Education, 194

Facts on File Encyclopedia of the 20th Century, The, 253

Facts on File News Digest: CD-ROM, 105

Familiar Quotations, 244

Famous First Facts, 77, 127

Far East and Australasia, The, 190

Feminist Companion to Literature in English: Women Writers from the Middle Ages to the Present, The, 242

Fiction Catalog, 132, 236

Film and Video Finder, 146

Film Encyclopedia, The, 232

Fine Arts: A Bibliographic Guide to Reference Works, Histories, and Handbooks, 220

Flags and Arms Across the World, 128

Fodor's Modern Guides, 261

Forthcoming Books, 133

Foundation Directory, The, 77, 127

French-English Science and Technology Dictionary, 210

General Periodicals Index, 102

General Periodicals Index, Academic Library Edition, 102

General Periodicals Index, Public Library Edition, 102

General Periodicals on Disc, 103

General Science Index, 207–208

Geographical Review, 261

Geography and Cartography: A Reference Handbook, 258

Geologic Reference Source, 207

Geological Society of America, *Bulletin*, 216

Glossary of Geographical Terms, A, 259–260

Glossary of Linguistic Terminology, 199

Golden Bough: A Study in Magic and Religion, The, 180

Goode's World Atlas, 121

Government Documents Catalog Service: GPO on CD-ROM, 153

Government Reference Books: A Biennial Guide to U.S. Government Publications, 153

Grande Encyclopédie, La, 95

Granger's Index to Poetry (See *The Columbia Granger's Index to Poetry*)

Graphic Arts Encyclopedia, 221

Gray's Manual of Botany, 213

Great Composers, A Biographical and Critical Guide: 1300–1900, 229

Great E B: The Story of the Encyclopaedia Britannica, The, 90

Great Song Thesaurus, The, 227

Great Soviet Encyclopedia: A Translation of the Third Edition, 95

Greek and Latin Authors: 800 B.C.-A.D. 1000, 247

Greek-English Lexicon, 87

Grzimek's Encyclopedia of Mammals, 212

Guide to American Poetry Explication, 248

Guide to Basic Information Sources in Chemistry, 206

Guide to Critical Reviews of United States Fiction 1870–1910, A, 210

Guide to English and American Literature, A, 236

Guide to Microforms in Print: Author-Title, 146

Guide to Microforms in Print: Subject, 146

Guide to Popular U.S. Government Publications, 153

Guide to Reference Books, 132

Guide to Reference Materials, 132–133

Guide to State Environmental Programs, 189

Guide to the Literature of Art History, 219

Guide to the Literature of the Life Sciences, 207

Guide to the Study of Medieval History, A, 252

Guide to Theatre in America, A, 230

Halliwell's Film Guide, 231

Hammond Atlas of the World, 121

Hammond Barnhart Dictionary of Science, 208

Hammond Gold Medallion World Atlas, 121

Handbook of American and Canadian Churches, 178

Handbook of American Popular Culture, 189

Handbook of American Women's
History, 255
Handbook of Denominations in the United
States, 179
Handbook of Latin American Studies, 183
Handbook of Mathematical Tables and For-
mulas, 213
Handbook of Modern Accounting, 188–189
Handbook of North American Indians, 189
Handbook of World Philosophy: Contempor-
ary Developments Since 1945, 168
Handbook to Literature, A, 243
Harper Dictionary of Contemporary
Usage, 203
Harper Concise Atlas of the Bible, The, 178
Harper Dictionary of Modern Thought,
The, 167
Harper Dictionary of Opera and Oper-
etta, 225
Harper Handbook to Literature, The, 242
HarperCollins Dictionary of American Gov-
ernment and Politics, 185
HarperCollins Dictionary of Economics,
The, 185
HarperCollins Dictionary of Sociology,
The, 185
Harper's Bible Dictionary, 175
Harper's Dictionary of Music, 224–225
Harrap's New Collegiate French and En-
glish Dictionary, 86
Harrap's New Standard French and English
Dictionary, 86
Harvard Encyclopedia of American Ethnic
Groups, 186
Harvard Guide to American History, 252
Harvard List of Books in Psychology, 170
Harvard Theological Review, 179
Hawley's Condensed Chemical Diction-
ary, 209
Henderson's Dictionary of Biological
Terms, 209
Historic Architecture Sourcebook, 221
Historical Abstracts, 261
Historical Atlas, 257
Historical Atlas of South Asia, A, 256–257
Historical Statistics of the United States Co-
lonial Times to 1970, 155

Historical Atlas of the Religions of the
World, 178
History of Religions: An International
Journal for Comparative Historical
Studies, 179
Holidays and Anniversaries of the
World, 127
Holman Bible Dictionary, 176
Home Book of American Quotations,
244–245
Home Book of Bible Quotations, The, 177
Home Book of Quotations, The, 245
Humanities Index, 230, 238–239, 252

Illustrated Dictionary of Place Names,
United States and Canada, 260
Illustration Index, 219
International Encyclopedia of Linguistics,
The, 199
Index Medicus, 170, 208
Index to Book Reviews in the Humanities,
An, 240
Index to Legal Periodicals, 184
Index to Poetry by Black American
Women, 238
Index to Publications of the United States
Congress, 154
Information Please Almanac, Atlas &
Yearbook, 127
Information Finder™ by World Book, 93
Institutions of Higher Education: An Inter-
national Bibliography, 193
Instruments in the History of Western
Music, 227
International Cyclopedia of Music and Mu-
sicians, The, 226–227
International Dictionary of Philosophy, 171
International Directory of Philosophy and
Philosophers, 168
International Encyclopedia of Communica-
tions, 199
International Encyclopedia of Linguistics,
The, 199
International Encyclopedia of the Social Sci-
ences, 186
International Handbook of Universities, 194
International Who's Who, 112–113

International Who's Who in Music and Musicians' Directory, 229

Interpreter's Dictionary of the Bible, The, 176

Introduction to United States Public Documents, 153

JAMA: The Journal of the American Medical Association, 216

James & James Mathematics Dictionary, 209

Jazz Handbook, The, 228

Journal of American History, 258

Journal of Economic History, 192

Journal of General Psychology, 172

Journal of Geology, 216

Journal of Higher Education, 195

Journal of Modern History, 258

Journal of Negro History, The, 258

Journal of Philosophy, The, 169

Journal of Physical Education, Recreation, and Dance, 234

Journal of the History of Philosophy, 169

Junior Book of Authors, The, 246

Junior High School Library Catalog, The, 132

Kessing's Contemporary Archives: Record of World Events, 190

Kodansha Encyclopedia of Japan, 186

Lange's Handbook of Chemistry, 214

Larousse Dictionary of Painters, 222

Larousse World Mythology, 180

LC Classification Outline, 50

Library of Congress Catalogs: National Union Catalog, 131

Library of Congress Catalogs, Subject Catalog, 1950–, 131

Library of Congress Subject Headings, 63, 67–68

Linguistics: A Guide to the Reference Literature, 198

Literary History of the United States Bibliography, The, 236

McGraw-Hill Dictionary of Modern Economics, 185

McGraw-Hill Dictionary of Physics and Mathematics, 209

McGraw-Hill Dictionary of Scientific and Technical Terms, 209

McGraw-Hill Encyclopedia of Energy, 213

McGraw-Hill Encyclopedia of Environmental Science, 213

McGraw-Hill Encyclopedia of Ocean and Atmospheric Sciences, 213

McGraw-Hill Encyclopedia of Science and Technology, 212

McGraw-Hill Encylopedia of the Geological Sciences, 212

McGraw-Hill Encyclopedia of World Art, 220

McGraw-Hill Encyclopedia of World Biography, The, 113

McGraw-Hill Encyclopedia of World Drama, 231

McGraw-Hill Handbook of Essential Engineering Information and Data, The, 213

McGraw-Hill Modern Scientists and Engineers, 215

McGraw-Hill Yearbook of Science and Technology, 214

Macmillan Encyclopedia of Architects, 222

Macmillan Encyclopedia of Computers, 211

Magazine Article Summaries, Full Text Select, 103

Magazine Index, The, 103

Magazine Index Plus, 103

Magazines for Libraries, 131

Magill's Bibliography of Literary Criticism, 248

Magill's Quotations in Context, 245

Masterpieces of Catholic Literature in Summary Form, 177

Masterpieces of Christian Literature in Summary Form, 178

Masterpieces of World Literature in Digest Form, 243–244

Masterpieces of World Philosophy, 168

Masterplots, 243–244

Masterplots II: Drama Series, 244

Mathematical Reviews, 217

Melloni's Illustrated Medical Dictionary, 211

Mental Health Book Review Index, 170

Merriam-Webster Online Dictionary The, 85

Merriam-Webster's Collegiate Dictionary, 85

MIT Dictionary of Modern Economics, The, 185

MLA International Bibliography (CD-ROM), 198–199, 237

MLA International Bibliography of Books and Articles on the Modern Languages and Literatures, 198–199, 237

Modern American Literature (A Library of Literary Criticism), 247

Modern American Usage: A Guide, 203

Modern American Women Writers, 246

Modern British Literature (A Library of Literary Criticism), 249

Modern Language Journal, 204

Monthly Catalog of United States Government Publications, 151, 153

Monthly Checklist of State Publications, 153

Morris Dictionary of Word and Phrase Origins, 201

Municipal Yearbook, 154

Music Index, 224

Music Index on CD-ROM, The, 224

Music Reference and Research Materials: An Annotated Bibliography, 224

Music Since 1900, 228

Musical Quarterly, The, 229

Musicians Since 1900, 229

Mythologies of the World: A Concise Encyclopedia, 181

Mythology: An Illustrated Encyclopedia, 180

Mythology of All Races, Greek and Roman, The, 180

National Atlas of the United States of America, The, 122

National Cyclopedia of American Biography, The, 115

National Geographic Atlas of the World, 77, 121

National Newspaper Index, The, 105

Natural History, 216

Nature, 216

NBC Handbook of Pronunciation, 202

Negro Almanac, The, 189

Negro in America: A Bibliography, 187

Nelson's Complete Concordance of the Revised Standard Version of the Bible, 175

New American Dictionary of Music, The, 227

New Cambridge Bibliography of English Literature, The, 238

New Cassell's French Dictionary: French-English, English-French, 86

New Catholic Encyclopedia, The, 177

New Concise Dictionary of American Biography, 114

New Dictionary of American Slang, 203

New Dictionary of Birds, A, 209–210

New Encyclopaedia Britannica, The, 93

New English Dictionary on Historical Principles, A, 81–82

New Grolier Multimedia Encyclopedia, 76, 94

New Grove Dictionary of American Music, The, 224

New Grove Dictionary of Jazz, 225

New Grove Dictionary of Music and Musicians, The, 225–226

New Grove Dictionary of Musical Instruments, The, 225

New Grove Dictionary of Opera, The, 226

New Harvard Dictionary of Music, The, 225

New International Atlas, 121–122

New Kobbé's Complete Opera Book, The, 227

New Milton Cross: More Stories of the Great Operas, The, 227

New Oxford Atlas, The, 122

New Oxford Companion to Music, The, 225

New Quotable Woman From Eve to the Present, 245

New Random House Encyclopedia, The, 94

New Revised Velázquez Spanish and English Dictionary, The, 88

New Standard Jewish Encyclopedia, The, 177

New Strong's Exhaustive Concordance of the Bible, The, 175

New York Public Library Book of Chronologies, The, 255

New York Public Library Book of How and Where to Look It Up, The, 127

New York Times, The, 78

New York Times Atlas of the World, The, 259

New York Times Biographical Service: A Compilation of Current Biographical Information of General Interest, The, 113–114

New York Times Index, 105

New Yorker, The, 97

Newsbank, 105

Newsbank Electronic Index, The, 105

Newspaper Abstracts on Disc, 105

NICEM Media Indexes, 145

Notable American Women 1607–1950: A Biographical Dictionary, 114–115

Notable American Women; the Modern Period: A Biographical Dictionary, 115

Notable Black American Women, 113

Notable Women in the American Theatre: A Biographical Dictionary, 232

Ocean World Encyclopedia, 212

Official Catholic Directory, 116

Official Congressional Directory for the Use of the United States Congress 1809–, 154

Official NBA Basketball Encyclopedia, The, 234

Online, 147

Opera Companion to Twentieth-Century Opera, The, 228

Opera News, 229

Ottemiller's Index to Plays in Collections, 237

Oxford American Dictionary, 86

Oxford Bible Atlas, 178

Oxford Classical Dictionary, The, 210–241

Oxford Companion to American History, The, 255

Oxford Companion to American Literature, The, 242

Oxford Companion to American Theatre, The, 231

Oxford Companion to Canadian Literature, The, 243

Oxford Companion to Classical Literature, The, 242

Oxford Companion to English Literature, The, 242

Oxford Companion to Film, The, 231

Oxford Companion to French Literature, The, 241–242

Oxford Companion to Musical Instruments, The, 227

Oxford Companion to Popular Music, The, 227

Oxford Companion to Ships & the Sea, The, 128

Oxford Companion to the English Language, The, 204

Oxford Companion to the Theatre, The, 232

Oxford Companion to Twentieth Century Art, The, 222

Oxford Companion to World Sports and Games, The, 233

Oxford Dictionary of Art, The, 220

Oxford Dictionary of Current Idiomatic English, 202

Oxford Dictionary of English Etymology, The, 200

Oxford Dictionary of English Proverbs, The, 245

Oxford Dictionary of Modern Quotations, The, 244

Oxford Dictionary of Music, The, 225

Oxford Dictionary of New Words: A Popular Guide to Words in the News, The, 202

Oxford Dictionary of Quotations, The, 162

Oxford Dictionary of the Christian Church, The, 176

Oxford Encyclopedia of Trees of the World, The, 212

Oxford English Dictionary, The, 82,
84, 201
*Oxford English Dictionary, Second Edition,
on Compact Disc*, 76, 84
Oxford English-Russian Dictionary, The, 87
Oxford Guide to English Usage, The, 204
*Oxford Illustrated Encyclopedia of the Arts,
The*, 221
Oxford Russian-English Dictionary, The, 87

PAIS on CD-ROM, 184
Paperbound Books in Print, 133
*Penguin Companion to World Literature,
The*, 243
Penguin Dictionary of Decorative Arts, 220
*Penguin Encyclopedia of Popular Music,
The*, 226
Peoples Chronology, The, 255
Periodical Abstracts on Disc, 103
Peters Atlas of the World, 122
Peterson Field Guide Series, The, 214
*Peterson's Annual Guides to Four-Year Col-
leges*, 194
*Peterson's Annual Guides to Graduate
Study*, 194
Peterson's Guide to Two-Year Colleges, 194
Phi Delta Kappan, 195
*Philosopher's Guide: To Sources, Research
Tools, Professional Life, and Related
Fields, The*, 166
*Philosopher's Index: An International Index
to Philosophical Periodicals and Books,
The*, 166–167
Philosophical Review, 169
*Philosophy: A Guide to the Reference Litera-
ture*, 166
Play Index, 239
PMLA, 204
Poetry, 250
*Poetry by American Women, 1900–1975:
A Bibliography*, 237
*Poetry Explication: A Checklist of Inter-
pretation Since 1925 of British and
American Poems, Past and
Present*, 248
*Poetry Handbook: A Dictionary of
Terms*, 242

Political Handbook of the World, 188
Political Science Quarterly, 192
Pollution Abstracts, 217
*Popular Music, An Annotated Index of
American Popular Songs*, 224
Praeger Encyclopedia of Art, 221
*Prentice-Hall Great International Atlas,
The*, 122
*Princeton Encyclopedia of Classical Sites,
The*, 254
*Princeton Encyclopedia of Poetry and Poet-
ics*, 241
Princeton Handbook of Poetic Terms, 241
Proquest Newspapers, 105
Psychiatric Dictionary, 210
Psychological Abstracts, 78, 163, 172
Psychological Review, The, 172
Psychology Today, 172
PsycLit, 172
Public Access Microcomputers, 146
Public Affairs Information Service, *Bul-
letin*, 183
Public Library Catalog, The, 132
"Putnam's Nature Field Books," 214

Quotation Database, 245

*Rand McNally Atlas of the Oceans,
The*, 215
*Rand McNally Commercial Atlas and Mar-
keting Guide*, 259
*Rand McNally Cosmopolitan World
Atlas*, 122
*Rand McNally Encyclopedia of World Riv-
ers*, 260
*Rand McNally Historical Atlas of the
World*, 256
Rand McNally Premier World Atlas, 122
Random House College Dictionary, The, 85
*Random House Dictionary of the English
Language, The*, 84–85
Random House Encyclopedia, The, 94
*Random House Encyclopedia: Electronic Edi-
tion*, 94
*Random House Webster's College Diction-
ary*, 86

Reader's Adviser: A Layman's Guide to Literature, 132
Reader's Companion to American History, The, 255
Readers' Guide Abstracts, 103
Readers' Guide to Periodical Literature, 77, 103
Readers' Guide to the Great Religions, A, 174
Recorded Classical Music: A Critical Guide to Compositions and Performances, 224
Reference Encyclopedia of the American Indian, 186
Reference Sources in History: An Introductory Guide, 252
Religion Index One: Periodicals, 174–175
Religious Periodicals Directory, 174
Research Guide to Philosophy, 167
Resources in Education, 196
Robert's Rules of Order, 77, 128
Rock On: The Illustrated Encyclopedia of Rock 'n Roll, 226
Roget's International Thesaurus, 203
Rolling Stone, 229

Science Abstracts, 163, 217
Science and Engineering Literature: A Guide to Reference Sources, 206
Science Citation Index, Compact Disc Edition, 208
Scientific American, 163, 216
Scientific and Technical Books and Serials in Print, 206
Scientific and Technical Information Sources, 207
Sculpture Index, 219
Selective Bibliography for the Study of English and American Literature, 236
Senior High School Library Catalog, The, 132
Sewanee Review, 250
Short Story Index, 239
Simon and Schuster Book of the Ballet, The, 232
Simon and Schuster Book of the Opera: A Complete Reference Guide, 1597 to the Present, The, 228

Simon and Schuster Encyclopedia of World War II, 254
Social Science Citation Index, 184
Social Sciences Index, 184, 258
Social Sciences Reference Sources: A Practical Guide, 183
Sociological Quarterly, 192
Solar Energy Handbook, 213–214
Sources of Information in the Social Sciences, 183
South American Handbook, 190
Southern Literature 1968–1975, 237
Speech Index, 239
Sports Encyclopedia: Pro-Football, The, 234
Sports Illustrated, 234
"Standard Catalog Series, The," 132
Standard Periodical Directory, The, 131
Stateman's Yearbook, The, 126
Stateman's Yearbook World Gazetteer, 123
Statistical Abstract of the United States, 155
Statistical Record of Black America, 189
Statistical Record of Women Worldwide, 189
Statistical Yearbook/Annuaire Statistique, 155
Statistics Sources, 183
Stedman's Medical Dictionary, 211
Subject Guide to Books in Print, 133
Supplement to Music Since 1900, 288
Supplement to the Oxford English Dictionary, A, 84, 201
Survey of Musical Instruments, A, 228
Symbol Sourcebook: An Authoritative Guide to International Graphic Symbols, 127

Thames and Hudson Encyclopaedia of 20th Century Music, The, 225
Thesaurus of ERIC Descriptors, 195
Thesaurus of Psychology Index Terms, 172
Third Barnhart Dictionary of New English, 201–202
Times Atlas of the Second World War, The, 256
Times Atlas of the World, 259
Times Atlas of the World, Vol I–Vol V, The, 120–121

*Times Atlas of World Exploration,
The*, 122
Times Atlas of World History, The, 256
Times Index, The, 105
*Timetables of History: A Horizontal Link-
age of People and Events, The*, 255
*12,000 Words: A Supplement to Webster's
Third New International Dictionary*,
85
Twentieth Century Authors, 247
*Twentieth Century Short Story Explica-
tion*, 249

Ulrich's International Periodicals Directory,
131–132
*Union List of Serials in Libraries of the
United States and Canada*, 132
United States Energy Atlas, The, 215
*United States Government Organization
Manual*, 155

Van Nostrand's Scientific Encyclopedia, 211
Vertical File Index, 146–147
Video Source Book, The, 147

Walker's Mammals of the World, 214
*We the People: An Atlas of American Eth-
nic Diversity*, 190
Webster's American Biographies, 115
Webster's Dictionary of English Usage, 204
*Webster's New Biographical Diction-
ary*, 113
*Webster's New Dictionary of Syno-
nyms*, 203
Webster's New Geographical Dictionary,
77, 123
Webster's New World Dictionary, 86
*Webster's New World Dictionary of Media
and Communications*, 203
*Webster's New World Secretarial Hand-
book*, 128
Webster's Sports Dictionary, 234
*Webster's Third New International Diction-
ary of the English Language*, 76, 85
Webster's Word Histories, 201
*Westminster Dictionary of Christian Ethics,
The*, 176

Who Was Who, 115
Who Was Who in America, 115
*Who Was Who in America, Historical Vol-
ume, 1607–1896*, 115, 257
Who's Who, 77, 116
Who's Who Among Black Americans, 116
Who's Who in America, 112, 116
Who's Who in American Art, 223
*Who's Who in American Politics,
1981–1982*, 191
Who's Who in Religion, 179
Who's Who in Theatre, 232
Who's Who in the World, 116
Wildflowers of the United States, 214
Wilson Authors Series, 247–248
Wilson Business Abstracts, 184
Women: A Bibliography, 183
*Women in American History: A Bibliogra-
phy*, 252
*Women in Psychology: A Biobibliographical
Sourcebook*, 171
Women in Science, 215
Women in Western European History, 252
*Women Philosophers: A Bio-Critical
Sourcebook*, 168
Women's Studies Encyclopedia, 241
*Words on Cassette: A Comprehensive Bibli-
ography of Spoken-Word Audio
Cassettes*, 147
*World Almanac and Book of Facts,
The*, 127
World Artists 1950–1980, 222
World Authors, 247
World Book Dictionary, 94
World Book Encyclopedia, The, 94
World Education Encyclopedia, 193–194
World Encyclopedia of Peace, 186–187
World of Learning, 195
*World Philosophy: Essay-Reviews of Major
Works*, 168
*Worldmark Encyclopedia of the
Nations*, 188
Worldmark Encyclopedia of the States, 188
World's Major Languages, 198

Yearbook of the United Nations, 155, 190
Year's Work in English Studies, 249–250